"As a practicing clinician I was thrilled to read this book. It is refreshing to find a guide for therapy that starts at the very foundations of any therapy – with ethical guidelines, and listening skills – then logically and sequentially builds on these, through a detailed explanation of the model, to its applications. Gordon applies this approach, which sees clients as complex beings with internal struggles, from basic problems to the more difficult. Throughout, he gives clear step-by-step guidelines, with a multitude of clinical examples; at every step emphasizing the key tenets of this approach – respect, acceptance, negotiation, integration.

"It illustrates great concepts for use intrapersonally first, and then maybe there is hope for use interpersonally and internationally!"

Barb Wood
Psychologist, Family Therapist, Hypnotherapist in Queensland, Australia

"Dr Gordon Emmerson's new book contains a wealth of information that will help counselors to build on their already well developed skills. Ego-state therapy enables the practitioner to assist the client in determining the cause of their problem, the root cause, and to effectively deal with it. The theory and examples are explicit and easy to adopt. Borrowing 'energy' from a negative part and giving that energy to a part that needs it is nothing short of brilliant. I've used ego-state therapy with clients for a number of years and I feel sure that this valuable book will influence many to also use this most effective technique."

Lyn Macintosh
Counselor, Hypnotherapist, NLP Master Practitioner
Fellow, Australian Society of Clinical Hypnotherapists

"In this innovative book Dr Emmerson clearly explains and demonstrates, with numerous case examples, powerful ego-state therapy techniques to practitioners who seek permanent character changes for their clients in shorter periods of time.

"Emmerson shows how to activate and work with covert states without inducing hypnosis. This is a significant contribution to the entire field of psychotherapy."

John G. Watkins, PhD
Past President, The International Society For Clinical and Experimental Hypnosis

"Gordon Emmerson's earlier book on *Ego State Therapy* (Crown House Publishing, 2003) already evidences his skill and experience in dealing with ego states, and should be a 'must read' for counselors and hypnotherapists alike. Now he takes ego-state therapy to a new level as a psychotherapeutic orientation with *Advanced Skills and Interventions in Therapeutic Counseling*. The author's combination of wisdom, intelligence and compassion evident throughout his latest book also make it a 'must read' for any caring counselor around the world. In my opinion, history should record Gordon Emmerson as a master of ego-state therapy."

C. Roy Hunter, MS, FAPHP
Author of *Hypnosis for Inner Conflict Resolution: Introducing Parts Therapy*

"*Advanced Skills and Interventions in Therapeutic Counseling* is a practical guide for students and professionals to understand not only the basic principles of counseling but also the development of ego states and ego-state therapy. The new ideas on personality development give a different perspective and a fresh look at diagnosis. This step-by-step guide from the basic principles of ego-state therapy to the advanced skills of practical application can be very useful for training. Clear examples of the therapeutic process with a wide range of disorders and trauma; provide a way to utilize these skills in the process to healing. Definitely a valuable contribution and an asset to the bookshelf!"

Stefanie Badenhorst, DLitt
Director, Milton Erickson Institute, Western Cape, South Africa and guest lecturer, University of Stellenbosch, South Africa

"*Advanced Skills and Interventions in Therapeutic Counseling* is the most refreshing text of its kind to appear in many years. Dr. Emmerson thoroughly reviews the fundamentals of the counseling process while bringing to light key new approaches overlooked in other sources. The writing style is clear, concise, and stimulating."

Professor Arreed Franz Barabasz, EdD, PhD, ABPP
Editor, *International Journal of Clinical and Experimental Hypnosis*

Advanced Skills and Interventions in Therapeutic Counseling

Gordon Emmerson, PhD

Crown House Publishing Limited
www.crownhouse.co.uk

First published by

Crown House Publishing Ltd
Crown Buildings, Bancyfelin, Carmarthen,Wales, SA33 5ND, UK
www.crownhouse.co.uk

and

Crown House Publishing Company LLC
6 Trowbridge Drive, Suite 5, Bethel, CT 06801, USA
www.crownhousepublishing.com

10 digit ISBN 1845900170
13 digit ISBN 978-184590017-5

LCCN 2005931938

There is a cause for every unwanted emotion or reaction.
This book is about understanding the cause and facilitating change.
When there is an internal dissent, the goal is a peace within.
When there is an unwanted reaction, the goal is resolution
and empowerment.

Prologue

The purpose of this text is threefold:

1. to present a brief and useful theory of personality that will guide the counselor in assessment and therapeutic interactions with clients;
2. to provide a clear means of assessing clients' concerns so the counselor can identify the best course of therapy; and
3. to provide brief and powerful therapeutic techniques, with examples.

Also covered in this text is a short but provocative discussion of ethical issues, and a presentation of some of the more general but important counseling skills.

Advanced Skills and Interventions in Therapeutic Counseling is written for advanced students and professionals. It provides the reader with an understanding of the personality, and reviews fundamentals of the counseling process, such as the setup of the counseling room, attending behavior, and advanced active listening skills. It gives the reader a means to assess clients so the direction of therapy is clear, and it provides illustrations for each general direction of the therapeutic process.

Unlike the DSM-IV-TR where *clients* are diagnosed into categories, the counseling assessment procedure provided in this book assesses each client *issue* into a category. Client problems are presented as falling into two main divisions, internal dissent and situational concerns, and into a number of subdivisions. A flowchart is provided to assist counselors to determine the best direction for therapy for each issue. Then clearly illustrated counseling interventions are presented to demonstrate the various directions therapy may take.

Among the therapeutic interventions that are covered are depression, sexual abuse, relationship issues, obsessive-compulsive behavior, anger, trauma, crisis intervention, grief and loss, and suicidal ideation.

With this book, the reader gains an integrated approach to therapeutic counseling, from personality theory, to applying that theory in assessing client problems, to the techniques to intervene. The counseling procedures presented and illustrated in this book facilitate the counselor to determine the origin of unwanted emotions and behaviors without psychodynamic interpretation and the interventions are designed to address the cause of the clients' concerns.

Contents

Examples of Therapeutic Techniques

Examples of working with some specific problems

Advanced Skills and Interventions in Therapeutic Counseling

Chapter 1

Therapeutic Counseling and Ethics

What is therapeutic counseling?

Professional therapeutic counseling is the process whereby a trained individual assists another individual, or group, in some type of personal problem resolution or desired personal growth. But is that all therapeutic counseling is? I think not, and I hope not. In order for change to occur there needs to be a particular interaction between the counselor and the client, based at least partly on the will and intent of each. If the client does not want to participate in counseling, effective counseling cannot occur. Likewise, if the counselor does not have the will to help, counseling will be of diminished value.

The desire to be a counselor is not one shared by all individuals. During training, I have heard various accounts of the reasons students decide to become counselors. One common account is, "It seems like I am always helping people with their problems, so I thought I might as well make it a profession." I have found, almost without exception, that students in counseling see the profession as more than a way to earn income: they see it as a way they can help others. There is something about helping others that appears to fulfill some of their own needs. This desire to help appears synergistic, since studies have shown that clients who believe their counselors care about their improvement make the best progress (McCabe and Priebe, 2004).

Therefore, counseling seems to be more than a mere exchange of conversation and professional techniques. Speaking in terms of individual counseling, two people come together, one with a desire for change and the other with a desire to help facilitate that change. At least in part, the interaction created by this common desire seems to be important in the outcome, the amount the client is able to make desired change (McCabe and Priebe, 2004).

One of the hardest clients to have, and one of the hardest to help change, is the client whom someone else has talked into coming to counseling. Unless the client wants to be there, is ready for change, and is ready to engage with the counselor, it is difficult for any counselor to be of assistance.

So, for the most effective counseling to occur, there needs to be the coming together of two people with a common goal, one to change and one to help in that change. The client has taken a sometimes large step in coming in to see the counselor. The motivation for change has become greater than the reticence to come in, the expense and the time. Often, the client will arrive in a vulnerable state, unable to understand or see a way forward. The client may fear sharing what is inside, while hoping to have the courage to do what is necessary to feel better or grow.

The counselor is a person who has chosen the helping profession because it helps to fulfill something that is needed. The counselor has the opportunity to be invited into the inner world of the client. It is an honor to be trusted enough for inner fears to be shared. Almost to a person, the counselor earnestly wants to take on the mandate of helper and be of real assistance to the client.

Counseling, while focused on the issues of the client, is a working together of two people for the benefit of both. The will of both has importance to the final outcome. Still, beyond wanting to help, it is important to have powerful and effective tools to facilitate change. It is hoped that the tools offered in this book will assist counselors in a real way toward achieving the positive outcomes they want for their clients.

Ethical issues

Adhering to appropriate ethical principles is the responsibility of every counselor. The counselor is a person who is given information and insights into the inner life of the client. The client is often vulnerable and trusting, and rightfully looks to the counselor for direction on ethical issues as they pertain to the counseling setting. Determining the appropriate ethical course of counseling is not easy, and cannot ever be fully delineated in any text. Often, context must be considered in the choice of the most ethical course of action.

While this section on ethics is not intended to be a thorough overview of ethical principles, it would be remiss not to highlight some of the most important ethical considerations. These considerations are divided into five categories below, the ethical person, confidentiality, maintaining boundaries in therapy, dual relationships, and duty of care.

The ethical person

Ethical guidelines must be interpreted and applied to real situations and real people. It is my belief that before a counselor can truly be ethical, he or she must do more than merely attempt to logistically apply guidelines to counseling situations. Contextual interpretation is often necessary, and only an ethical person can make interpretive judgments in an ethical manner. The ethical or honorable person will be able to seek and choose what is internally deemed "right" over "personal gain". Personal curiosity, need for power, desire for money, need for relationship, or any other self-serving need should be relinquished in favor of "doing the right thing". The ethical person has an inner sense of honor and peace and a positive knowledge that "Who I am" is more important than "What I want". The ethical person will be able to honor the client and make appropriate distinctions in difficult decisions. It is also important to understand ethical guidelines and to be able to discuss with another appropriate professional ethical dilemmas.

Confidentiality

One of the most important aspects of ethics and counseling is confidentiality. Clients often share with their counselors information and aspects of themselves that they either rarely share, or have never shared, with another person. It can be very frightening to open oneself, however fragile, trust, and tell it like it is. It is tragic if clients, after trusting, hear their story from someone else. It is often this fear that prevents clients from sharing their innermost feelings. It is appropriate to explain to a new client what confidentiality means in therapy, and to assure the client that there exists the utmost respect for maintaining that high-level confidentiality.

Breaching confidentiality

It is good to outline to the client when confidentiality might ever be breached, and when it would never be breached. Generally, it is the responsibility of the counselor to breach confidentiality if clients, in the professional opinion of the counselor, are at real threat of hurting themselves or someone else. For example, if the client is determined to commit suicide, and it is the professional opinion of the counselor that this danger continues to exist, it is appropriate to breach confidentiality to maintain the safety of the client. Likewise, if it is the professional opinion of the counselor that the client is likely to hurt someone else, then confidentiality should be breached. As is the case in most ethical dilemmas, a blurred line will exist concerning when an ethical breach of confidentiality is necessary. The next paragraph illustrates this.

Consider a client who informs the counselor that he is HIV-positive and that he is having unsafe sex with a partner who is unaware of his diagnosis. If the client cannot be convinced by the counselor that his partner should be told, this is an example when confidentiality should be breached for the safety of another. But consider a continuum of diagnoses a client might have when he is having unsafe sex with a partner who has not been told: HIV, hepatitis, herpes, chlamydia, the flu, the common cold. Where on this continuum should the counselor stop breaching confidentiality? That final determination must rely on the professional judgment of the counselor.

When should confidentiality not be breached? It is generally agreed that clients should be able to disclose their past, even when laws have been broken, without concern that confidentiality will be breached. In this way, counseling can be available to all people and confidentiality will not be a concern unless the counselor considers the client a current threat. Therefore, irrespective of what clients have done in their past and what they might be prosecuted for, the counselor should not breach confidentiality, unless the counselor has the opinion that this person is currently a real threat. As an aside, most priests are technically unable to breach confidentiality even when a current threat is believed to exist. Local laws vary according to what courts can subpoena, and those laws may vary from ethical guidelines, or from the personal ethics of the counselor.

With whom can cases be discussed?

It is generally considered appropriate, and to the benefit of the client, for counselors to be able to discuss their cases with other counselors who work at the same setting, with supervisors, or with co-supervisors. When discussing cases, if possible, the identity of the client should not be revealed. Cases should not be discussed with other counselors who are friends and do not work at the same setting. Cases may be discussed with specific individuals when the client gives the counselor special permission, or upon a request by the client.

It is also considered appropriate that cases can be discussed in educational settings where therapy is taught, and in professional print, such as journal articles and books. These professional case presentations should never occur if the client could be identified in any way. And, if the client is to be presented in print, it is appropriate to first consult with the client and gain permission for this type of presentation.

Maintaining boundaries in therapy

It is very important in therapy for the client to feel a *safe haven* has been found. Any aspect of feeling personally threatened by the counselor should be avoided. Clients, female and male, may have suffered from abuse, even those clients who have not presented this as an issue. While this should not be assumed, it is best to treat every client in the manner that sets crystal-clear boundaries between the counselor and the client. Obviously, there should never be any touch, comment, or joke that would lend itself to misinterpretation. As has been said already, clients often come to therapy feeling vulnerable, and they may have good reason to feel vulnerable if they have previously been mistreated.

The counselor should always maintain a professional demeanor, and should position the chairs in therapy at a safe distance to allow the client a feeling of space. While most counselors understand that any overt sexual remark would be inappropriate, some are insensitive to remarks that can leave the client feeling uncomfortable. Counselors should avoid remarks such as, "You look nice today," or, more obviously, "You wear that top very well." Comments such as, "Have you been working out?", "Have you lost weight?", and "You are a very attractive person" should be avoided. Comments such as these can blur the boundaries in the professional relationship between the counselor and the client. They may cause the client to begin looking at the counselor in a different way, either more threatened by the counselor, or more attracted to the counselor. Either can be devastating to the therapeutic relationship.

If the looks of the client have a direct bearing on the client's problem, careful wording should be used when referring to this. For example, it can be OK to say to a client, "It sounds like some men have been attracted to you more because of how you look than because of who you are." This statement is much preferred to, "You're a good-looking person and it's natural that men will be attracted to you." The client could hear the second statement as, "My counselor thinks I'm sexy"—and that is the context that should not be part of therapeutic relationships. Muscles, legs, physique, and other aspects of the body should not be commented on by the counselor. While it could seem friendly to offer compliments, the risk is too great that well-meaning compliments might be misinterpreted. The goal is for the client to feel as totally safe, secure, and respected in as professional a manner as possible.

It is not unusual for a client to develop attachment feelings to their counselor, even when the counselor has maintained excellent therapeutic boundaries. This is understandable, as clients may be coming from failed relationships where respected honesty is minimal, and clients may also have a real need for a close relationship beyond that of the counselor–client therapeutic relationship. It is the responsibility of the counselor to make sure that the boundaries stay in place, both literally and subjectively. This can be tricky.

If the client develops emotional feelings for the counselor, therapy is compromised. The client will not as freely disclose and will not be able to maintain a focus on what brought him or her to therapy if there is confusion about feelings for the counselor. If the client is developing nonprofessional emotional feelings for the counselor, it can be devastating to the client should the counselor overtly state this in an attempt to establish professional boundaries. The client can feel embarrassed and rejected, and the ability to do good therapeutic work can be greatly compromised. One might say, "But I believe the counselor should always be honest with the client." Not when that honesty could ruin the therapeutic relationship, or cause the client to feel *grossly* uncomfortable. Obviously, a counselor should never say to a client, "I think you're a sexy person," even if this is viewed as an accurate statement.

A much better way to deal with a client who the counselor believes has developed an emotional attachment in therapy would be with a statement such as the following. "I noticed this is our fifth session. I always like to review confidentiality and some of the aspects of therapy at this time with my clients. After a short review of confidentiality I also like to talk about aspects of the therapeutic relationship. It may seem silly and I know you know this, but obviously there can never be any other kind of relationship between the counselor and the client than a purely professional therapeutic relationship. I always hold this to be of extreme importance." I continue by telling the client how important it is to maintain very clear boundaries in the therapeutic relationship, and that those boundaries continue even after therapy. It is important that these comments be made in an off-hand casual manner. Another point that I make with my clients is that, even after therapy finishes, if in the future my client wishes to return to work on the same problem further, or another problem, that is quite OK. By clearly defining the therapeutic relationship in this way, and by couching it among other aspects of therapy, it can be possible for the client to understand that no relationship beyond the therapeutic relationship is possible, thus allowing therapy to continue unimpeded.

It is probable that even a presentation such as this, at least at some level, indicates to the client that the counselor has an understanding of the client's feelings, but within such a presentation the client's self-respect can be maintained.

What if the counselor develops an emotional attachment to the client? Like anyone else, counselors are human. If the counselor develops an emotional attachment to the client this should not be mentioned. As long as it does not interfere with therapy, therapy can continue. But, if the counselor's emotional attachment to the client interferes with therapy, it is appropriate to refer the client to another counselor. It is considered inappropriate for the counselor to disclose to the client why this referral is required, as this would place upon the client an inappropriate emotional burden. When making the referral, the counselor should make sure the client understands that it is not because of the client that the referral must be made. Sometimes a loving lie is more appropriate than the truth. During World War II when the Gestapo asked, "Are there any Jews upstairs?", the loving lie was to say, "No." When the client wonders, "Why do you want to refer me?", the loving lie is to say something like, "I have personal issues that in no way have anything to do with you, but that require me to occasionally refer clients. I'm working on those issues. I hope you can understand."

Another aspect of maintaining boundaries in counseling relates to philosophical, religious, political, and social differences. Often clients view the world in a different manner than the counselor. Unless clients are hurting themselves or someone else, or if clients are allowing themselves to be hurt by someone else, the counselor should attempt to work within the client's worldview. Religion and politics have a place outside the counseling office, but the counselor should not use the powerful role of therapist as a soapbox to forward a personal belief structure. If a counselor feels so strongly about a belief structure that he or she is unable to leave it outside counseling, then all that counselor's clients should be made aware of the type of counseling that will be offered prior to the first session. Christian counseling, feminist counseling, and other types of counseling that offer teaching a counselor-held belief structure can be offered to those who seek it when they are informed from the onset. Some clients actively seek counselors with particular belief structures. But, generally, clients should be able to have multicultural, multisocial perspectives without feeling pushed or pulled by the person they sought out for counseling.

What about accidentally meeting the client in the supermarket? What is the appropriate way to handle this situation? A number of years ago, and still today in some cultures, going to a counselor was a badge of dishonor. You must be crazy if you have to see a counselor—that was a prevailing idea. Thankfully, this is no longer the prevailing idea. Often individuals talk about their therapy and counselor openly and with just about anyone. Still, there are those who prefer to maintain secrecy about visiting a counselor. This is their right. Because of this, when accidentally meeting a client outside of therapy it should be the client who sets the level of recognition.

The counselor can match the level of recognition set by the client. If the client chooses to walk by and not speak, it is best if the counselor does the same. If the client chooses to speak openly, or even to say a few words then the counselor can respond in a similarly friendly fashion.

Dual relationships

One of the trickiest and fuzziest aspects of ethics and counseling is that of dual relationships. It is generally considered inappropriate to have any relationship with the client other than the therapeutic relationship. It is further generally considered inappropriate to take on a client where there has been any significant relationship with that individual, or where there is future promise for a significant relationship with that person. For example, it would be inappropriate for a university lecturer to take on the client who will likely be a student in that lecturer's class. It would not be appropriate for the person who has disclosed their innermost thoughts and fears to have to sit in a class with their counselor, or ex-counselor, looking at them from the front of the room.

As with all aspects of ethics, these considerations are sometimes blurred. For example, would it be inappropriate for a counselor to provide a one-session quit-smoking hypnosis technique to someone who is known? If the technique contains no aspects of personal disclosure and is confined to the stopping of smoking then this would probably be OK.

What about the client who lives in a small rural town, who is unable to travel to another city for counseling, and who knows all the counselors in the town? Is this client to be deprived of therapy because of the rural logistics? Probably not. Here, as in all ethical dilemmas, the decision of the counselor should be based on the context of the issue. The rights of the client should be respected, and the decision that is made should not be based on the personal or business needs of the counselor.

An interesting question in relation to dual relationships is, "Is it possible for a client and a counselor to have any type of relationship other then the professional client–counselor relationship after the conclusion of therapy?" Some therapists say no. Some therapists say, "As long as the client understands that no therapeutic relationship can again be entered into, then it is OK to have a friendship with an ex-client." Here again, context needs to be considered. If the therapeutic relationship has been one in which the client looked upon the therapist as a "guru", then any attempt at a friendship after therapy would probably be unethical. But, if the client, for example, was a counselor themselves and saw their counselor as an equal professional (less power imbalance) providing facilitation for their growth, then it may be ethical for the two to have a friendship after the conclusion of therapy.

In some legislative districts laws dictate a specified length of time before sexual activity can occur between an ex-counselor and a client. While these laws are understandable, and preferred, it is strange to imagine two people sitting watching their watches to see when their two-year deferment has finished. These types of relationships, while they are known to occur, should be discouraged. Obviously, if during therapy the counselor finds it impossible to view the client in a professional way, the client should be referred, as described in the section above, to another counselor without troubling the client with the issues of the counselor.

Duty of care

Duty of care refers to the professional responsibility that the counselor has toward the client. For example, it would be unethical for a counselor untrained in dissociative-identity disorder to offer therapy to a client with multiple personalities. It would be ethical to refer this client to a counselor trained in, and able to attend to, this disorder.

The writing of appropriate case notes also falls within duty of care, as does the appropriate keeping of these notes. In other words, clear and legible notes should be kept for each session that a client is seen, and those notes should be kept in such a way that ensures that no other person will have access to them. Case notes should therefore always be kept under lock and key.

An aspect of keeping case notes that is often not considered is, "What will happen with the notes upon the death of the counselor?" Counselors should make provision for the appropriate storage or disposal of their client case notes should something unforeseen happen to the counselor. An excellent way to make such a provision is for co-supervisors to share keys with the understanding that the clients and clients' notes of each would become the responsibility of the other in the case of unforeseen circumstances.

Co-supervision itself is an aspect of duty of care. It is difficult, if not impossible, to have a caseload of clients and do justice to each client without being able to discuss cases with a respected colleague. At the conclusion of supervision training, co-supervision should be seriously considered. Co-supervision offers the counselor an ability to debrief with a respected colleague, and an ability to gain insight into challenging cases.

Chapter 2
Theoretical Orientation

All counseling is based on some theoretical orientation. This is the case even if the counselor is unaware of the orientation he or she is using. Many counselors base their work on a person-centered orientation developed by Carl Rogers. This orientation holds that clients have a natural tendency to be self-healing and it is the counselor's role to be a good listener. Person-centered theorists contend that, by listening and reflecting in an understanding and respectful way to what the client says, they will ensure that the client will gain a better understanding of his or her concerns and will naturally become more mentally healthy.

Some counselors hold a cognitive behavioral orientation. These counselors look more to define the problem and educate or train the client into new coping skills to obtain a positive outcome. Within this orientation the counselor is generally not interested in working within a historical context. Problems are seen to stem from either faulty thinking patterns, or from behavioral learning that needs to be supplanted with new learning.

The claim that this theoretical orientation is "preferred" because of research evidence is problematic, due to the amplified number of studies being conducted upon this orientation and the alpha* probability that at least 5 percent of these studies will show positive results merely by chance.

It is very important to have a theoretical orientation that can act as a basis for problem solving with clients. Without such an orientation, it is easy for a counselor to get lost in the client's problem and not know which way to go. The theoretical orientation lays the groundwork for assessing clients' problems and determining appropriate solutions. This section will briefly present a theoretical orientation of the personality and offer some justification for the

---

* At an alpha of .05, random data in 100 studies will demonstrate five significant results merely due to chance, and it is generally only the significant results that are published. The journal reader sees five studies indicating that cognitive behavioral therapy (CBT) provides positive results with a particular problem and is unaware of the original number of studies where this result was not produced. This is not the fault of the researchers, but the exorbitant number of CBT studies compared with the number of studies from other orientations, and the problem that significant results are the ones that are published, make it difficult to determine the relative value of various orientations.

validity of this orientation. My own experience with this orientation and the feedback received from others who have adopted it has been extremely positive. Clients, also, easily understand the theory and report appreciation for having the more personal insights that it offers.

The counseling techniques presented in this book are based on a different theoretical orientation than that of person-centered or cognitive behavioral therapy (CBT). The orientation presented here is grounded in ego-state theory. Ego-state theorists hold that the personality is made up of different parts: for example, one may hear comments such as, "Part of me wants to continue in school; part of me wants to quit" or "Part of me has to check the locks over and over, and part of me hates that part." It is important to understand what ego states are, and by gaining these understandings the counselor will be able to devise appropriate interventions when new problems arise.

According to ego-state theory, the personality is not a homogeneous whole, but is a group of parts that the individual moves into and out of throughout the day. The power of using an ego-state orientation in counseling is that the counselor can focus work on the particular part of the personality with the problem. Gaining access to "where the problem is" is an excellent method of facilitating change where it needs to happen. Too often, clients talk intellectually about a problem to a therapist. An intellectual ego state discusses a problem that another, fragile, ego state experiences. The fragile part of the client that has the problem is not attended to directly, and the course of therapy is extended. The following sections will describe ego states and ego-state personality theory. The interventions provided in this book will be based on and underpinned by an ego-state theoretical orientation.

Ego states

My ego is my "me-ness", what I think of as me. When I think of who I am and point my finger to myself I am pointing at my ego. This is my sense of "me". (It is interesting that when most people point at themselves and think, "me" they point at the top center of their chest.) The state that I am in at the time when I am pointing is one of my ego states. If I am angry at a friend and I say to that friend, "I hate you, I don't like you, I don't ever want to see you again," I am speaking from a state that is angry. I am speaking from an anger state, and because I have my ego in that state, it feels like me, therefore I keep using the word I, I, I. Later, if I am in a different state that appreciates my friend I may think and say things like, "I don't know why I said those things.

You are my best friend. I will always like you." Here again, while I am in the state that appreciates the friendship my experience is, "This is me, this is my ego." This is an example of two separate "ego states".

We all have a number of ego states. When someone says, "I don't like that part of me," what they are really saying is that one of their states (the one that is talking) does not like another state. When an obsessive-compulsive individual checks locks again and again, and then later earnestly wishes that such checking did not occur, two separate ego states are obvious. When that person is checking locks the ego present is, "I have to check, I have to check." And, when that person wishes he or she did not check locks the ego again is present in a different state: "I really wish I didn't do that." Sometimes one state wants to rest and watch TV and be a couch potato, and another state wants work to be done. All individuals have different ego states, and they switch between them throughout the day.

It is powerful to use ego states in counseling. It is important for the counselor to be able to talk to the ego state that has the problem, not to an intellectual ego state that is aware of the problem and can talk about it, but has little power to change it. Learning about and working with ego states allows the counselor to recognize the problem, gain access to the appropriate states, and work to resolve the problem. Often, ego states do not get along, and this can cause an unsettled internal dissonance. Some ego states are assertive and some ego states are passive. Counselors working with a knowledge of ego states can assist clients to bring their resources to their needs, to use assertive states when they are most appropriate and other states when they are best to fill the needs of the client.

The following sections will outline ego states, where they come from, and ego-state personality theory. It is important to review these sections thoroughly in order to apply the techniques presented in this book. It is imperative to have a good understanding of the personality from an ego-state perspective to work most successfully with this therapeutic approach.

Development of ego-state therapy

Paul Federn, a contemporary of Freud, was the first to write about ego states. Federn theorized that the personality was composed of a group of parts he called ego states, and while an individual is experiencing and acting from one of those parts that part has ego identity. That is, when a person is in a compassionate state he or she will think, "I feel compassionate toward others," and when that same person is in a rejecting state the thought might be, "I don't trust or like others." The ego, the I, is experienced in each state.

While Federn (1952) defined and theorized about ego states, he did not build a therapy using this theory of personality. Federn practiced therapy as a psychoanalyst, in line with the prevailing therapeutic orientation of his day.

In order to complete training as a psychoanalyst, an Italian, Eloardo Weiss (1957), underwent psychoanalysis with Paul Federn. During this process, Federn shared his views of personality with Weiss. Weiss, likewise, later psychoanalyzed the American, John Watkins, so he could complete his training as a psychoanalyst. When John Watkins learned about ego states from Weiss, the work he had been doing as a therapist gained an understandable therapeutic theoretical underpinning (Watkins and Watkins, 1997).

John G. Watkins had used hypnosis as chief psychologist of the Welsh Convalescent Centre with returning soldiers from World War II (Watkins, 1949). He had learned that by hypnotizing soldiers with psychosomatic symptoms, he could bring forth traumatized states. When this trauma was alleviated the psychosomatic symptoms would most commonly disappear. He recognized the switching of states in his clients but at that stage did not have a theoretical understanding that enabled him to understand his observations. It would be later that he and Helen, his future wife, would lay the groundwork for ego-state therapy.

In the mid-1970s, Hilgard and Hilgard defined hidden observers (1975). They had found while doing experiments on hypnotic deafness and hypnotic analgesia that, while the conscious personality indicated no awareness of sound when the participant achieved hypnotic deafness, a subpersonality could respond to sound using finger signals. The same response was evident in relationship to pain. Participants who reported no conscious feeling of pain when a hand and arm were submerged in ice water responded with finger signals that signified that some unconscious part did indeed feel the pain.

John Watkins recognized Hilgard's hidden observers to be what he, Weiss, and Federn called ego states. Watkins and Watkins (1990) replicated the Hilgards' experiments using hypnosis, and spoke directly with the subpersonalities that had an awareness beyond that of the conscious state. Participants in both the Hilgards' and the Watkinses' experiments were not multiple-personality individuals who suffered from dissociative-identity disorder (DID). In the Watkinses' experiments, participants were previous clients of Helen Watkins, John's wife. The Watkinses (1990) had wondered if previously discovered ego states (during Helen's work with the subjects when they were her clients) would emerge as "hidden observers" responding to hearing and feeling when the conscious state of the participant was hypnotically deaf or hypnotically anaesthetized. This was indeed the case. Ego states that Helen had mapped and named were able to respond as hearing states when the participant was hypnotically deaf, and were able to respond as states that experienced pain when the participant was hypnotically anaesthetized.

Beginning in the mid-1970s, John and Helen Watkins published on ego-state therapy numerous journal articles, book chapters, and, in 1997, the book, *Ego States: Theory and Therapy*. They can be considered the father and mother of ego-state therapy.

A number of other authors have published on ego-state techniques and theory, in the form of both journal articles and books. Among those authors who have greatly contributed to our understanding of ego states are Maggie Phillips, Clare Frederick, Shirley McNeal, Moshe Torem, Waltermade Hartman, George Fraser, and Michael Gainer. In 2003, the First World Congress on Ego-State Therapy was held in Bad Orb, near Frankfurt; attendance numbered in the hundreds. Also in that year the book *Ego State Therapy* (Emmerson, 2003) was published.

Prior to the current book, other than the presentation of a small number of journal articles, publication on ego-state therapy has related to its use in combination with hypnosis. Through teaching graduate counseling students ego-state techniques without hypnosis, it became clear to this author that the power of understanding ego-state theory and working with ego states makes this approach more powerful than any therapeutic approach I have taught. Feedback I have received from graduate students indicates they have little difficulty learning and using ego-state counseling techniques (without the use of hypnosis). Indeed, some individuals trained in hypnosis preferred to use ego-state techniques without using hypnosis, reporting that it brings excellent outcomes.

It is hoped that this book will, along with other works, bring the power of ego-state techniques to general counseling therapeutic practice. This book is meant to provide an avenue for counselors and psychologists who have not been trained in hypnosis to attain the effectiveness of ego-state techniques for their clients.

Ego-state personality theory

Ego-state personality theory is based on the concept that the personality is not one homogeneous whole, but is composed of a number of sections or parts. These parts are termed ego states because, when a state is out, or conscious, we identify that part of us as "me". That is, we consistently have ego identification with the conscious state. There is an underlying awareness of our different parts, as evidenced by our language. Statements such as the following are illustrations of this:

- I don't like that part of me.
- Part of me wants to do one thing and another part wants to do something else.
- There is part of me that loves him.
- I just can't find peace within myself.
- It's like having two voices in my head, each telling me a different thing.

Freud saw the personality as divided into three parts: the id, ego, and superego. Jung, also, saw the personality as compartmentalized, both in his views on archetypes (such as the mother archetype, the mana, the shadow, and the persona) and in his construction of the animus and anima (the male and female parts). Therapists who use transactional analysis see the personality as being composed of five parts (two parent parts, the adult part, and two child parts). These five personality parts are termed *ego states* by transactional analysts, and every person is viewed as having the same five parts.

While the terminology appears similar, ego-state theorists pose a more dynamic view of the personality. Individuals are seen to have a multiplicity of parts, specific to the person. No two individuals are seen as having the same ego states structured in the same fashion.

The origin of ego states

Ego states form during the development of the personality. Especially during early years, but even later in life the brain is a dynamic changing organ. It is primarily during the development of the brain in the early years that ego states form. An ego state is a neural pathway of dendrite and axon connections and trained by recurring synaptic firings. It is created through training repetition.

Animal studies have made it clear that the brain grows according to stimulation. The brains of animals that have been raised in a deprived environment weigh less than the brains of animals that have been raised in an active environment. Axon and dendrite growth, as well as the development of synaptic connections, varies according to both the amount of stimulation and the type of stimulation. Schrott (1997) overviewed a number of studies, both animal and human, that indicate that the brain develops "profoundly" in relation to the stimulation it receives.

Muir and Mitchell (1973) demonstrated how the brains of kittens develop in early life in relation to vision. During the first five months of life the vision of kittens was confined to contours of a single orientation (using special lenses), either vertical or horizontal. Kittens that were raised where they could view a vertical orientation of their surroundings during their first five months were later less able to see horizontal shapes, and kittens that were raised where they could view a horizontal orientation of their surroundings during their first months were later less able to see vertical shapes. Numerous other animal studies confirm that the brain develops according to the particular type of stimulation it receives (Wilkinson and McGill, 1995; Blakemore and Price, 1987; Parfitt et al., 2004; Wark, and Peck, 1982; Buisseret, Gary-Bobo, and Imbert, 1982).

Not only do brains grow according to stimulation, but existing synapses fire more easily with repetitive practice. The first time something is attempted, whether it is a physical activity or mental learning task, ability is normally low, but with repetition the same activity or task may become easy and commonplace (Wolpaw, 2001).

Ego-state personality theory is based on the evidence that the brain is formed and is trained through repetition. During early childhood, if the child is nurturing to a parent and receives positive feedback for this nurturing behavior, the child may return over and over again to this nurturing behavior to receive the positive feedback. This repetition of nurturance can create a nurturing ego state, that is, a neural pathway made by axon and dendrite connections and trained synaptic firing that may be activated in the future when the person wants positive feedback. Physiological brain growth and training from repeated practice creates this neural pathway, this ego state.

If, in a particular family, a child wants attention and tells a joke, then gets positive feedback, a subconscious message to that child may be, "If I need attention, doing something funny may help." If that child, over and over again, tends to get positive feedback from telling jokes and doing funny things when attention is wanted, that child may develop a "joking" ego state.

17

Later in life, when that child or adult needs attention, he or she may tell a joke or do something funny, because the joking ego state is activated. But suppose a child, in a different family, wants attention and tells a joke, and this child is told, "Be quiet and stop being silly." If this happens enough where no repetition of joking is established, then this child will not develop the joking ego state.

If the child learns, in a family where there is a lot of yelling and screaming, that withdrawing and being quiet results in "keeping out of trouble", and if this withdrawing occurs repetitively to the benefit of the child, then a withdrawing ego state may develop. In childhood, and later in life, when this person is confronted with anger or loudness, this withdrawing ego state may emerge, giving the person the feelings of being frightened and having to be quiet.

Ego states, therefore, are theorized to be physiological. They are a result of brain development. They are a result of axon and dendrite development early in life, of dendrite development later in life, and of the synaptic training learned through repetition at any time in life. They become a part of the personality. Each person has an undetermined number of ego-state neural pathways, numbering at least in double digits. Ego states can be divided roughly into two types, *surface* (used often) and *underlying* (rarely used), and the state from which a person is currently experiencing life is called the *executive state*. The next two sections will further define these basic and central terms.

The executive state

When an ego state is out it is said to be *executive*. When the child with the joking ego state is in the process of joking, the joking ego state is executive. When the person with the withdrawing ego state is feeling and experiencing withdrawal, the withdrawing ego state is executive. At any time a person says "I", the "I" refers to the executive ego state, and other ego states at that time are nonexecutive. Nonexecutive states may be observing the interaction the executive state is experiencing, or if they are more underlying they may be unaware of this interaction. The person who finds no memory of having driven for the past ten minutes has changed executive ego states, and the one that has just become executive was not observing the interactions of the state that was just previously executive. The person who changes ego states from a relaxed state that studied for a test to a more stressed state that takes the test is switching the executive to a state that has some level of communication with a state previously in the executive. Therefore, an amount of memory will be available for testing, but not as much as would be available if the person were to take the test in the ego state that studied for the test.

Surface and underlying states

The personality is composed of a number of ego states, some that are executive often, while others may not have been executive for many years. The ego states that are often executive are called surface states, while those states that are rarely executive are called underlying states. An individual may be in one surface ego state while driving to work, and in another surface ego state while at work. Yet another surface ego state may be executive when that person reads a book, or watches television at home.

Ego states have varying levels of communication (or information transfer) between themselves. Surface states normally communicate and share information easily. What a person says while in a reactive, angry ego state will probably be remembered when that person is in a more reflective and calm ego state.

It is possible for some ego states to have poor communication between them. Occasionally, a person may have read a couple of pages, and then upon switching states may have no memory of what was just read. Ego states that have poor communication are said to be more *dissociated* from each other.

Underlying states include child states that have stopped coming to the executive. When a person has little memory of events during a time period of childhood, the ego states that were being used most during that period have become underlying states. The neural pathways that form them are still there, but are rarely activated. A visit to a childhood home may bring a child state to the executive that has been underlying for a number of years. Underlying states may have current roles, even though they rarely come to the executive. Sometimes these states take on bottled anger or frustration. They can also be responsible for some physical symptoms, such as migraine headache (Emmerson and Farmer, 1996).

Ego states and alters

Dissociative-identity disorder (DID), or multiple-personality syndrome as it is commonly known, is the result of the communication between ego states breaking down. This normally occurs when, during relatively early childhood, severe and chronic abuse is experienced. As a subconscious coping mechanism, the child learns over time to forget what happened the night before. Over many months, or years, this training to break the communication between the ego states can be successful, thus transforming ego states into alters. Alters are the subpersonalities the person experiences who is suffering from DID. While there may be groups of alters that can share communication, alters generally communicate poorly, if at all. Adults with multiple-personality syndrome may have no memory of what they did all morning. They may meet someone who talks openly about their exploits on Friday night together, and they may have no memory of ever having seen this person. The communication between at least some of their parts has been broken. That is, the synaptic connections that had connected the ego states, through trained underuse, have stopped firing. All individuals have some underlying ego states that communicate poorly, both with other underlying states and with surface states, but the persons with DID have surface states that communicate poorly with each other.

The unconscious

The nonclinical individual will have underlying ego states that do not communicate with the surface states. This is why we do not have ready access to the full range of childhood memories. This is why the unconscious exists. Unlike Freud's view of a large and mysterious unconscious, ego-state theorists see the unconscious as merely underlying ego states that are not either currently in the executive or currently communicating with the conscious (executive) state. The unconscious can be brought to the conscious by activating underlying ego states one at a time, bringing them to the executive.

The individual who, while walking down the street, smells something that brings back a flood of childhood memories has activated an underlying ego state. This childhood ego state may not have been in the executive for a number of years. The individual who is regressed during hypnosis to an earlier age has brought to the executive an underlying ego state.

Introjects

While ego states are physiological neural pathways created over time, introjects are the internalized impressions of other people as they were perceived at a given point in time. A client will have an introject (internalized impression) of each current friend, will have an introject of a parent or guardian from when the client was five years old, and will have a different introject of that same person as he or she is perceived in today's life (if currently living).

A client can even have an introject of an imagined person who has not been met.

Ego states and introjects are very different, although they share some commonalities. The client experiences the world from an ego state, not from an introject, although an introject may be role-played by the client and the client can get an impression of the feelings of an introject while role-playing that introject. Ego states cannot be eliminated since they are a physiological part of the client, but the introject of a perpetrator can be asked to leave. An ego state can gain resolution from pain and empowerment, but it cannot leave.

Each introject is an internalized, learned impression. An ego state of the client can speak directly to an introject (imagined in an empty chair or standing across the room). For example, while a child ego state of the client that was abused is in the executive, that state can demand that the introject of a sexual perpetrator leave (a remembered or imagined setting). This rising above the previously held fear is empowering and therapeutic, when the client ultimately overcomes a fear that has been maintained since childhood of an introject (internalized impression).

Introjects can be impressions of loving individuals the client knows or has known during different points in life, and these introjects can be positive resources in counseling. A client may have a feared introject and a loving introject of the same person. One ego state of the client may have experienced trauma from the individual, while another ego state may love and appreciate the same person. This is evident when considering a person who currently both loves and fears another person, for example, a partner or child.

In Freudian terminology, transference is when the personification of the previously known introject is transferred to and upon the therapist. Ego-state therapy and personality theory focus directly upon surface and underlying ego states, and introjects. Therefore, transference is not considered an issue. Ego states are given an opportunity to express directly, and the introjects the client holds are directly explored. Also, because ego-state therapy is brief, and the ego-state therapist makes no concerted attempt to hide self, only minimal transference develops.

Later development of ego states

Most ego states develop in early childhood, as the brain is rapidly developing. All ego states develop to satisfy some need. Ego states may develop later in life, although the repetition of behavior takes longer. Later development is rare. Most surface states are ego states that developed in early childhood and have been used rather consistently since that time. These states can evolve and mature through years of use. Childhood states that have been executive little since childhood (underlying states) tend to talk and act more like children (i.e. the adult may talk and act like a child when one of these states is executive). Some childhood states become executive only rarely: for example, to play, to cry, to withdraw, or to hug.

It is common for individuals to develop new ego states during sustained periods when there is no current state capable of coping. Adolescence is the time that new ego states are often developed, given the trials of this period. In adulthood, the macho man who loses his wife in childbirth may develop a nurturing ego state he has not previously had, while bringing up the child. It is hypothesized that a combination of new dendrite growth, new synaptic connections, and the training of existing synaptic connections facilitates this new neural pathway in its development.

Pathology and ego states

Ego states may be normal functioning, which is nonpathological, or they may be pathological, that is vaded, retro-functioning, or conflicted.

Normal functioning states function with positive roles to the benefit of other states and the person. It is the goal of therapy for all states to become normal functioning.

Vaded ego states are overcome by negative experience to the point where they can no longer conduct their role. These states may interfere with the life of the individual when they come to the executive. If an ego state experiences a trauma, and is not able to receive some type of crisis intervention after the trauma (that is, talking with someone who understands, being able to more fully express, and gaining some perspective on the event), then that ego state becomes vaded, and while vaded, each time it comes to the executive that individual will re-experience negative emotions associated with the trauma. The brain has a need for closure. If a person has difficulty remembering the name of the friend, a restless uneasiness may be experienced until that name is acquired. In the same way, when a trauma has been experienced without closure, the experience of the trauma dominates the feelings of the state that was executive during that trauma until closure is realized. Therefore, when a current life situation stimulates an ego state to the executive that has not experienced closure from a trauma, a neurotic response will occur. This is what Freud called a *situational neurosis*. In order for the neurotic symptomology to cease, the ego state that experienced the trauma may be brought to the executive so that the traumatic feelings can be resolved. Trauma resolution can free a vaded ego state so it can resume its normal role and cease causing neurotic reactions.

Retro-functioning ego states exhibit old roles that are opposed to other states or opposed to the benefit of the person. States that manifest uncontrolled anger, pathological lying, or psychosomatic symptoms are examples. Ego-state negotiation can facilitate a retro-functioning state to take on positive roles. It is possible for a state to be both retro-functioning and vaded, and when this is the case the state will also benefit from trauma resolution.

Conflicted ego states have a positive role but are uncooperative internally. A state that wants to work and a state that wants to rest may be conflicted. The statement, "He is at war with himself" illustrates a person who has ego states that are conflicted, that do not get along. It is not unusual for a person to make the statement, "I hate myself when I do that." Further examples include one ego state of a person very much wanting to stop smoking, while another ego state very much enjoys smoking. Ego states may disagree on "working and leisure", on "eating and dieting", on "assertiveness and passiveness", and on a multiplicity of other dimensions. This internal struggle of conflicted states may become psychologically debilitating. Obsessive-compulsive disorder is an example of where warring conflicted states reflect pathology. Ego-state negotiation that results in conflicted states learning the value of each and learning to compromise and communicate can facilitate conflicted states to become normal functioning. If a conflicted state is vaded it will also benefit from trauma resolution. It is possible for a state to be conflicted, retro-functioning and vaded.

Malevolent ego states

Individuals sometimes hurt themselves and others. They are sometimes at war within themselves. Ego states that appear angry and malevolent sometimes exist within a personality. One example of how a malevolent ego state might develop is that of the child raised in a violent home, who may develop a fighting, violent state for protection. This fighting, violent state is a coping mechanism for a difficult environment. Later, this fighting and violent state may no longer be needed to cope on a daily basis, but may still know only the role of fighting and violence. It can be a malevolent ego state, and it may be violent against other states, or violent against other people.

Emmerson and Farmer (1996) reported a malevolent ego state in their study on menstrual migraine. This aggressive state, which had started as a protector for the child, disliked another ego state of the woman that was emotional and "soppy". In order to stop the emotionality of the woman, the malevolent state would cause her to have migraine headaches when the "soppy" ego state came to the executive. A negotiation with the malevolent state and others resulted in a fivefold decrease in the number of migraines. Malevolent ego states may cause self-harming behavior or rude behavior that, on the surface, appears difficult to understand.

Malevolent ego states are retro-functioning, in that they have roles that are opposed to other states or opposed to the benefit of the person. They may also be vaded. They are almost always conflicted with other states.

Ego states and physiology

When individuals who have multiple-personality syndrome change personalities, or alters, there is often a clearly defined physiological change. This underlines the connection between mind and body. It is also true that, when individuals change ego states, physiology can change.

It is not unusual for an individual to feel ill and to experience low levels of energy, then to feel a real shift in energy levels and wellness following a change in ego states brought about by an opportunity to play a sport, or even to read a good book. When ego states are switched back to the state that had previously felt ill, the same feeling of illness and low energy levels may be again experienced.

Michael Gainer (1993) reported that a woman suffering from reflex sympathetic dystrophy (a degenerative muscle illness that normally has a very poor prognosis for improvement) did not experience symptoms of this disease while in three of her ego states. While in other ego states, she had a range of severe symptoms. Gainer, using ego-state therapy, was able to find a connection between the illness and a traumatized ego state. The patient was able to become free of all symptoms across her states when the childhood trauma was resolved.

A time-series study by Emmerson and Farmer (1996) describes an ego-state intervention that facilitated the reduction of average migraine days per month from 12.2 to 2.5 in a sample of women who were chronic sufferers of menstrual migraine. The participants in this study also demonstrated significant reductions in depression and anger.

Maggie Phillips (1995) discussed the use of ego-state therapy for somatic symptoms. She concluded in her article that uncovering memories held by childhood ego states, and working with those states, can have a beneficial effect on physiology.

Overview of ego-state personality theory

The personality is composed of a number of parts, called ego states. Ego states are physiological neural pathways of axon and dendrite synaptic connections that are formed through the repeated practice of useful coping techniques. Each ego state has its own function and abilities, according to the practice that has formed it. When any one of these ego states is in the executive, that executive state is the conscious state invested with ego. States that are not in the executive at any one time are part of the amalgam of the unconscious. Bringing one of these underlying ego states to the executive brings underlying memories to the conscious. The individual is the composite of all of his or her ego states. A metaphor for the personality and its ego states is a country that has a number of state governments. Each state is a part of the country, and, while the states of the country differ, they combine to form the nature of the country as a whole.

For an individual, there is no one ego state that is that person, although some states may be executive more than others. While an individual is conscious, life is always being experienced from an executive ego state. There will be other surface states aware of the experience of the executive state, and there will be underlying states that are unaware of the current experience. The occasional ability of the hypnotized subject to have partial amnesia after a hypnosis session demonstrates the lack of communication among some underlying states and surface states. One of the ego states that was executive during hypnosis did not communicate with the surface states.

Ego states differ and they vary in how they experience the executive. While one state may be intellectual and demonstrate almost no emotion, another state may be reactionary and emotionally laden. While one state may be able to focus intensely on study and work, another state may have skills in relaxation and leisure. While one state may be fragile and able to greatly appreciate safe nurturance, another state may be crusty or assertive.

Ego states have the ability, with help, to evolve and to alter the experience and feeling of trauma to the experience of security and safety. Ego states have the ability to take on new and different roles. When an individual learns his or her states, there can also be an ability to select the preferred state to match a specific need: for example, an assertive state for expression, a fragile state to receive love, an intellectual state for study and exams, or a light-hearted state for social interaction. Ego-state counseling techniques facilitate the resolution of internal trauma, the resolution of internal conflict between states, and the ability of the client to better understand the array of useful states that are available and the best times those states may be used.

Ego-state theory and techniques in the context of other psychotherapies

Many clients believe that when they go to see a counselor or psychologist they will receive generally the same type of therapeutic techniques regardless of whom they see. Any student of psychology realizes that this is not the case. Major differences exist between both the theories and techniques of various psychotherapeutic approaches. This section will briefly overview major psychotherapeutic approaches and will place the techniques presented in this book in the context of those approaches.

Three main streams exist in psychological counseling: (1) psychodynamic; (2) cognitive behavioral; and (3) phenomenological (sometimes called humanist).

The psychodynamic stream

The psychodynamic stream, in large part, derives from the work of Sigmund Freud. Freud believed that the mind was composed of the conscious and the unconscious. A central theme of psychodynamic psychotherapies is the belief that it is important to bring information from the unconscious to the conscious in order to help the client. According to Freud, neurotic responses result from unresolved issues of the past. A neurotic response is a response that is inconsistent with the current situation. The individual who becomes extremely angry when criticized is exhibiting a neurotic response. Freud thought that bringing the unconscious to the conscious was beneficial in extinguishing neurotic responses. He experimented with hypnosis as a means of gaining access to the unconscious, but Freud was a poor hypnotist and the development of hypnotic therapy at his time provided him with little instruction. Therefore, he came to the conclusion that hypnosis worked with too few clients to be beneficial.

Freud developed a process of using free association, dream interpretation, transference, the breaking down of transference, and interpretation to assist clients in moving information from the unconscious to the conscious so that they could become aware of why they had neurotic responses. It was felt that this awareness would help extinguish the neurotic responses. Psychoanalysts were trained to interpret covert information so they could explain to the client why neurotic responses occurred. Clients who did not agree with the interpretations of the psychoanalysts were sometimes said to be in denial. In order to be able to make clear and unbiased interpretations, psychoanalysts were encouraged to finish a course of psychoanalysis themselves as clients so that their own unresolved neuroses would not blur their interpretations.

The process of psychoanalysis included the therapist's remaining a blank slate to the client so that the client could say absolutely anything without fear of being found out by someone they knew, and to enhance transference. It was felt that, by investigating the thoughts and feelings the client transferred onto the therapist, important information could be revealed about the client. Had the therapist been personable and self-revealing, the process of transference would have been confounded.

Carl Jung, Alfred Adler, and others added their own theories and therapeutic interventions into the psychodynamic stream. Each of these underlined the importance of the unconscious, and movement of information from the unconscious to the conscious for the benefit of the client.

Ego-state theory accepts Freud's contention that early traumas can cause neurotic reactions later in life. Unlike Freud's contention that the unconscious is vast and mysterious, ego-state theory holds that the unconscious is merely ego states that are not currently in the executive (i.e. out). Unconscious material may be retrieved by facilitating an underlying ego state to come out into the executive, bringing with it its memories.

Ego-state techniques differ vastly from Freud's techniques. There is no emphasis for the therapist to remain a blank slate to the client because transference is not considered important. Because ego-state therapeutic techniques work quickly with most clients, therapy does not continue long enough for transference to become an issue. Therefore, ego-state therapists may be personable and, if it is felt it would be beneficial to the client, self-revealing.

A further major difference between most psychodynamic psychotherapy and ego-state therapy is that ego-state therapists do not interpret to the client. It is contended that the therapist's interpretation to a client would most usually be wrong, and even if correct would often not be accepted. During ego-state therapy, the client gains insights into the cause of neurotic responses through experiencing the emotion of those responses in therapy, and then bridging to the original cause of those emotions. Therefore, neither the therapist nor the client needs to interpret why a response occurs.

Ego-state therapy fits most closely in the psychodynamic stream of psychotherapies because it involves a process of moving information from the unconscious to the conscious, even though ego-state therapists work with clients in a more personable, noninterpreting fashion more often associated with phenomenologists.

The cognitive behavioral stream

Cognitive behaviorists, unlike psychodynamic psychotherapists, believe that looking into the past is of little value. Cognitive therapists believe that the manner in which people think results in their feelings and actions. They contend that, because two people can be exposed to the same event and react to it differently, the difference must be in how they interpret the event. Therefore, emphasis is put on altering the interpretation that clients have of events in order to affect their emotional reaction and behavioral response.

Behavioral therapists believe that psychological problems are the result of faulty learning, through either classical conditioning or operant conditioning. They contend that both the thought responses and emotional responses of clients are the result of behaviors, and that behaviors are the result of conditioning. Therefore, they emphasize homework assignments given to clients that will provide new learning opportunities, and thus enable clients to respond in a preferred emotional fashion to life events.

Many therapists work both with cognitive reframing and behavioral homework such as systematic desensitization. This CBT type of therapy does not attempt to resolve issues from the past, but provides clients with coping skills to deal better with psychotherapeutic issues. The focus of these therapies is surface-based rather than based on underlying, covert, unconscious psychological processes.

While ego-state therapists see value in some cognitive behavioral interventions for surface-based issues such as childhood tantrums or difficulty in responding to a demanding employer, their surface-based techniques are viewed as inadequate to properly help clients whose problems stem from unresolved trauma. A short case illustration can clarify this point.

Mary (pseudonym) presented with the problem of having never been able to enjoy amorous behavior with a partner. Each time her partner either touched her in a sexual fashion or gave her compliments that could be interpreted as sexual, Mary would become extremely distressed and would want to get away from him. She presented as loving her partner, and wanting to be able to have caring, intimate relations with him, of the types her friends described. Ego-state techniques were used to assist Mary in experiencing in the counseling room the negative emotions she had when her partner complimented her on her looks. A bridging technique (which will be explained later) was used to determine the traumatic incident associated with Mary's neurotic response of having a negative emotional reaction to her partner's compliments. The bridging technique took Mary to a frightening sexual incident that she experienced with two older male cousins when she was a little girl. The frightened ego state came into the executive, and this frightened-little-girl ego state was encouraged to express directly her feelings to her cousins (introjects) as she remembered them at the time (expression was in the counseling room with Mary imagining her young cousins there, as she had her eyes closed). The little-girl ego state rose above her fear to express these feelings, and was later congratulated and further empowered by more understanding from one of Mary's adult, nurturing states. (These techniques are presented later.) Mary, free from the fear and misunderstanding of an unresolved child state, was able to begin enjoying a sexual relationship with her partner, and reported reveling in the sexual experiences and being surprised about what she had missed during her life to that point.

While behavioral systematic desensitization could have helped Mary to get through her sexual encounters with a lowered level of trauma, it is most likely that, without addressing her traumatized ego state, she would not have been able to feel free of her past and revel in her experiences with her partner. Cognitive reframing might have helped Mary to accept herself, even though she did not enjoy sexual experiences, or it might have helped Mary to look at sex in a different way and gain some level of improvement, but again it is unlikely that, without addressing her traumatized ego state, she would have been able to feel free of her past and revel in her sexual experiences. Therefore, it is the contention of ego-state therapists that cognitive behavioral interventions fall short of facilitating the release of the trauma that can interfere in the current experience of living.

The phenomenological stream

Phenomenologists see clients as too dynamic to pigeonhole. They most often prefer to make no formal diagnosis, and they prefer to work with each client as an individual. Clients are thought to deserve an individualized response for their problems, because every two clients differ. Change is seen to come through the process of therapy, rather than through interpretations or training. In the case of person-centered therapy, individuals are seen to be naturally healthy and to have an ability to naturally *become* healthy, given the right environment for growth. That environment includes unconditional positive regard, congruence (honesty), and empathy. Psychological problems are thought to be the result of the deprivation of a healthy environment.

Gestalt therapists attempt to assist clients to gain better levels of understanding by attending to the emotions they have in the here and now. Therefore, like cognitive behavioral therapists, Gestalt therapists prefer to leave the past in the past. If a client says she feels like a little girl, a Gestalt therapist might say, "But you know you are not a little girl." An ego-state therapist would want to hear from that little girl, to help resolve the issues of that ego state so that it would not interfere with the adult's experience of life.

Some Gestalt techniques are extremely similar to ego-state techniques. Gestalt therapists might ask a client to address another part of him- or herself in an empty chair, or might ask a client to speak to their mother or father or partner in an empty chair. Gestalt and ego-state therapies differ in their interpretations of these techniques, with ego-state therapy providing a theoretical understanding for the process. Another difference is that with ego-state therapy the client may speak from a childhood ego state, about a past event, thus varying from the "here and now" paradigm of Gestalt therapy.

Existential therapy, another phenomenological therapy, encourages clients to take control of their own lives by understanding the power of their own decision making. There are few similarities between this therapy and ego-state therapy, as existential therapy deals mostly with thoughts and attitudes, while ego-state therapy deals directly with the unwanted emotional symptoms.

Ego-state therapy is similar to phenomenological therapies in that the process that occurs in therapy is viewed as important in creating the change. Ego-state therapists also view clients as dynamic individuals, each possessing specific ego states arranged in a way that no one else has. Unlike person-centered therapists, ego-state therapists use a range of techniques to facilitate finding an ego state that needs resolution, or to negotiate a respectful understanding between ego states.

Table 1. Psychotherapeutic orientations

	Psychodynamic therapies	Cognitive/behavioral therapies	Phenomenological therapies	Ego-state therapy
Theory—problems stem from	Unconscious material from childhood	Faulty thinking or faulty learning	Lack of personal awareness due to nonopen/honest environment	Unresolved issues or internal dissent between states
Therapy focuses on	Bringing unconscious material to light	Reframing and homework assignments; does not focus on the past	Therapeutic process of open expression	Locating ego states that need resolution or better internal communication
Therapist responds to client as	A person who needs help with insight and interpretation	A person who needs help reframing and relearning	An equal who needs respect and encouragement to express	An equal who needs assistance in resolution or state negotiation
Level of interpretation to clients	Interprets to clients why problems exist	Explains faulty thinking or learning	Does not interpret, allows clients to interpret	No interpretation by clients or therapists
Techniques used	Free association, discussion, interpretation	Teaching new ways of thinking and behaving	Empathy, positive regard, congruence, some empty-chair work	Negotiation between disputing states; expression and empowerment of unresolved states
Therapist	Remains distant from "patient" and unrevealing	Is a teacher/negotiator/trainer	Is warm, and sometimes is self-revealing	Is a tactical assistant to help resolve and negotiate
Focus on surface or underlying issues	Underlying issues	Surface issues	Surface and underlying issues	Surface and underlying issues
Goal	Resolve neuroses by understanding why they exist	Learn to change or accept problems by thinking of them differently, or by new learning	Gain clarity and self-healing by openly and coherently expressing problems to the counselor	Resolve unwanted symptoms by empowering unresolved states and gain a peace within by ego-state negotiation
Length of therapy	Long-term	Medium-term	Medium- to long-term	Generally short-term

Role of ego-state theory in counseling

Understanding that the personality is composed of a group of relatively distinct parts allows the counselor to more easily assess the client's concerns. As the client begins to understand personality in the same way, there is often some relief that, "It is only *part* of me that is a having a problem"—while the other parts are doing quite fine.

The counselor will be able, rather quickly, to assess the client's concern as one relating to some type of internal dissent, or one relating to an unwanted response to a situational cue. With this understanding, a direction for therapy can be planned. Later in this book, the challenge of assessing clients presenting concerns and determining the best course of therapy will be discussed.

Once a theoretical understanding of the client's presenting concerns has been conceptualized, and the direction of therapy is determined, work related to the communication, negotiation, and resolution of ego states may begin. These techniques will be discussed later.

Chapter 3

Basic Counseling Skills and Techniques

While the primary purpose of this book is to present advanced theory and techniques for working with problems such as depression, addictions, and trauma disorders, the importance of demonstrating good basic counseling skills cannot be underrated. Good basic skills are a necessity for being an effective counselor. They give the client trust in the counselor and in the counseling process. They make it easier for the client to disclose important information. Without good basic skills, the counselor will not have an opportunity to apply the best and most appropriate advanced techniques.

Attending

Attending means many things in counseling. All have to do with the counselor's fostering a therapeutic relationship conducive to positive outcomes. The clothing the counselor wears, the preparation of the room, the body language and voice tones, the interest shown in the client, and the ability to maintain a focus in the client's world all potentially influence the therapeutic outcome.

Attire

Whether or not we think it should, dress matters. The professionally dressed person is taken more seriously than the person less professionally dressed. This is not to say that one should overdress, but the counselor who is underdressed may be dismissed by the client in a way that impedes any real progress. Attire should be slightly more professional than what would normally be thought of as casual in the context where counseling occurs.

Therefore, if the counselor works in a downtown business where professionals normally wear suits, the counselor will likely be able to do the best work if also dressed in a suit. If the counselor works with inner-city youth, a more casual, but respectable, attire would be best. Counselors working in public or private schools often find their level of dress is more dictated by the expectations of parents who visit with the counselor, than by the more liberal expectations of the students. They find that to do a good job their level of dress needs to be accepted by both parents and students.

The level of dress should be professional, and should not be noticed as "out of the ordinary" by clients. Provocative attire should be avoided, as a focus in the counseling setting should be on the client. The desire to "dress well" normally results in the appropriate selection of attire.

Preparation of the room

The first thing a client sees when coming for counseling is the counselor. When he or she is greeted with a professionally dressed person, an appropriate tone is set. The second thing that the client notices is a counseling room. If the client sees a room that is disheveled, untidy, and unkempt, there may be notions of nonprofessionalism, and "What am I doing here?" If, on the other hand, the client enters and finds a neat and tidy room, a tone is set that says, "This person knows what they're doing, they are professional, and I may get real help here."

The client should be provided with a comfortable chair that is either the same as, or on par with, the counselor's chair. There should be a box of tissues in easy reach, and a wastebasket also in easy reach. The client should not be expected to focus on the counselor with a bright window or light behind, making it difficult to focus. Lighting should be bright, but not glaring. It may be useful to have a small clock in easy vision so that the counselor can glance at it and ensure the session is adequately timed. The counselor's and client's chairs should be a comfortable distance apart, with the client's chair not directly in the corner of the room. It is important for the client to feel comfortable in the room, not cornered and not crowded. This understanding becomes even more clear when considering the possibility that abuse issues may arise in counseling. When possible, it is preferred for the counseling room to be of an appropriate size so it doesn't feel cramped. Regardless of the size of the room, a feeling of space should be encouraged. In a metaphorical sense, the client should be given room to grow.

Body language and voice tone

It is important that clients feel that counselors want to hear them. A counselor who sits leaning back in a chair looking in different directions and paying little obvious attention to what the client says shows a lack of interest. Examples of bad body language include crossing the legs or arms, facing a direction away from the client, looking at things in the room other than the client, looking at a clock, and making repetitive movements with the fingers or feet.

The counselor who faces the client, leans slightly forward, maintains good eye contact, and shows real interest in what the client is saying indicates good body language. It makes a big difference that the client feels attended to. It should be noted that a cultural context should be considered. Clients from some Asian cultures generally prefer less direct eye contact, and more distance from the counselor. Clients from some European countries, for example, France, prefer the counselor to sit closer to the client than would be normal in most Anglo countries.

The voice tone of the counselor is important in helping the client feel attended to. Voice tone is further discussed under 'Active listening' below, but generally the voice should have energy and should reveal a real interest in hearing what the client has to say.

Interest shown to the client

One of the most important things clients can understand when entering counseling is that the counselor is really interested in them, in their concerns, and in their improvement. It is impossible to illustrate the general tone of showing interest to a client by presenting a checklist. It is better to maintain the positive intent to show interest in a way that ensures that the client understands that the counselor cares. The counselor is the employee of the client. The client is paying for the time of the counselor. It is important that the counselor be there for the client, and show the client respect and attention. Any form of arrogance will be distancing and will disrupt the therapeutic relationship. Wearing the appropriate attire and the preparation of the room are for the client; the attention and the interest are for the client; and the therapeutic relationship is for the client. The client needs to feel that the counseling room and the counselor provide a safe, caring, and understanding haven. The client needs to feel positive about stepping into the counseling room, about seeing how the counselor is dressed, and about the interest shown by the counselor. When these aspects of counseling come together and the client can feel comfortable and relaxed and attended to, then the proper milieu is set for therapy.

Maintaining focus in the client's world

There is an aspect of being a good counselor or therapist that cannot be undervalued. It is what John Watkins (2003) called "resonance", what Frederick Perls (1965) called "contact", and to a lesser extent what Carl Rogers (1951) called "empathy". It is when the counselor can, to some extent, lose him- or herself and enter into the client's world. It is at this time that the counselor can become intuitive, can hear and see things that otherwise might be missed, and can communicate naturally in a way that can be heard.

If, when I have a client, I am thinking about how well I am doing as a counselor, if I'm thinking I'm doing a good job, I'm doing a bad job, I wonder how I should be doing this, or anything else about myself, I am not maintaining focus in the client's world. I am in my world, and I will miss what is going on with the client. When I am thinking that I may fail, I am not in my client's world. It is when these personal thoughts of the counselor enter that refocusing needs to occur.

It might be helpful to think of the location of the focus in counseling as an object that exists somewhere in the room. If I am thinking something about me, the focus object is located somewhere inside my own body. If I am thinking about something outside the counseling room, obviously the point of focus is outside the counseling room and prevents any proper attending to the client. If, on the other hand, I am thinking partly about the client and partly about my technique or about me, then the focus object might be halfway between the client and me. If it is my intent to really understand the client's world, and I listen intently while paying respect to the client, and if I try to experience the client's world in order to feel the perspective the client feels, then I am more approaching placing the focus in the client's world. It is at this time that the point of focus is inside the client.

When we drive a car we look at the road. We don't focus on the steering wheel and the brake and the gearshift. It is by focusing on the road and thinking about where we are going that we, as drivers, respond the best. In the same way, it is important to be with the client. Think of where the point of focus is, and think about where the client wants to go. Have an earnest desire to help, and, when you seem to be lost, forget yourself and place your point of focus inside the client's world. It is from this reuniting with the feelings and concerns of the client that a natural direction for therapy normally follows.

The importance of this "maintaining focus in the client's world" cannot be overestimated. When proper focus is in the client's world, a client feels attended to, and the counselor is far more able to understand and gain insights about the client. Useful intuition seems to go hand in hand with the ability to maintain focus in the client's world. I say to my students, "Learn as many techniques as you can, then, when talking with a client, enter into his or her world with the intent of helping, and follow your intuition." Regardless of the technique you use, this may be the one most important factor in being an effective counselor. It is a gift to be the person who is asked for help. It is an honor to be trusted with the innermost thoughts of another person. It is our responsibility to respect that gift by attending to the client.

Active listening

Active listening is a valuable tool that counselors from any orientation can use. It is not easy to learn and there appears to be a real art in being a good active listener. It is often misunderstood in regards to what good active listening entails. Basically, active listening is hearing what the other person is communicating and responding to the client what has been heard. Good active listening goes beyond the word content of what has been said, and reflects emotion, body language, and content. It is best to learn active listening by attempting to ask no questions and by supplying no answers or suggestions. Of course, during a real counseling setting questions and answers will sometimes be used.

Benefits of active listening

Clients often feel misunderstood. They often feel, "No one really knows me." Often, others have tried to tell them what to do with little understanding of their feelings, with little knowledge of their capabilities or of what they have already tried. Clients can feel that they are not talking with someone who hears them, but parallel to someone who has little understanding of them.

Counselors often get an idea about what the client's problem may be and then ask questions to determine whether the problem is what the counselor supposes. Too often, it is not. Questions can take clients away from what they really want to talk about to the inquiry the counselor wonders about.

Active listening can be beneficial by both allowing clients to feel heard and understood, and by allowing the clients to continue their explanation directly to the root of the problem, without being stopped or pointed toward different directions with questions.

Consider the female client who states in the sad tone, "My marriage isn't what I thought it would be." The active-listening statement, "It sounds like there's something that's upsetting you about how your marriage is going" will allow the client to continue to explain what the problem is. But the question, "What did you think marriage would be like?" moves the client away from the problem to a discussion on what good marriage is. The counseling interview in each case is illustrated below:

Non-active listening

Client: My marriage isn't what I thought it would be.

Counselor: What did you think marriage would be like?

Client: I think marriage should be where two people can share their love, equally.

Counselor: Do you think it's ever possible for two people to share their love equally?

Client: No, I guess that would be impossible.

Active listening

Client: My marriage isn't what I thought it would be.

Counselor: It sounds like there's something that's upsetting you about how your marriage is going.

Client: My husband has been spending a lot of time away from home at night, and I don't know where he is. [Crying.]

Counselor: I can see this is really hard for you. It must be horrible not knowing where he is.

Obviously, this example is biased to illustrate a problem with questioning. But it is very true that questions often take the client away from the problem, rather than help define it. Questioning is a cognitive, mental process that keeps the client in an intellectual state, while active listening is a process that reflects words and emotions, facilitating the client to communicate in the ego state that needs help.

The client in the *non-active*-listening example above does not feel heard or understood, and is not encouraged to be self-revealing. The client in the *active*-listening example above feels heard and understood, and therefore is encouraged to reveal a deeper level. Clients often test the counselor to see how much can be said and how much can be understood in a sensitive way.

If the counselor passes these tests, then clients feel comfortable to reveal a deeper level, a level that otherwise would have been too scary.

Active listening, used skillfully, can facilitate clients to quickly get to their problem, as they understand it. It can, further, allow many clients to verbalize their problem in a way they have not before, and this can help them understand themselves at a deeper level. While this is therapeutic in its own right, it is my belief that this person-centered approach is best used as a tool integrated with more powerful therapeutic tools, rather than being the central focus of counseling. Still, the benefits that active listening provides—in helping clients to feel understood and to communicate more quickly their concerns—are important. It is well worth the time to practice and learn active-listening skills so they may be used at any point in therapy when they seem appropriate. The following paragraphs offer some basic pointers to becoming a good active listener.

Good active listening

There are at least three things to be aware of when attempting to practice active listening. They are (1) the affect of the client, (2) the body language of the client, and (3) the words of the client. They will each be discussed below.

Be aware of the affect of the client

Noticing the emotion level of the client is more important than hearing the content of the words. This is not to say that the content of the words is unimportant, but the emotion of the client is most important. Clients do not come to therapy because of how they are thinking. They come to therapy because of how they are feeling. Even if individuals are thinking quite strangely, if they are emotionally secure about this they will generally not come to therapy. It is the state of feeling emotionally upset, isolated, and depressed, or grieving that brings most clients to therapy. When the emotion of the client is reflected with a good active-listening response, the client has finally found someone who hears and understands. The following is an example of a non-emotive response and an emotive response.

Non-emotive active-listening response

Client: My son doesn't know what he's doing when he takes those drugs [said with tears welling up in the eyes].

Counselor: Your son doesn't have the maturity and knowledge to make good choices at this time.

Client: No, he doesn't. He's making horrible mistakes.

Counselor: The mistakes he's making could affect him for the rest of his life.

Client: Yes, he could ruin his life.

Emotive active-listening response

Client: My son doesn't know what he's doing when he takes those drugs [said with tears welling up in the eyes].

Counselor: I can see that you really love your son [said with a sensitive, caring voice].

Client [starting to cry]: He's everything to me since my partner died. If anything should happen to him I don't know if I could make it.

Counselor: That must be horribly scary to love someone like that and not know how to help them.

Client: It is! I love him so much and he won't listen to me.

The non-emotive active-listening response above indicates an example of responding only to the words and not the feeling of the client. Often, this is what people think of when they think of active listening, but it can be much more. When the client makes a statement and shows emotion, and if the emotion itself is reflected to the client, the client normally feels much more heard and understood. An important key in making a good emotive active-listening response is to make sure that your voice, the voice of the counselor, reflects an element of the emotion demonstrated by the client. You do not have to reflect the complete emotion of the client at the same level, but it is very important for the client to hear in your voice an understanding of the emotion that has been shared. For example, if the client says, in an upset and teary voice, "I've just found out my cat is dying," a monotone, professionally stated response, "I can see you love your cat," will not be heard in the same way as a caring, sensitively said response, "*I can **see** you love your cat.*"

Likewise, if the client says in an angry, loud voice, "**My boss is really getting under my skin**," the monotone, professionally stated response, "It sounds like your boss is bothering you," will not be heard in the same way as an understanding, slightly loudly stated response, "**Boy, it sounds like your boss is really bothering you!**"

The importance of reflecting, during active listening, an understanding of the emotion of the client cannot be understated. Counseling is a completely different experience for the client when he or she feels emotionally recognized and understood by the counselor. When clients feel emotionally understood they are much more willing to share and talk at a deeper level about their concerns.

Be aware of the body language of the client

While it is most important to be aware of the affect of the client, often clients present in a non-emotional tone, at least at first. The words of the client are very important, and will be discussed in the following subsection. But even more generally honest than the words of the client is the body language of the client. It is sometimes the case that the body language of the client and the words of the client say the same thing, but it is also sometimes the case that the body language of the client and the words of the client say two different things. When this occurs it is best to trust the body language. It is sometimes the case that clients are unaware that their own words are less than accurate.

Consider the client who says, "My partner and I have a great relationship. It really couldn't be better." And, at the same time the client is saying this, the fists are being clinched. An active-listening response that did not consider the body language might be, "It sounds like you and your partner are really meant for each other." But an active-listening response that incorporates the body language could be, "I'm a little confused. I hear you say you're enjoying your relationship, but when you talk about your partner I can see you clinching your fist." When confronted with this in a statement of confusion, the client will often look inside and give a more thorough and accurate account of the relationship. It may be that this statement of confusion will allow the client a deeper understanding of his or her own feelings.

Therefore, body language should be reflected to the client. If there is a long pause and the client appears to be thinking more about something outside the window than about the concern that brought him or her to therapy, a good active-listening statement might be, "I get the feeling that you have moved away from your problem, and aren't really present right now." If the client is rocking forward and backward when talking about a certain person, an active-listening response might be, "I really want to hear what you have to say, because it seems to me you're in an important place right now with what you're talking about."

Be aware of the words of the client

Often, all we have are the *words* of the client. This is the case when the client is presenting with very little affect. A large part of active listening will be reflecting the content of the words. It is often not easy to determine how to reflect the words you have just heard. This is especially the case after a client talks for two minutes nonstop and you have to determine what to reflect from several paragraphs of listening. If the client talks for a few minutes, it can be useful to jot down two or three things you will want to reflect upon over the course of the session. Still, the question is, "What do I reflect and how do I say it?"

I tell students to think about what they would say they heard from this person if they were going to write about it in a letter to a friend. I say, "Tell me what you would say to your friend about what you just heard—if confidentiality wasn't an issue. What would you say the problem is?" When asked this question, the student can often say in their own words what they just heard. They can say an excellent active-listening response that could be reflected to the client.

Counselors should not attempt to rephrase the words of the client. They should attempt to put in their own words the meaning of what they heard the client say. A poor active-listening response to "I am not happy at work" is, "It sounds like you don't enjoy your work." A better response is, "It sounds like there's something happening at work that's upsetting to you." The second response illustrates an interpreted understanding of what the client has said, not just a remake of the same words. When the client hears an interpreted understanding, there is a greater sense of being heard, and the client feels more able to continue to describe the problem at a deeper level.

In order to offer an interpreted response (to clarify, not a Freudian interpretation of the problem), the counselor needs to (1) hear and understand what the client has said, (2) think about the meaning of that to the client, and (3) reflect that meaning back to the client. The following are some examples of interpreted and noninterpreted responses and active listening.

> **Client**: I don't understand why I can't make the grades in university that I did in high school.
>
> **Noninterpreted response**: It's not clear to you why your university grades are not as good as your high school grades.
>
> **Interpreted response**: As much as you try, you're just not able to make the grades you want.
>
> **Client**: When my girlfriend said she doesn't trust me, I get really angry.
>
> **Noninterpreted response**: You get angry when you're not trusted, especially by your girlfriend.
>
> **Interpreted response**: There's something about the way you're expressing your anger to your girlfriend that you don't feel comfortable about.

> **Client**: It's been ten years, and I'm still not over my father's death.
>
> **Noninterpreted response**: Even though your father died ten years ago, you're still having trouble in the grieving process.
>
> **Interpreted response**: You're concerned that you shouldn't be grieving the way you are after such a long period.

The above examples illustrate a deeper understanding of the client's concerns when interpreted responses are offered. It is very difficult to learn this type of active listening. Students of this process can expect to be disillusioned and frustrated when attempting to feel comfortable and spontaneous while learning this level of active listening. Just as the first efforts at learning a new sport are clumsy and awkward, learning active listening can be expected to be clumsy and awkward. Students find it difficult not to ask questions and not to solve the problem for the client, but being able to accurately reflect the emotion and the meaning of what has been heard and understood is an excellent therapeutic tool to have.

Statements of confusion

One powerful aspect of active listening is what I call statements of confusion. Most of us enjoy helping someone out of the state of confusion. It feels quite fun and empowering. Questions can feel interrogating and, as stated above, can direct the client away from the central issue. Consider the following question:

> **Client**: My husband has really been upsetting me.
>
> **Counselor**: What has he been doing?

The client may not feel comfortable at first, telling about what her husband has been up to. And, as stated above, questions can direct the client away from the central issue, away from the straight line to the core of the problem, as they understand it. Consider the following statement of confusion made in response to the same client statement:

> **Client**: My husband has really been upsetting me.
>
> **Counselor**: I can see there's something disturbing going on between you and your husband, but I'm still a bit confused and I guess I don't understand what's happening.

Here are some further examples of statements of confusion:

> **Client**: When I come home from work I just feel like lying down and I have a lot of work I have to do.

> **Counselor**: It sounds like you're having an internal conflict. I would love to hear what both parts are saying. [This statement expresses a need to know, not a question.]
>
> **Client**: I can't stand being alone. When I'm alone I feel like I have to panic. I think there's something really wrong with me.
>
> **Counselor**: I really want to understand this because I can see it's really upsetting to you. I'm a bit unclear, though. You said you feel like you *have* to panic.

Another variation on the last example would be just to say, "You feel like you *have* to panic." Restating a phrase of the client using the voice tone of not understanding is making a statement of confusion. In the previous example, it may seem like a semantic variation between, "I would love to hear what both parts are saying," and "What are both parts saying?" In truth, sometimes a question works just as well as a statement of confusion, but also sometimes it works not nearly as well. Over the course of a counseling session, statements of confusion will elicit much more information, and more revealing information than questions.

Obviously, there are times when questions should be asked, and there are times when answers should be given to a client. While a good response to, "I would really like for you to tell me if you think I should leave my husband," might be, "I don't know your world enough to answer, but I can hear that you're feeling a need for a decision to a really important question," it would not be a good response to the question, "I really want to know where a women's refuge center is in my area," to say, "I can see you would really like to know your area better." That, of course, would be silly.

Even though questions and answers are sometimes what best satisfy the demands of communication, learning the art and the skills of good active listening will enhance the abilities of the counselor, irrespective of the therapeutic orientation followed. It will help the client feel heard and understood, and will assist the client to more quickly and easily share difficult thoughts and feelings.

Starting and ending a session

To paraphrase Frank Herbert in his book, *Dune*, "Beginnings and endings are fragile things." This is true not only in life but in counseling, and in each single counseling session. While the heart of the session is where real work is done, the ability for that work to be done and the impression about the work that has just been done is determined by how the session was started and how the session was ended.

Beginning the session

Until the time when the client sits down at the beginning of a session, it is appropriate to make casual small talk. Because clients have not come merely for small talk, it is best to begin focusing on the session when the counselor and client sit down. I like the question, "What are you ready to change today?" When the client answers this question, a contract for change has already been made. The statement, "How can I help you?" removes power and responsibility from the client and places the responsibility for change upon the counselor. Of course, it is impossible for the counselor to change the client, as change has to come from the client. The statement, "What would you like to focus on today?" signifies that something can be talked about today, but that change will not necessarily occur. Of course, phraseology by itself cannot effect change, but it is an important ingredient.

While the client is giving initial information to the counselor, a good question is, "Is there anything you haven't told me that might be helpful for me to hear?" This question often results in deeper and useful information. It is also good at the beginning of the session to check with clients in relation to how they have been since their last session. This gives feedback to the counselor and it helps the client feel attended to.

If it is the first session, information on confidentiality and other logistical-type information should be presented. It is possible to allow the client to read about this before entering the counseling room to save time, and then to ask a short question to see if it was clear. It is also appropriate during the first session to let the client know the theoretical orientation that is presupposed by the counselor. For example, the counselor might say something like, "I believe we are all naturally made up of a group of parts—part of me wants to do this and part of me wants to do that. One part might really want to continue in school, while another part might really want to quit. I feel it is important to spend time talking directly with the part that needs change, rather than just talk intellectually about the need for change to an intellectual part." Normally, that is about all that needs to be said to inform the client about work from an ego-state orientation. It is always good to ask, "Are there any questions?"

It is OK to have a plan for a session, but it is best to be guided by the current needs of the client. There is little that is less beneficial than a counselor guiding a session away from the current needs of the client. The use of that question, "What are you ready to change today?", will help the client feel included in the direction of the session.

Bringing the session to close

Near the end of the session, it is good to review what has been done during the session. This recaps for the client the progress of the session, and reminds the client of opportunities for change that have been highlighted within the session. If ego states have been named (see page 51) it is good to use those names in this end-of-session review. And it is always good to ask the client if there are any further questions.

It is not unusual for the client to make a statement something like, "I'm not sure whether this will change anything." This statement appropriately comes from a doubting ego state of the client. It is almost never good to argue with the client to any degree. This entrenches the client away from the view of the counselor; therefore, it would be an inappropriate statement to say, "I think you'll see some really positive changes." A statement such as this could set up a resistance in the client, resulting in a need to prove that no positive changes will occur.

A much better response to "I'm not sure whether this will change anything" is something like, "I don't know if anything will change, either. It can be really nice to be surprised." The first sentence here agrees with the client; therefore, the chance of resistance is minimized. The second sentence, "It can be really nice to be surprised," indicates that a positive result may occur, and the result may be so positive that the client will be surprised. Again, subtle phraseology such as these examples is not enough to ensure a positive result, but positive phraseology said in a way to minimize resistance will ensure a better chance for positive results.

When the client and the counselor stand up at the end of the session, it is a time to leave the session behind and return to cordial small talk.

The last session

What if the client is finishing therapy with the counselor? The last counseling session in a series is normally referred to as *termination*—not really the best term. There are a few important things to remember when having the last session with a client. If the client has been seen for a number of weeks or months, it is good to lead up to the last session rather than end therapy abruptly. Sometimes it is good to space therapy out to biweekly sessions or monthly sessions before having the last session. The client should be encouraged to consider how the support of therapy will be replaced by other positive aspects in the client's life.

During the last session, the client should be informed that further therapy is available at a later time if the client chooses. It is not unusual for clients to fear that the counselor will no longer see them after the last session, if a further need presents. It is good to review what has been done during the course of counseling. It is good to talk about the original goal, and how the client has progressed. And it is good to focus on progress as something that will continue into the future. For example, rather than see progress as ending at the end of therapy, it is good to focus on it with the client as a continuing process that the client now has the tools to maintain.

Chapter 4

Advanced Counseling Skills and Techniques

The chapter on basic counseling skills covered aspects of listening and attending. This one provides instruction in how to speak with individual ego states and introjects, and it begins by providing instruction relating to the therapeutic value of these techniques. Being able to gain direct access with the part of the client that has the problem is a powerful tool in counseling.

While what ego states are, where they come from, and their lasting nature has been discussed earlier, in order to best understand the techniques for communicating with ego states it is useful to review an aspect of the nature of ego states. Each ego state is a part of the personality, and, while executive (conscious and out), each state thinks of itself with *ego identity*, that is, it thinks it is the person. Therefore, talking to a single ego state is like talking to an individual. It is important to speak respectfully to each and every ego state that is spoken with. If any ego state believes, or feels, that you, the counselor, do not like or respect it, it will not work with you in a positive way, and it may even hide or not speak with you. Speaking respectfully to all states will be discussed further, while the first instruction will be provided in terms of how to access and speak with each state individually.

Accessing ego states

It is not difficult to access individual ego states and speak with them separately. It is important to learn to recognize ego-state switching so individual states can have a better opportunity to express themselves more fully. For example, if a client says that there is a part that would really like to quit smoking and another part really enjoys smoking, two parts are evident. The counselor can be aware of which of the two parts is speaking by watching the content of the words and the expression of the client while the client is talking. Statements such as "I know I really have to quit: my health's suffering and it's stupid, the amount of money that I'm spending on smoking" obviously indicate that the state that wants to quit has the executive. If the client then says, "But, I really enjoy a cigarette, and when I'm with my friends who smoke it's really hard for me to turn down an opportunity to smoke with them; a cigarette is also really good after a meal," the counselor can see that the client has switched to the state that enjoys smoking.

A good way to begin talking with ego states individually is to use multiple chairs. For example, the counselor might say to the above client, "While you're in this chair I want to hear only from that part of you that wants to quit smoking. When you change to the other chair, I will have an opportunity to hear how you like to smoke, but in this chair I want to hear only from a part of you that really wants to quit." If, while speaking from the quit chair the client begins telling a reason why smoking is good, the counselor should stop the client and say, "Remember, in this chair I only want to hear how you want to quit, and you'll be able to tell me the good things about smoking when you sit in the other chair.

In working with ego states, it is very important for the counselor to continue to monitor the client so that each ego state can be heard individually. This way, each ego state will be able to be heard, and will be able to have its needs met. As the counselor gains more proficiency in noticing ego-state switching, a number of chairs may be used so that all ego states involved in the presenting concern of the client can be heard.

Continuing with our example, the counselor should talk with the ego state that wants to quit smoking until it has had a good opportunity to express all the reasons quitting is good. Then, the counselor can say something like, "OK, now I want you to sit in this chair [pointing to the other chair] and as you sit in this chair, I only want to hear the good things about smoking. I want to hear only from the part of you that smokes." Conversation with the smoking state should continue until this ego state has a full opportunity to express itself. Every state needs to be able to express itself fully for the best outcome to occur.

It may be the case that more than one ego state will share the same opinion. For example, when the client is talking about reasons to quit smoking, the counselor may notice that, while the reasons are about health and fear of dying (emotive), the client has a different affect than when the reasons are about saving money (intellectual). It is best, when this is the case, to set out another chair so both the emotional health-conscious state and the intellectual money-conscious state may be fully expressed. This is especially important when determining whether each state is satisfied with the conclusion. If multiple states are talking from the same chair, one state may express satisfaction while another would not.

Naming ego states

It is helpful and important to get a name for each ego state while working with it. It is best if the state can name itself. In order for this to happen, the question, "What can I call this part of you?" is best asked after talking with a state for a few sentences in order to make sure that the ego state to be named is currently executive. It would not be appropriate to ask the state that wants to quit smoking for a name for the state that wants to continue smoking. A name might be given that the smoking state would be dissatisfied with, and it is important for all states to feel respected during therapy.

States sometimes have difficulty giving themselves a name. When this happens it is okay to suggest a possible name, such as "Health", but it is always appropriate to check with the state to see if the suggested name is acceptable. For example, "This part of you I'm talking with right now seems concerned about your health. Is it OK if I call this part of you, Health?" It is interesting that sometimes when a state is asked, "What can I call this part of you?", a personal name is given such as Jane, Sue, or Mary—a name that may have nothing to do with the name of the client. If this occurs, the personal name that is given can be used to refer to the state.

It is important to keep good notes so that you will be able to remember which names go with which ego states. If you are working with a number of ego states using a number of chairs it can be helpful to write the name of each state on a piece of paper and place it on the chair. This way, both the counselor and the client can keep track of all states in the conversation.

Good note taking is imperative when doing work with ego states. It can be helpful to circle the name of each state on the page and write the attributes of that state next to the circled name. This way, when the counselor wants to talk to the state that is concerned about health, the client can be asked to sit in that state's chair and, as he or she sits down, the counselor can say something like, "Now I want to talk just with Health, the part of you that is really quite upset about what cigarettes are doing to your body, that part that would like to breathe more deeply and live longer. Health, what do you think about …?"

It is somewhat surprising and interesting how quickly clients are able to speak directly from their ego-state parts. It is common for clients to express surprise about this at the end of the session. When clients change ego states, as they change chairs, their affect often changes dramatically. It may be that while a client is in one ego state, he or she will appear fragile and teary, and while expressing from another ego state the same client will appear aloof, cold, and distant. This switch in affect can occur very rapidly as the client changes chairs, when the counselor asks to talk with each state by calling its name.

The technique of having a client switch chairs has been used in other therapies, and was first discussed in ego-state therapy by Helen Watkins. Gestalt therapists have a technique where clients are asked to switch chairs so they can experience talking to different parts of themselves, or to a different person whom they know. This usage of chairs is very similar to that presented in this book. A major difference between the work of Gestalt therapists and that of counselors working from an ego-state framework is that Gestalt therapists work only in the here and now, while ego-state therapists often facilitate the resolution of a past trauma by assisting a childhood state to assertively express to an introject that had been feared.

It is important while accessing ego states to speak directly to the ego state that is being accessed. For example, it would be inappropriate to say, "What does that part of you that wants to quit smoking think?" or, "Tell me about the part of you that wants to smoke." That would be asking for one ego state to report what another ego state is thinking or feeling. This would not allow the accurate expression of the "smoking" ego state, and would not facilitate a positive outcome in counseling. In talking with the "smoking" ego state the question should be direct, and asked only when the client is in the appropriate chair: "Smoking, what do you think?" If, at any time the counselor notices the answer is coming from a different state, the counselor can say something like, "I think I was hearing from another part there, right now I just want to hear directly from Smoking. Smoking, what do you think?"

Let us review some of the things we have learned about accessing ego states:

- The counselor should first observe the client, noticing the client speaking from more than one ego state.
- It is important for the counselor to be able to notice switching of ego states.
- A separate chair should be placed for each ego state talked with about the topic.
- Each ego state should be named so it can be referred to and spoken with again.
- Good note taking, including the name and the nature of each state, is imperative.

- Additional chairs should be added as additional states are noticed in the conversation.
- Speak with each state respectfully, and never denigrate one state to another.
- Speak directly to each ego state, making sure you are hearing directly from that state.

Speak respectfully to all states

Each ego state has its own intellect and emotions. Some ego states are extremely emotional and have little logic, while others may be very logical with little emotion. Therefore, each ego state can form its own opinion about the counselor. This should not be surprising, as ego states form differing opinions about people in the life of the client. For example, one ego state may really appreciate a parent, while another ego state may resent that same parent. One ego state may view a person as someone who would make an excellent marriage partner, while another ego state may hold the opinion that "I should stay away from the person."

Because ego states form their own opinions about the therapist, it is very important to always speak respectfully to and about each state. If an ego state has a less than positive impression of the counselor, it will not work with the counselor in a positive way. It may even choose not to communicate with the counselor at all. It is important to talk with each state with respect, even if that state has been problematic for the client (such as a state that has become violently angry). It is also important when talking with states to always speak respectfully about other states.

It is not unusual for one state to dislike another state. An ego state can have extremely negative feelings toward another state. For example, a client may have an ego state that is emotional and reactionary and sometimes embarrasses the client with its emotional expression. Another ego state may speak very disparagingly about this overly emotional state, and when this occurs it is important for the counselor to be able to hear what is being said, but not to also speak disparagingly about the overly emotional state.

Here is an example.

Client: Every time he tries to talk with me, I become like a blubbering idiot. I can't speak, I sweat, and act really silly. I hate myself when I'm like that.

(Inappropriate comment) Counselor: I can see why you don't like that part of you. That would be really embarrassing when that happens.

Advanced Skills and Interventions in Therapeutic Counseling

(Appropriate comment) Counselor: It sounds like you have the ability to be fragile and sensitive. That can be a great asset at the right time, but right now that part that can be fragile and sensitive seems to be coming out when it is uncomfortable, and that makes you uncomfortable too.

This example illustrates two different ways of responding. The first comment by the counselor initially sounds empathetic and understanding. And it is empathetic and understanding for the ego state that is upset about the overly emotional response. The problem with this comment is, the ego state that has been responding in an overly emotional way has already been feeling fragile and out of control. That ego state, upon hearing another ego state, and the counselor, disparaging it will feel even more fragile and out of control. It will not be helped, and it may not be willing to cooperate with the counselor when asked to do so.

The second comment by the counselor is also empathetic to the ego state that is talking. This comment shows an understanding that it is not easy for the speaking state when the fragile ego state acts in a way that makes a person look silly. But the second comment also demonstrates an appreciation and understanding for the overtly emotional ego state. When hearing this appreciation and understanding, this overtly emotional ego state will feel more comfortable, respected, and will be more willing to work in a positive way for a resolution that all states will appreciate.

It can be challenging for the counselor to speak about and to an ego state in a positive way, when that state sometimes acts aggressive and uncompromising. For example, a state that has had a role of being aggressively angry may feel that that is the only role it can fulfill. It may know that other states dislike it, and disapprove of it, but it may believe it is important and has to fulfill its own role. Still, the best way to promote positive change is to find a way to work with the state, rather than against it. When one is speaking directly with such a state, comments such as the following may be used:

- I can see you're very powerful. I don't think I can help this person without your help.

- I know you originally came about to help this person. I want to help, too, and I really need your help to be able to do that.

- It must not feel good to not be liked by other parts of this person. Wouldn't it be nice to be liked and appreciated by all parts? [Normally, a state will at first answer with something like, "They will never like me no matter what I do," or, "I don't care what they think." These seemingly intransigent attitudes can change very quickly.]

- What if we find an important role for you where you can be liked by all parts and you can help this person at the same time?

- It may not seem possible yet, but you can either do the same thing you have been doing in the past, only do it less, or you can learn to do something new.

- Is it OK with you if I ask some of the other states if they can accept you, if you take on this new role?

When working with states that have appeared to be malevolent, it is important to maintain focus, and not give up. Often, initially, the states may appear unchangeable. It is amazing how quickly the states can take on new roles, or can continue with the same role in a diminished fashion. The goal here is for all states to appreciate each other and get along; to achieve a peace within. For example, a state that has been overtly angry and aggressive in a way that has been problematic for the client may agree to continue with its ability to defend the client, but only at the appropriate time. If the client is being physically attacked, for instance, then this angry, aggressive state may use adrenaline to defend the client, but it may be that at other times an assertive state will be able to express anger with more composure. At the end of this negotiation, it would be important for the angry, aggressive state and the assertive state to agree to work together. Such an agreement can result in very rapid change for the client. An example of this type of negotiation is included in the section on working with anger (see page 152).

When working with ego states

There are some general guidelines that are useful to understand when working with ego states. First, let's review how to access ego states.

Accessing ego states—a review

1. While talking with the client notice at least two separate ego states.

   This is most easily done by noticing when the client holds separate opinions on the same subject, especially when there is a different amount of affect associated with each opinion. For example, "Sometimes I just hate him" and, "He's really not a bad guy."

2. Place an extra chair next to the client and tell the client, "When you're sitting in this chair I want to hear only from that part of you that ... Then,

later, when you sit in the other chair, I will want to hear from that part of you that ..."

This is the first step in isolating the ego states so that each may be expressed and understood. At this point, it is important to speak clearly as a professional telling the client what you are telling him or her to do. If you speak reluctantly, or ask the client tentatively something like, "Is this something you would like to try?" then the client may have little confidence in the procedure and a negative outcome is almost assured.

3. Next, speak directly to each state when the client is sitting in the appropriate chair. Make statements such as, "Tell me how you feel about this," not, "Tell me what that part of you feels about this." Do not accept replies from the client from an alternative ego state. For example, if the client says, "When I am like that I feel ...", then stop the client and say something like, "No, I want to hear directly from ... While you are in this chair tell me how you feel. I will want to know how the other part feels when you move back to that chair.

Counselors who have tried using a switching-chairs technique and found it not useful have, almost without exception, fallen short on this step. They have not made sure that they are speaking directly to the state they are intending to speak with, and/or they have not made sure that the client is speaking directly from that state. This process will not work unless ego states can be spoken with directly, and can be heard individually.

Remember, speaking with ego states is just like speaking with people, because each state you are speaking with is a part of a person, a part that has been executive and speaking as that person at some time in the past. Speak respectfully and clearly, and have as an aim that all states will get along with you, and will get along with all the other states of the client. If one state has a need, or has a fear, it is good to assist that state in gaining resolution. The counselor is the facilitator for all states to have their needs met in a manner that every state can appreciate.

Working with introjects

An introject is an internalized perception of another person. We may have many different introjects for a single person whom we have known. For example, a client may have an introject of her mother when the client was five years old, another introject of her mother when the client was fifteen years old, and another introject of her mother as she is perceived today.

It is very powerful to work with clients by facilitating them to focus directly on their introjects. Clients may be asked to speak to an empty chair in which introjects have been associated, or clients may be asked to speak directly from their own persona of an introject, with the client role-playing the introject.

Speaking to an introject

There is something about a client speaking directly to an introject that connects the client with his or her feelings much more than when the client merely speaks *about* an introject. For example, if the counselor directs the client to, "Tell me what you would like to say to your mother," useful information may follow, but the client will usually speak in an emotionally detached manner, and the feelings of the core issue may be missed.

Alternatively, the client may be directed to focus on an empty chair sitting across from him or her, and told, "I want you to invite your mother as you perceive her into that chair. Just tell me when you're ready, when you feel the essence of your mother is there in that chair." When the client is ready, say, "Now, go ahead and tell her exactly what you would like to." Here, when the client is speaking directly to the mother, often the real issues emerge. There is something about speaking directly to an introject, rather then telling what they would *like* to say to an introject, that connects clients to their feelings. The emotional ego state that has had difficulty communicating is brought to the executive, and it has an opportunity to achieve clarity, understanding, and resolution.

Clients may become emotional, and may have difficulty speaking directly to an introject. When this happens, it is important for the counselor to support and encourage the client to continue. Things may be said, such as, "This is your opportunity to say exactly what you feel. I am here to support you in this safe place. Now, go ahead and tell her exactly what you feel. Now is the time you can tell her those things that have been difficult to say in the past."

It cannot be stressed too much that it is extremely important for the client to speak directly to the introject, rather than saying back to the counselor something like, "Well, I guess I would tell her that ..." Here, the counselor should stop the client and say something like, "No, say it directly to her. Say it to the essence of your mother sitting right there in that chair."

It may sometimes be helpful if the counselor also speaks to the introject. For example, if the client is having difficulty verbalizing that he or she is angry at the introject, the counselor may say something to the introject such as, "Can you hear what she's saying? The things you've done have really upset her. She's angry with you." Then, the counselor would look back to the client and say, "Now, what else do you want to tell her?" This can be especially helpful if the client is talking to the introject of a perpetrator, and the client is too afraid to begin speaking with the introject. The counselor can verbally disempower the perpetrator by speaking to the introject in a strong and scolding manner. Then the counselor can say to the client, "Now you tell him. Say anything you want." This will be further discussed below (see "Speaking to the introject of a perpetrator", page 62).

Speaking as an introject

One of the most powerful aspects of working with clients when they are communicating with an introject is the client's ability to take on their internalized persona of the introject and reply back to the client. (It is recommended that clients be asked to speak as the introjects only of persons with whom they want a stronger or more understanding relationship.) Often, when this happens the client gains a new understanding of the ability of the introject to hear and understand the client, and the client gains a new understanding of the feelings the introject may have. Of course, these understandings are based on the client's internalized perception of the introject, but, in my own work and from the feedback of my colleagues and students, I have found these internalized perceptions to be more than adequate to assist in problem resolution. The client can speak as an introject (for example, can speak back to the client from the chair of the introject—as the mother of the client). After a client has spoken to the introject of his or her mother in an empty chair, the client may be directed to sit in the mother's chair and speak back to the client's chair.

There is a real difference between those times when the client is speaking as the introject from their own perspective, and when they are speaking as the introject from the perspective of the introject. I know this sounds confusing at first, but it is important to understand this distinction. The next two paragraphs will illustrate this: the first paragraph will illustrate the client speaking from the perspective of the introject, and the second will illustrate the client speaking from the perspective of the client.

1. Clients speaking from the perspective of the introject

Clients who speak from the perspective of the introject will be sensitive to the feelings of the introject. They will not be trying to illustrate how the introject is wrong. They may more easily be viewed by the counselor as the real person of the introject. When the counselor observes the client speaking from the perspective of the introject, it does not appear that the client is acting out a role. Often, new information about the relationship between the client and the introject, information that the client has not yet offered, becomes part of the conversation. The conversation seems to be coming from the heart, not from the head.

2. Clients speaking as the introject from the perspective of the client

Clients who speak as the introject, but from the perspective of the client, are not sensitive to the feelings of the introject. They often appear to be acting a role that is designed to illustrate the negative aspects of the introject. The client appears to be thinking about what can be said, rather than saying it spontaneously. The conversation seems to be coming from the head, not the heart.

How the counselor can facilitate conversations with introjects

Initially, the counselor will need to direct the client to change chairs, and take on the chair and the persona of the introject. This normally occurs after the client has had an opportunity to express him- or herself to the introject. The counselor may say something like, "That was very good, what you said. I'd really like to hear what your mother has to say about that. I'd like to hear just exactly how she heard that [pointing to the chair of the introject]. I want you to sit over here, and as you sit down I want you to be your mother. I want to hear directly from the essence of your mother. [Then, as the client sits down …] Mother, James said some things to you that could be really hard for you to hear. Mother, what do you think about what James said?" Other statements of the type that the counselor may say to the introject include:

- How are you feeling right now, Mother?
- Life is hard for you, isn't it, Mother?
- What's going on in your life?
- What would you like to say to James?

- Just go ahead and tell him directly how you're feeling now.
- What do you really feel about James?
- Can you tell him that?
- Go ahead, and tell him now [pointing to the chair the client was sitting in before assuming the persona of the introject]. Tell him directly.

It is important for the counselor, when speaking to the introject, to speak directly to it as if it were the real person. Never say things like, "What would your mother say now?" Statements such as this direct the client back into a mental process of calculating what Mother might say, rather than speaking directly from the internalized perception of the introject. It is the interplay between the internalized perception of the introject and the client where the problem lies. It is, therefore, imperative for the client to speak as the introject, and directly to the empty chair of the client.

After the client has expressed from the internalized perception of the introject, i.e., after the introject has spoken, the client may be asked to move back to his or her chair (the client's chair). Then the counselor may say something like, "Boy, it sounds like your mother really does have some problems of her own. She's having real difficulty understanding what you feel. What do you think about what she said?"

Here, the counselor plays the role of mediator, but, of course, is mediating in favor of the best outcome for the client. It is the counselor's role to promote expression from the client (while the client is in the client's chair) to the introject, and from the introject (while the client is in the introject's chair) to the client. Often, the outcome is an increased understanding, and a "mending of fences". This is probably the most preferred outcome.

It is also not unusual for the outcome to be that the client gains an understanding that the introject will never be able to be who the client wants that person to be. By gaining this understanding, the client is better able to settle with the issue, and to accept that the introject is imperfect. This outcome also assists the client in problem resolution.

Following an interchange using the two chairs where the client is able to speak and say what is needed to be said, and the client also speaks as the introject, the client will most usually comment about an increased level of understanding. Often, the client also comments about being surprised concerning some new level of insight. Interestingly, clients will often report during later sessions a much improved level of communication between themselves and the person who was introjected during a session.

What should the counselor do if the client is having difficulty speaking as the introject? It is somewhat common for the client to speak as the introject, but from the perspective of the client, as discussed above in the section, "Clients speaking as the introject from the perspective of the client". If the counselor sees that this is happening, the client should be stopped, and asked to return to the chair of the client. Then the counselor can say something like the following:

> **Counselor**: I had the impression that, while you were talking from your mother's chair, you were making a case against your mother. That can be a good way to let me know your feelings and I would like to hear that case from your chair (that you're in now), but what I really want to hear right now is your mother's perspective. It's like being an actor and really taking on and living the role, where you sort of forget who you are and you feel like the other person, telling her point of view. In a way, it's like my being able to hear from her, using all the things you know about her. I want to hear what she thinks and what she feels. Now, do you have any questions? [After questions, if any, are answered:] Good. Now, sit again in your mother's chair, and as you do I want to hear directly from Mother, from her perspective.

Normally, a clarification like this is all that is needed to help a client understand what is wanted, in terms of being able to speak as an introject from the introject's chair.

Remember, introjects may be personae of individuals whom the client knows at the present time, the personae of that person as they are today, or personae of that person as they were a number of years ago. For example, if the client reports feeling like a little child who is not listened to by her father, the client may be asked to invite the father of the little child into the other chair, not her father as he is today. It can be that a child ego state has a need to be expressed to her childhood father. When this is the case, it is important for the counselor to be very clear that the father being invited into the other chair is the father of the child, the father who lived at the time of the child, not the father as he is today. This is very important, as often a resolution needs to occur for a child state with that child's father, and often no resolution needs to occur with the father of today. Of course, mother and father are being used as examples only. Introjects may be internalized impressions of any individuals.

Speaking to the introject of a deceased person

It is also possible for the client to speak to the introject of the deceased person. The client is speaking with their internalized perception of this individual. It is even possible for the client to speak to, and with, the introject of a baby, living or deceased, or to the introject of an aborted fetus. The counselor needs to be prepared for clients who speak with loved deceased persons to be very emotional while doing so. Therefore, this type of work should not be begun by counselors who have difficulty dealing with highly emotional clients. But, if the counselor is able to be understanding and allow the client to be emotional, cathartic work can be done. Often, in a single session, an issue that has plagued the client for a number of years can be greatly relieved. The following paragraphs will provide some examples of this type of work.

Speaking to the introject of a fetus

It can be extraordinarily traumatic for a woman to lose a fetus in any way. The client who has lost a fetus may find it is difficult to grieve appropriately. There may be much that seems incomplete and unsaid. In the case of abortion, guilt may be involved, and in any case sorrow may be deep and unrelenting.

The normal grieving process should be allowed and encouraged. But, years after the loss of the fetus, a profound feeling of nonresolution may be still experienced by the client. When this is the case, it can be extremely helpful to facilitate an opportunity for the woman to express herself to the persona of the unborn fetus, and also to hear in reply what the introject of the unborn fetus has to say. Often, counselors will be at first reluctant to allow the introject of the fetus an opportunity to speak, fearing something might be said that could be hurtful or harmful to the woman. While it is possible that this could occur, it has never occurred with one of my clients, nor have I had a student or colleague report to me that it has occurred with one of their clients. As a matter of fact, when the woman is able to express herself openly to the introject of the fetus, the response from the fetus has always been loving and positive. Theoretically, this makes sense, because the introject is internalized as an innocent and loving being.

Speaking to the introject of a perpetrator

It can be extremely beneficial for a client to speak to the introject of a perpetrator. This work is normally done after bridging from a current unwanted reaction has located unprocessed feelings related to a perpetrator (see "Bridging from the unwanted symptom to the cause of the problem", page 65). It is by rising above the previously held fear and saying exactly what the client has always wanted to say that empowerment takes place. Still, there are some cautions that should be recognized when encouraging a client to speak to the introject of a perpetrator.

With most work where the client is directed to speak with introjects, it is common to place an empty chair so that it is facing the client, and encourage the client to think of the essence of the other person sitting in that chair, before asking the client to say to that person what he or she has to say. It is also common to ask the client to move over and sit in the chair of the introject so that the client can respond as the introject, and thereby better understand the dynamics of the encounter.

When working with the introject of a perpetrator, it is important for these common techniques to be altered. For example, rather than ask the client to imagine the essence of the perpetrator in an empty chair, it is better to ask where in the room the client would prefer to imagine the essence of the perpetrator. This leaves more space between the client and the perpetrator, and allows the client to feel more safe.

It is not my practice to ask the client to move to the location of the perpetrator and respond as the introject. It is better to allow the client to stay well away from where the perpetrator is, and encourage the client to say everything he or she would like to say to the perpetrator. Normally, after expressing to the perpetrator, the client is asked if it would be better for the perpetrator to leave, and, if the client agrees, the client is then encouraged to tell the perpetrator to, "Get out!"

Because it is so empowering and therapeutic for the client to express to the perpetrator, it is not my practice to ask the client, "Would you like to talk to the perpetrator now?" When posed with this question, some clients would answer, "No," and the chance to gain empowerment would be delayed. It is better to help make sure the client is able to become empowered over the perpetrator by saying something like, "Where in the room can you imagine [the perpetrator] being right now?" If the client appears too frightened to imagine the perpetrator as being in the room, the counselor can say something like, "Remember, I'm right here with you on your side. I can say something to him first if you like."

It is not unusual for a client to, at first, express an inability to speak to the perpetrator. Clients may say things such as, "I'm too afraid," or, "He's too big." At this point, the counselor has an opportunity to direct the session in one of two ways. The counselor could say that it's OK, you don't have to talk. If the counselor does this, the client has revisited a fear and has not overcome it. The client may be closer to that fear than he or she was prior to coming in for counseling, and to end this part of the session without the client's achieving empowerment may leave the client feeling worse than before the session began. This is obviously not the preferred option.

The other option is for the counselor to professionally help the client rise above the fear and say exactly what the client would like to say to the perpetrator. This is the much preferred option as this leaves the client feeling empowered and safe. In order to help the client rise above fear, the counselor can say things such as:

- Remember, you're really safe within a counseling room. He's not really there, so this is our opportunity to say exactly what we want to him, safely.
- Do you want me to say something to him first?
- [If yes to the above question, said with strength, e.g.:] You bastard. You have no right to do what you did. I cannot believe what you did. You should not have done that. [Then said to the client:] Now you tell them what you want to! Tell them anything you want!
- What would be helpful to you to be able to say what you want to say to him? Would you like him to be really small, or behind a thick bulletproof glass? You can have anything you want. This is our scene and we have the power here. How do you want him to be?

After the client has said everything he or she would like to say to the perpetrator, it is good to say, "That was really good. Now, do you want him here or do you want him to leave?" The answer to this question is almost without exception something like, "I want him to leave." The counselor can then say, "Good! Tell him you don't want him here. Tell him to get out. Tell him to go!" Next, it is good to confirm with the client that the perpetrator has gone. "What happened?"

It is important for the client to rise above the fear and say everything that the client wants to say, before asking the perpetrator to leave. Almost always, after the client has risen above fear and said to the perpetrator everything the client wants to say, the perpetrator will then leave immediately when the client asks him to do so. This makes sense because the introject of the perpetrator has been disempowered by the client's rising above the previously held fear. On the rare occasion that the introject of the perpetrator does not leave when the client asks, the counselor can also demand that the perpetrator leave: "Didn't you hear her? She does not want you here. You have to get out now! Just leave! We don't want you here! Go, now!"

An important aspect about communication with an introject of a perpetrator is that the client understands there is support from the counselor. The counselor is strong, is a professional, and is clear.

There is something that appears almost magical when the client rises above previously held fear and expresses to an introject of a perpetrator. The fear has existed because the client has previously been unable to rise above it. When the client is able to rise above the fear and say everything the client wants to say, then the fear disappears. Obviously, fear cannot exist when nothing is feared.

Bridging from the unwanted symptom to the cause of the problem

There is a reason for everything, so there is a reason that clients respond to a situation in a manner they do. If the client responds in a manner that seems inconsistent for the situation, that means the client has an internal tender spot that has been touched by that particular situation, and the touching of a tender spot causes the client to respond in a way that is undesirable to the client. This tender spot is an ego state that is carrying an unresolved issue. An ego state of the client has become vaded, overcome by negative experience to the point where it can no longer conduct its role, to the point where the state interferes with the life of the individual when it comes to the executive. This lack of resolution is what often brings clients to counseling.

Below are some examples of clients who have responses that are inconsistent with the situation at hand. These are indicators of vaded ego states.

- The client becomes extremely nervous when stepping into an elevator.
- The client has an unwanted response during sexually intimate situations.
- The client becomes extremely upset when criticized by an authority figure.
- The client becomes extremely nervous when attempting to speak in front of the group.
- The client finds it impossible to be assertive.
- The client fears spending or handling money.

These examples constitute only a small portion of the manner that clients can respond in a way that is inconsistent with situational stimuli. And, in each situation, the clients respond in the manner they do because some earlier incidents in their lives have not been processed.

Advanced Skills and Interventions in Therapeutic Counseling

Therefore, it is important to be able to determine the cause of an unwanted symptom. The cause of the unwanted symptom will be a situation that has occurred in the client's life where resolution was not achieved. Often, the client has not discussed the unresolved issue with another person. And often the client is not consciously aware of which issue is connected to the problem at hand. The client may or may not have a conscious memory of the incident when coming to therapy. It appears to be unimportant whether the client has a memory of the incident or not.

Bridging is the process of using the negative emotions of a client to bridge back to the original time that the ego state acquired these emotions. Bridging is important because when the original trauma is found it can be resolved, thus freeing the client of future interference from that trauma. Bridging is appropriate when a client presents with a difficulty to which the client responds in an abnormal manner.

Steps in bridging

- Gather detailed information concerning:
  - when the problem was experienced,
  - multiple sensory cues associated with the problem, and
  - how the problem was experienced.
- Use the detailed information that was gathered to facilitate a current experience of the unwanted symptoms, then say:
  - How old do you feel right now?
  - Go to when you were that age and tell me if you are inside a building or outside.
  - Are you alone or with someone else?
  - Tell me exactly what is happening.
- After bridging, it is good to get a name for the ego state that is speaking, so you will be able to talk with that state directly and call it back at a later time.
- Trauma Resolution is the next step.

The counseling process of bridging is detailed in the section entitled "Determine the precipitating cause of the unwanted symptoms" on page 175. An example is given, and illustrated to assist the reader in gaining more full understanding of this important process.

Basically, the process includes assisting the client to experience the unwanted symptom in order to place the client into the ego state that is unresolved. When the client is obviously experiencing the present through this unresolved ego state, bridging to the original incident is possible.

Resolving a trauma

Locating the cause of the unwanted symptom is only the first step. It would do little good to merely locate the cause of the unwanted symptom. The second important step in facilitating the cessation of unwanted symptoms is to help resolve the trauma the client has been carrying.

Once the trauma has been located, it is important for the client to be able to express, i.e. to say everything that the client would have liked to have said during the original occurrence. This rising above fear and expression is very important. Once the client rises above fear and says everything that he or she wants to say, there is a great sense of empowerment. Steps and examples to help the counselor assist the client in this step of expression begin on page 107.

Following expression, it is important for the client to feel free of whatever provoked the fear. Whether it was a perpetrator, a misunderstood person, an animal, the dark, or anything else, the client needs to feel internally free.

The final aspect of helping a client resolve a trauma is assisting the client to feel comfortable and relieved. Following the client's verbal expression, and removal of the provoking element, it is important for the client to be able to feel relaxed, comfortable, and empowered.

Therefore, the process of resolving a trauma involves locating the ego state that has been traumatized and that has carried fear. This will be the ego state that comes into the executive in the client's current life causing the client to feel the unwanted symptom. In counseling, this traumatized ego state is brought to the executive by assisting the client to vividly describe a moment when the unwanted symptom was experienced. When the client talks in detail about an incident where the unwanted feelings were experienced, the traumatized ego state comes into the executive and bridging may occur to locate the original cause of the unwanted symptoms, i.e. the time when the ego state became traumatized. After locating this original trauma, the counselor can help the client with expression, removal, and relief so the ego state that had been traumatized no longer has to carry the feelings of fear and disempowerment.

For detailed instructions on resolving a trauma, see "Facilitate a resolution to the trauma the client has been carrying" on page 107.

Chapter 5

Assessing the Client's Problem

One of the most difficult aspects of helping clients is determining the most appropriate direction for counseling intervention. Adding to this difficulty is the fact that clients often do not come to counseling with a clear view of what they want to change, or even of what their problems are. During the first part of counseling, time should be spent on getting as clear an understanding as possible concerning what the client wants to change. Useful questions are, "What are you ready to change?" and, "What was the final thing that happened that helped you decide you wanted to come to counseling?" Clarity on what the client wants to change is important for both the counselor and the client, and it is the first step in assessment.

The issue the client first raises will likely not be the only issue that is focused on in counseling, and may not be the central issue facing the client. Therefore, the counselor needs not only a strategy to determine the initial course of intervention, but also to be flexible enough to continue to assess the client's issues throughout the therapeutic intervention, consistently evaluating each issue the client poses in order to assess the appropriate course of counseling in an ongoing manner. This chapter presents a method for continually assessing clients' concerns so therapy can be properly directed.

DSM-IV-TR diagnosis

Clinical psychologists often use the DSM-IV-TR to assess and diagnose clients. This process of diagnosis can be useful, although some studies indicate a low reliability among different psychologists who diagnose the same clients (Harrison, 2001). Humanist psychologists, such as person-centered and Gestalt therapists, often view clients as too individually dynamic to diagnose into the pigeonholes of the DSM-IV-TR. They generally prefer to think of clients as individuals necessitating tailor-made responses for their needs.

A major difference exists between a DSM-IV-TR diagnosis and ego-state assessment. While the DSM-IV-TR diagnosis places the client into a category, the ego-state assessment places *each problem* of the client into a category. Ego-state assessment is merely used to help determine the course of therapy for each presenting concern, and is not seen as a label for the client. If the therapist has reason to also diagnose a client using the DSM-IV-TR, of course, this diagnosis may be used in conjunction with the ego-state assessment.

The counseling assessment method

The assessment method presented here is relatively straightforward, and allows the counselor to determine the appropriate course of therapy by first assessing whether the presented problem is related to a type of internal dissent (cognitive dissonance) or to a difficulty in responding to a situational concern (see Figure 1). Counseling clients are seen as needing work with one of, or a combination of, six things.

1. **Internal dissent.** For example, two or more states are not agreeing – no peace within. One state may want to rest while another state may want to work.
2. **Difficulty with a situational concern that is connected to an unresolved issue from the past.** For example, the client is responding to a current situation in a manner that is inconsistent with a normal response to that situation.
3. **Difficulty dealing with a situational concern related merely to a current difficult problem.** For example, the client is having difficulty managing a relationship with a teenage son or daughter.
4. **Needing information or education.** For example, about what can be expected during grieving, or about finding what community services are available.
5. **Needing help to bring resources to needs.** For example, the client is interested in improving performance.
6. **Medical referral.** For example, the client presents issues that may require medication, or medical attention.

While most client concerns can be viewed as relating to one of these six areas, it may be helpful to present a flowchart that demonstrates assessment. Figure 1 may be used as a guide to assess each concern the client presents in counseling. The first step of assessment is to determine whether the presenting concern is one of internal dissent or difficulty with a situational concern.

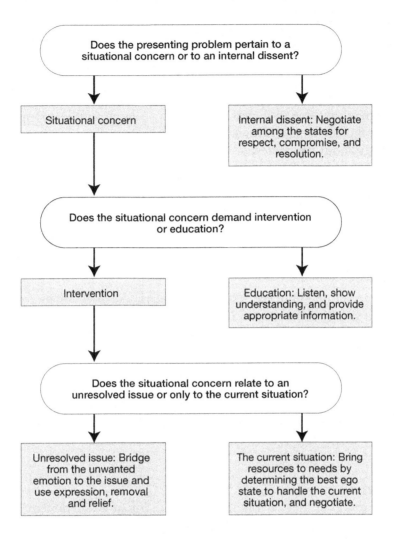

Figure 1: Assessment/intervention flowchart

An internal-dissent issue

An example of an internal-dissent issue is the problem clients sometimes present of procrastination. One of their states has work that needs to be done and wants that work to be done, while another state wants to rest or play, resulting in cognitive dissonance or an internal dissent. Clients who have an internal-dissent issue often have difficulty feeling settled and at peace with themselves. They may also suffer from headaches, resulting from the internal struggle for control. They have no peace within.

A situational issue

An example of the client having difficulty responding to a situation is the one who becomes too anxiety-laden to speak to a large public group. Another example is the client who is having difficulty in dealing with a teenage son or daughter. In both examples, a particular situation is associated with the problem of the client. There may be no internal struggle, just a problematic response to a situation.

While it is relatively easy to determine whether the primary presenting problem is a result of an internal dissent or situational concern, it may also be the case that a problem presented by a client has components of both internal dissent and situational response. When this is the case both types of issue will need to be addressed, in turn.

After a presenting concern has been determined to be related to internal dissent or a situational concern, it can further be assessed into subcategories. A situational concern can be divided into two subcategories: a current-context-situational concern or a situational concern that is based in an unresolved issue. It is not difficult to distinguish between these two types of concern, as the situational concern that is based in an unresolved issue is flagged by the client responding to a situation in a manner inconsistent with the stress that situation would normally cause. Future parts of this book will detail, with examples, how to distinguish between these two types of situational concern.

Education

It is often the case that clients need an amount of education to help them normalize their concerns. Probably, the most common example of this is in grief counseling. Many clients who come for help during the grieving process are poorly educated about what is normal in grieving. Sometimes these clients do need therapeutic interventions, but often they need to know that the experiences they are having in grieving are normal. Another example of a client who needs education is the one who needs to understand what community resources are available, especially in times of crisis. Hotlines, shelters, and other community resources are an important aspect of education that the counselor can provide for the clients. Therefore, while education is not considered to be a major part of the therapeutic counseling process, it is sometimes necessary and invaluable.

Recognizing personal resources

Clients often need assistance to recognize their own internal resources, and to learn how to bring these resources out when needed. For example, a client who has difficulty with public speaking may find it very useful to recognize an ego state that can speak comfortably and clearly. It can be the case that learning about internal resources and learning how to call these resources out is all that is needed to satisfy the client's goals. But it is often the case that, even when these resources are known, they cannot be used because an injured or traumatized ego state forces itself into the executive, preventing the preferred ego state from being able to be used. The section on bringing resources to needs illustrates techniques to help clients discover and use personal resources.

Medical referrals

Not all client issues are psychosomatically based. Clients will need medical referrals when the counselor determines that there may be an organic cause relating to the presented problem. Family history and personal history are key criteria to consider in determining the possibility of an organic cause. It is the responsibility of the counselor to refer a client for medical or psychiatric appraisal if there is a determination that a physiological cause may be related to the issue. Some other examples of necessary referrals include clients who fail to show positive response in counseling to chronic depression, clients who demonstrate psychotic or paranoid behavior, and clients who may pose a danger to themselves or to others. Obviously, any time a client poses a problem or an issue that is outside the training of the counselor, a referral to another professional is required. No amount of counseling may benefit a client whose psychology is being affected by physiology.

This assessment chapter is provided only as an aid to determine the direction of therapy. The reader will necessarily need to review sections related to each type of therapeutic intervention highlighted in this chapter. It is expected that after reviewing the sections on therapeutic interventions, a review of the assessment decisions presented in this chapter would be helpful. It will be by gaining a fuller understanding of the specific types of intervention that the reader will be more able to benefit from the assessment/intervention flowchart in Figure 1.

Chapter 6

Internal Dissent: Cognitive Dissonance

Many clients present with a primary concern directly associated to internal dissent. Therefore, every counselor should be well trained in methods to deal with this issue. The goal is "a peace within". Whenever clients feel as if part of them is pulling one way and another part is pulling another way, or as if, no matter how hard they try, they cannot make up their minds on an issue, internal dissent needs to be addressed.

In order to help clarify and illustrate the problem of internal dissent, a few client statements presenting this problem will be given:

- "Procrastination is a real problem for me. I really want to get my work done, but I seem to always wind up watching television." (One state wants to work and another state wants to rest.)
- "I don't know what's wrong with me. Sometimes I know I want to marry him, and at other times I look at him and I think I need to get out of this relationship as quickly as I can."
- "I really want this degree, but I just don't want to do the work."
- "Before I go to bed I have to check all the locks and all the water taps. Then I go to bed and have to get up and do the same thing again, and then maybe another time, and again. It's driving me batty. I really wish I could just go to bed and go to sleep." (One state has a need to check locks and taps and another state is tired and angry about all the checking.)
- "I hate myself when I talk to my mother like that. She really gets under my skin and I wind up saying things I really don't mean." (One state has feelings about her mother that are sometimes being expressed in a way that another state is embarrassed about.)
- "I just can't make up my mind if I want to go for this job or not. The extra income would be great, but I don't think I would like to work that much."

The commonality illustrated by all these concerns is that two parts of the client, two ego states, are disagreeing with each other, not respecting each other, and have found it impossible to come to an accommodation.

Almost every client has an issue concerning internal dissent. This is the case even if the primary presenting concern has to do with an unwanted response to a situational problem. For example, the client's primary concern may be the way he or she is responding to a boss at work (a situational problem), but a secondary concern may have to do with that client's ability to finish work at home, or to have leisure time. This secondary concern demonstrates two parts of the client that are disagreeing. One part wants to do the work while the other part really wants to have leisure time, and this internal dissent makes the client feel unsettled and experience a lack of internal peace.

Another example is the client who presents with an overt demonstration of anger as being the primary concern. The anger response to a situational cue is the primary problem, but there may also be an internal dissent concerning which part of the client, which ego state, will respond to this situational cue. Part of the client might prefer to respond in an assertive manner, part of the client may want to respond with overt anger, and another part of the client might prefer to respond with calm negotiation. Therefore, internal dissent or cognitive dissonance entails part of the problem involved with the presenting concern.

Helping the client resolve internal dissent

Internal dissent is caused by ego states that do not communicate well with each other, and/or that do not respect each other. Therefore, in order to resolve internal dissent, it is important for the affected ego states to have good communication, respect, and negotiation skills with each other. An example will help illustrate how the counselor can assist the client with internal communication, respect, and negotiation skills. For the purpose of this example let's take the first presenting problem illustrated above.

Julie: Procrastination is a real problem for me. I really want to get my work done, but I seem to always wind up watching television.

Counselor: It sounds like you're divided between wanting to get work done and wanting to watch TV.

Julie: I guess so. I'm just getting extremely behind on my work.

Counselor: Right now I'm hearing about two parts. I'm hearing about that part that really has a need to watch TV when you get home, but it seems like I'm hearing more from that part that's concerned about your work. I want to be able to hear from both parts so I'm going to put another chair right here [just across from the client]. In a moment, I will want to hear from that part that would like to watch TV, but it sounds like the part that is concerned about your work is really ready to talk now. So I just want to hear from that part that wants to get work done while you're sitting in the chair that you're in right now. Later, I'll hear from the part that wants to watch TV, but just go ahead now and tell me all the reasons you want to get your work done.

Julie: I'm just really far behind. I have this big report that has to be written, and I don't have enough time at work to do it. So, I have to work at home until I get this report finished, but something happens and I start watching TV.

Counselor: Remember, I just want to hear from the part that wants to do the work right now.

Julie: If I can just get started on it I know I can do it. It's not that hard. It just has to be done.

Counselor: This work part of you I'm hearing from now sounds very confident. I can see it really wants to get work done and has the confidence that you can do it. What word or term would describe this part of you—this work part of you?

Julie: I don't know, "Worker"?

Counselor: That sounds perfect. So, while I'm talking to this part of you that wants to work I will call you Worker. Worker, what do you think about this other part of Julie [the client] that wants to watch TV when she comes home?

Julie: Well, I guess I don't like it very much. It just takes over and I can't get anything done. I just wish it would leave me alone and let me get my work done.

It is surprising to many counselors how quickly clients are able to distinguish between their ego states. It is also occasionally surprising to clients.

Counselor: That must be frustrating. It would be nice for you to get your work done, but I'm sure that other part is very important also. Let's see if we can work something out. Worker, thank you for talking with me.

It is very important to always speak respectfully about all ego states. That way each and every state will be more willing to work for a successful outcome.

Counselor: Now, go ahead, Julie, and move to this other chair [pointing to the other chair], and as you sit down I want to hear only from that part of you that really wants to watch TV when you get home. [As Julie sits down:] Part, tell me what it is like to want to watch TV when you get home.

Julie: I've had a long day and I don't want to work anymore. I just want to sit down and veg out.

Counselor: That sounds really important. It sounds like you do important work making sure that Julie gets rest, because everyone needs some rest time. Everyone needs some time for the body to regenerate. What word or term would fit you? What can I call you, part?

Julie: "Exhausted".

Counselor: OK, Exhausted, tell me what you think about Worker.

Julie: She just wants to work all the time. She's very annoying. She won't leave me alone.

Counselor: But it sounds like you are the one who has the power when you get home.

Julie: I *do* [spoken proudly]. But she's not happy about it. She just wants to work all the time, and I'm really tired. I have to get some rest.

Counselor: You sound like a really important part, Exhausted. I think Worker is probably important also. I'm not sure if you understand it, but without Worker this person wouldn't make any money, and you might not even have the TV to watch. Are you aware of how important Worker is?

Julie: I don't know. I guess she is important, but she just will not leave me alone.

Counselor: That must be really annoying, because it is important for you to make sure this person gets some rest, but I was talking with Worker a few moments ago and she's really stressed.

Julie [interrupting]: She is always stressed.

Counselor: She feels she's behind on important work, and she doesn't think you listen to her.

Julie: I don't. If I did, I never would get any rest.

Counselor: Wouldn't it be nice if you could get rest and you could also be respected by Worker? I don't think she understands how important you are.

Julie: She doesn't.

Counselor: What if we can work out a way so you could have time to get rest, really good time without Worker bothering you, and Worker could have some time to get some work done, and you could both respect each other? You could be respected by Worker.

Julie: I don't think she will ever respect me. She just wants to work all the time.

Counselor: But wouldn't it be nice if you could have some time to rest without being bothered by Worker?

Julie: Yes.

Counselor: I think it might be possible for the parts to compromise and respect each other. Worker is a very useful state to have. She gets a lot of things done. This person needs her. If it wasn't for her you might have to do work yourself, and that's not your role. Is it OK with you if I talk to Worker to see if I can work something out?

Julie: You can try.

Counselor: Thank you. You're very helpful, and a very important part. Now, Julie, move back to this other chair and I want to talk with Worker again. Worker, did you hear what Exhausted said?

Julie: I heard.

Counselor: Exhausted is very important. Without Exhausted this person would probably break down, and then you would not be able to get any work done. You need Exhausted, but Exhausted believes you would like to work all the time. It seems to me that both of you are really important parts. It is important for you to be able to work, and it is important for Exhausted to be able to have some rest time. What do you think of that?

Julie: I can see that. It makes sense, but Exhausted just wants to watch TV all the time.

Counselor: Would you be willing to allow Exhausted some time to have some really good rest when you get home from work, if Exhausted will give you some time to get caught up on some of your work. That would mean that neither one of you has all the time, but you could both have time without being bothered by the other. And, you could get respect from Exhausted and the two of you could cooperate together. What do you think?

Julie: I can see how that would work, as long as I get enough time to get my work done.

Counselor: It will only work if you allow Exhausted time to rest. There may be some days that Exhausted needs more time, and other days that you need more time. The only way you will be able to work that out is if you respect each other and can talk about it on the inside. Would you be willing to give it a go?

Julie: Yes.

Counselor: Thank you, Worker. Now, Julie, please move back to the other chair so I can speak with Exhausted. Exhausted, I believe Worker is now seeing how valuable you are. She's willing to give you some time to rest when you will not be bothered, if you will give her some time to get some work done without being bothered. You are both very important. Are you willing to work with Worker on this?

Julie: As long as I get time to rest. I will work with her.

Counselor: That's great, Exhausted. I think the two of you will really be able to work this out. Just close your eyes for a moment and have an internal conversation with Worker, and see if you can come to some agreement. [Eyes close, pause.] What happened?

Julie: She said I could have some time to rest after coming home from work as long as she gets time to do her work.

Counselor: That's great. Now, in the future it would be good for the two of you to continue talking internally, because you both know how important the other one is. I want to say thank you to Exhausted and to Worker for working together in order to get a resolution. Now, I would like for both states to settle in where they belong and I want

> to ask Julie a question. You can open your eyes now. Julie, how are you feeling about this resolution?
>
> **Julie**: That was really interesting. I could feel both parts. They were so different. I think this could work.

A resolution whereby ego states are able to learn to respect each other and work together normally has immediate effects. Clients most often describe in following sessions a major change in what may have been a long-standing problem. In the above example, three ego states were spoken with, Worker, Exhausted, and the state that responded to the client's name, Julie. Because each person is always experiencing life from an executive ego state, there is no central ego state that has a priority as being the person. The state that responded to the name Julie was most likely a state that was troubled by the confrontation between the other two states, the state that decided to come to counseling.

The two ego states Worker and Exhausted had not been communicating together, and they had little respect for each other. They both wanted use of the same time, the time after work at home. This conflict caused an internal disharmony in the client. Often, when the client would come home, a struggle would be felt, as no resolution could be made. Sometimes struggles such as these can result in a physical headache as two states struggle for the executive. By facilitating each state to recognize the importance of the other, and to gain an understanding that each state could be respected by the other, it was possible to successfully negotiate between the two states. It was also possible for a line of communication to be made between two states that grew to respect each other in counseling.

It is not unusual for the client to express surprise at the end of a negotiation such as this one. Indeed, I have found when demonstrating this technique to students that often students will express surprise that different parts of a personality can speak almost like different people. Students are often amazed that it is so easy to speak to individual ego states separately, and to see a different level of affect or emotion from each. Often, it is not until they try the techniques with their own clients and receive positive feedback that they begin to understand the power of working with ego states. Clients will often later report observing a real change in the way they handle situations, without their having to continue to think about the issue.

It may be helpful now to describe some important features of working to resolve internal dissent.

1. Get a clear understanding of the division and of the states involved

First, it is important to interview the client and gain a clear understanding concerning the internal division that is being presented. In the simple example that was provided, it was clear that two states were not agreeing. One state wanted to do work when the client arrived home, and another state wanted to watch television. The client should be interviewed until the counselor understands the nature of the two states. What is it that each state wants, and what is the nature of the dispute. When the counselor has these understandings, it is time to hear from each state individually.

2. Make clear which state will sit in each chair

Often, when one is talking to the client, it is obvious which of the two states in the dispute is talking more. It is good to identify that state as a part of the person, and to indicate that you want to hear everything it has to say, and then you will want to hear what the other state has to say. Therefore, the state that has been talking more effectively is assigned the chair the client was originally sitting in, and the newly introduced chair will be the chair assigned to the other state. If it is not clear that either state is talking more when the problem is being described, the client may be asked, "The chair you're sitting in now, which of the two parts seems to be more comfortable in this chair?" The answer to this question will determine where each of the two states will sit during the session.

3. Listen to everything each state has to say

After positioning the states in the chairs, it is important for each state to be fully heard. It is also important that, while each state is being heard, if an argument from the other state is introduced, the counselor should interrupt and explain that, while the client is in this chair, it is important to speak only from the state that has been assigned to this chair. Therefore, in this third step, both states will be able to have a discussion with the counselor, and will be able to feel heard, understood, and respected.

4. Help each state to see the value of both states

It is important for the counselor to impress upon each state how valuable that state is, and also how valuable the other state is. It is good to ask each state how it feels about the other state and to express an understanding of that feeling, but also to express an understanding of the importance of the other state to the client. It is not unusual, at first, for states to have difficulty seeing the importance of another state. In fact, it is not unusual for a state to say about another state that it should just go away. There can be no resolution with this attitude, so an important part of the negotiation is for the counselor to find a way for each state to respect the value of the other.

5. Suggest how nice it would be to have the respect of the other state

It is often useful to suggest to a state how nice it would be for it to have the respect of the other state. Again, it is not unusual to get a reply that such a thing could never happen. The counselor should not be discouraged by this, and can say things such as, "Yes, I know it seems like it could never happen, but wouldn't it be nice if it did?" It is often surprising how quickly states that seemed to dislike each other can learn to cooperate.

6. Negotiate a way the states can work together

When each state has had the opportunity to get a vision of being respected by the other state, it is time to negotiate a manner in which the states can work together and respect each other. This negotiation is much like a negotiation between two people. The counselor needs to be flexible and to promote flexibility to both states. It is when a mutually agreed-upon solution is found that both states can begin to understand a partnership.

7. Suggest that the states communicate directly with each other

At this time, when a mutually agreed-upon solution is found, a suggestion should be made that the states talk internally together to see if they can work it out. This is a very important step. Often, the two states have had little or no communication prior to this time. By bringing the states together when a solution has been brokered, and by suggesting that they will continue to work together in a positive way, a productive line of communication is made for the future. Therefore, in the future, the states have an opportunity to work out solutions that will be mutually beneficial, with each knowing its own importance and the importance of the other; peace within.

8. Thank each state for working together to achieve a solution

It is good to thank both states for working together and for being helpful in achieving a solution. This is another technique in facilitating ego-state change. Ego states that are treated rudely will not want to be helpful, and those that are treated politely are more likely to be of assistance.

9. Debrief with the client

It is good to suggest that the ego states can settle into their new roles, and the client should be given an opportunity to debrief. Good questions during debriefing include, after a short pause, "What do you think of that? Could you feel a difference between the two states? How do think that will work for you? Are there any questions?" Of course, the questions and the debriefing will depend on the client and the situation.

It is not necessary to follow these steps in order, or completely. And, it may be that other steps are seen to be important by the counselor working with particular clients. These steps are illustrated merely as a guide for counselors who are beginning to work with clients on issues of internal dissent.

It is also common for more that two ego states to become involved in the resolution of internal dissent. When this is the case more chairs may be used.

It is important for the counselor to act as a professional who has a vision of what needs to happen in the session. If the counselor is timid or tentative about asking the client to switch chairs, then the client will be tentative and this will affect the outcome. The counselor should always speak in a clear, understanding, and instructive voice when telling the client to switch chairs. For example, statements such as "I want you to try this" should be avoided in favor of statements such as "Julie, right now I want you to move to this chair and as you do I want to hear only from that part of you that ..." Clear and direct instructions such as this will be followed, and not questioned. The client comes to the counselor seeking professional assistance. It is appropriate that a trained professional instill confidence in the client, confidence that the counselor knows how to direct and handle the session.

Working with the issue of internal dissent is somewhat more straightforward, and easier than working with situational concerns. It is therefore good for counselors new to this therapeutic approach to first practice working with internal-dissent issues with clients before tackling situational concerns, especially when unwanted situational responses stem from unresolved issues.

It is by becoming comfortable in learning to speak with individual ego states directly and learning to negotiate with them that the counselor will gain a natural skill and confidence. Later, when clients revisit a traumatized ego state, the counselor will be able to naturally respond in a manner that can help resolve the issues that state has held.

Chapter 7
Difficulty Responding to a Situational Concern

A common presenting concern of a client is that he or she is having difficulty responding to a situation. Examples of this include:

1. When my boss is disappointed with my work, I can't say anything and I feel like going home. I just feel as if I should not even be there.

2. My teenage son is driving me crazy. I'm doing the best I can to be a good parent but he shows me no respect and I'm afraid he may be doing things that could get him in trouble.

3. Ever since my husband left, I can't feel comfortable at home alone. I just freak out being there alone and I don't know what to do with my time.

4. When my brother tells me something, it seems like I'm able to hear what he's saying but, when my sister says the same thing, I get really angry at her.

5. When I try to get in front of a group and speak, I get so nervous I can't say anything.

6. There's just too much for me to do at work. It's really stressing me.

7. Each time I try to get in an elevator I freak out. I'll walk up the stairs, even if it's twenty floors.

The one thing that all these presenting concerns have in common is that some situation is giving the client a problem. Actually, there are two different types of problem caused by situations here (current-context-situational concerns and unresolved-issues-situational concerns). While it is impossible to tell for sure which type each question belongs to without more information, we can have an idea concerning how they may be divided.

A current-context-situational concern
A situational concern can cause a client difficulty merely because it is a difficult situation, and it would be a difficult situation for most people. The client's level of emotional distress is in line with what would normally be

expected with this type of problem. This type of situational concern is purely within the current context. Points 2 and 6 above are examples of this type of concern.

- My teenage son is driving me crazy. I'm doing the best I can to be a good parent but he shows me no respect and I'm afraid he may be doing things that could get him in trouble.
- There's just too much for me to do at work. It's really stressing me.

It is quite possible that clients with these concerns are in situations that would be stressful for anyone. And it is possible that these clients are having emotional distress brought about by the situations, and this distress is unrelated to unresolved issues in the clients' lives. Of course, as counseling proceeds, it could be that the clients' responses are partially associated with unresolved issues. But it may be that the response of a client is completely in line with the stressful situation. The client will need help in responding to a surface issue, not a problem where underlying issues need to be resolved.

In this case, the counseling techniques presented under "Current-context-situational concern" (page 87) would be appropriate.

An unresolved-issues-situational concern

Concerns 3, 4, 5, and 7 above indicate situational concerns that probably stem from unresolved issues in the past, and Concern 1 could easily reflect either a purely surface problem, or a problem related to an unresolved issue. Each of these statements indicates that the client is reactive when a particular button is pressed. A tender spot has been touched. Those tender spots reflect an event earlier in life that has not been resolved, an ego state that has not healed.

- Ever since my husband left, I can't feel comfortable at home alone. I just freak out being there alone and I don't know what to do with my time.
- When my brother tells me something, it seems like I'm able to hear what he's saying but when my sister says the same thing, I get really angry at her.
- When I try to get in front of the group and speak, I get so nervous I can't say anything.
- Each time I try to get in an elevator I freak out. I'll walk up the stairs, even if it's twenty floors.

These statements are characterized by a response that would not be considered normal for the situation at hand. For example, the statement "When I get in an elevator I just freak out" indicates that the client is not responding in a normal fashion to the situation of getting into an elevator. The client who says, "When I get in front of the group I get so nervous I can't say anything" further illustrates an example of responding to a situation reflecting an unresolved issue. It is not unusual for a person to have some degree of nervousness when talking in front of a group, but not being able to say anything would indicate the degree of nervousness is beyond what would normally be expected. The following sections will discuss counseling techniques for both current-context-situational concerns and unresolved-issues-situational concerns.

Current-context-situational concern

Everyone has current life situations that can be demanding, and that can seem impossible. It is not unusual for clients to bring to counseling current life situations that have placed them under stress. There are a number of strategies and techniques that can be helpful to individuals who are having current-context-situational stress.

The first role of the counselor in this instance is to hear and understand the problem the client is presenting. Good active-listening skills can be helpful in this process, since they may help the client feel understood and less isolated within their problem. But what clients often need is an increased ability to bring in their own resources to their own needs.

When confronted with a difficult situation, clients often respond from a reactive ego state. This can result in their feeling out of control. It may also result in their saying or doing something that may later be regretted. Feelings of stress and incompetence may follow. The counselor needs to be able to assist the client in hearing the problematic information in a way that is less stressful, in determining the best course of action, and then in responding in a manner that the client can feel positive about. Therefore, steps for assisting the client presenting with a current-context-situational concern may be presented as follows:

1. Hear and show understanding of the problem the client is presenting.
2. Determine the ego state that the client is in when the situational problem occurs.

3. Assist the client to find a more appropriate ego state to deal with the problem.

4. Assist the client to determine how he or she would prefer to respond.

5. Facilitate ego-state negotiation so that the client will be able to hear and understand the situational problem from an appropriate state, and so that the client will be able to respond from an appropriate state.

6. Debrief with the client.

These steps assist in empowering the client, and in helping him or her to bring internal resources to external needs. It is the client who will decide the best response, and it is the client who will be able to respond in a more natural and skillful fashion from an ego state that is better able. Each of the six steps will now be discussed in turn.

1. Hear and show understanding of the problem the client is presenting

It is in this step that the counselor makes a determination whether the problem being presented stems from a current-context-situational concern or from an unresolved-issues-situational concern. It is important that problems stemming from unresolved issues address those past issues (see "Unresolved-issues-situational concern", page 99). Otherwise, the steps taken in the session may be of limited benefit. For example, a client who is dealing with only a surface issue will be more easily able to bring to the executive ego states that have the ability to deal with those issues. But the client may not be able to bring to the executive talented ego states if, because of an unresolved issue, an ego state with negative feelings jumps into the executive. A client may not be able to bring a relaxed ego state into the executive when getting in an elevator if a traumatized state jumps into the executive, causing fear and panic.

A mistake many beginning counselors tend to make is to try to intellectually solve the problem of the client. This practically never works. If the problem were easily solved, the client would have solved it long before, and would not have brought it to professional counseling. It can be insulting to the client for a counselor to automatically offer solutions to a problem when the full context is not even understood. Even if the client listens to the counselor and takes the counselor's solution, it is most often thought of as "the counselor's solution". The client has little ownership, and if it does not work the counselor may be blamed. Solutions that come from the client, the person who has the most complete knowledge of potentials and possibilities, are more fully invested in and have a much better chance of providing a positive outcome. When clients supply their own solutions they are more likely to be able to solve their own problems in the future.

Therefore, the purpose of this step is merely to hear and understand, and reveal this understanding to the client. This, in itself, can be therapeutic, because, in order to help the counselor understand, clients have to clarify sometimes cloudy problems and may thereafter better understand themselves. Also, when the counselor demonstrates an understanding the client can feel less alone in his or her concern.

It is the information gathered in this first step of understanding that will enable the counselor to proceed with ego-state work.

2. Determine the ego state that the client is in when the situational problem occurs

It is important that, when listening to the client's problem, the counselor hear the ego state that is initially taking on the problem. To better explain this, an example will be used. Let's take a statement from the above list for this illustration.

> **Julie**: My teenage son is driving me crazy. I'm doing the best I can to be a good parent but he shows me no respect and I'm afraid he may be doing things that could get him in trouble.
>
> **Counselor**: It sounds like you're feeling like you've lost control.
>
> **Julie**: You have no idea. He expects to be fed and clothed, but other than that it's like I'm not even there. No matter what I say.
>
> **Counselor**: I can see this is really upsetting for you. It must be awful not to be heard by someone who you have raised. An example would really help me better understand exactly what's happening.
>
> **Julie**: This morning he was leaving for school, and I just asked if he had his lunch. He turned and looked at me and said, "As if you would care," and slammed the door behind him. I just started crying. I don't know what to do. I don't know what I can do.
>
> **Counselor**: I can see this is really difficult, and that it's hard on you. It's going to help me if I can get as accurate an understanding as possible of how you're feeling through this. [Pulls out an empty chair across from the client.] Would it be easier for you to imagine your son sitting in this chair, or standing next to it when you think of how you felt when were talking with him this morning?
>
> **Julie**: Standing next to it, I guess. He wasn't sitting down. He was on the move.

Counselor: OK, just imagine the real essence of your son standing next to the chair. He's leaving for school and you want to ask him about his lunch. Even before you ask him, how are you feeling?

Julie: I'm frightened. I don't know how he's going to respond. We just can't seem to talk anymore, about anything.

Counselor: OK, he's about to leave and you're frightened and you want to ask him about his lunch. Go ahead and ask him now just as if he were standing there.

Julie [in a tentative voice]: Andy, what are you going to do about lunch today?

Counselor: That was very good. Right now, I want you to feel what you're feeling like. I could hear it in your voice. You said you're frightened. Tell me more about how you're feeling right now as you ask Andy about his lunch.

Julie: I'm just really scared. I'm afraid he's going to bite my head off.

Counselor: Feeling scared, like you are right now, what can I call this state you're in? What can I call this part of you, this part you're feeling right now?

Julie: What do you mean?

Counselor: This part of you I'm talking with right now. Would the name "Frightened", or possibly "Timid" fit for that part of you.

Julie: "Frightened" would fit best.

Counselor: That's perfect. From now on, when I speak with this part of you, the part called "Frightened", I will address it directly using the name, "Frightened".

This example illustrates finding the ego state that is executive when the situational problem occurs. This is a very important step. Often, clients meet difficult confrontation with an ego state that is ill-prepared or inappropriate to handle that situation. The first step in helping the client meet the difficult situation from the preferred ego state is to identify the ego state that has been used in the past. In the example above, the ego state that has been named "Frightened" has been executive when the client attempted to speak with her son. This frightened ego state is probably not the best ego state she could use to talk with her son, either for herself or for him. It will be important for her to determine what ego state she would like to use in speaking with her son when she fears a confrontation.

3. Assist the client to find a more appropriate ego state to deal with the problem

To determine the most appropriate ego state it is important to determine how the client would like to be able to respond to the problem. This is the client's choice, and it is appropriate for clients to be able to define the kind of thing they would like to say, and how they would like to feel when they say it. Obviously, if the client says something like "I would like to punch his lights out," then the counselor needs to negotiate with the client a more appropriate response. Normally, though, clients choose appropriate responses that will work best for them. In order to illustrate the step, the above example will be continued.

Counselor: It seems to me that, when you respond from this part of you to your son, which I call "Frightened", it may not be good for you or for your son. When you're frightened, you feel fragile and worried, and you make it easy for your son to walk right by you, without respecting you. It might be nice if you could speak to your son from a part of you that is not afraid. What do you think of that?

Julie: Yes, that would be good, but he frightens me.

Counselor: I understand that. But, I bet you have parts of your personality that are never frightened. Right now, what I would really like to know is how you would like to feel when you talk with your son. You know how he's speaking to you now, and you know how he's responding to you when you speak with him. This has been very upsetting to you, and that's understandable. But, given the way he is now, how would you like to feel when he talks to you, and how would you like to feel when you talk to him?

Julie: I don't know. I guess I would like to feel confident, not afraid of him. I mean he's never hit me, and I know he never would, but I'm still afraid of him.

Counselor: That sounds reasonable, to want to be confident when you talk with him, and not afraid. Tell me about a time when you feel confident, a time when you are strong, when you have something to say and you expect people to listen. [See the section, "When the client has difficulty finding an ego state that can help another state", page 210.]

Julie: Well, when I'm at work I manage three people in my department, and I don't have any trouble telling them what to do.

Counselor: That's excellent. I want you to think about being at work right now and describe to me where you are, what room you are in, and what you're wearing. [This helps place the client into the assertive ego state she experiences while she is at work.]

Julie: I'm sitting behind my desk. It's a big desk. I have my blue suit on, and there are papers on my desk.

Counselor: Now, imagine that one of the people you manage is sitting in that chair right there [pointing to the chair across from the client] in front of you. How are you feeling?

Julie: I feel good.

Counselor: Who is that in the chair?

Julie: It's Ruth.

Counselor: What does she want?

Julie: She wants to know how to do something.

Counselor: How are you feeling right now, with her asking for your advice on something?

Julie: Strong. I know how it should be done.

Counselor: What can I call this part of you that feels strong, and confident?

Julie: You can call me "Strong".

Counselor: I will now speak directly with that strong part of you. I want to speak with it as if it is a person all by itself. It is a part of you. Strong, I can see you are a very confident part of Julie.

Julie: Yes, I am.

Counselor: Strong, I have a question I want to ask you. A few moments earlier I was talking to another part of Julie that was a nice part, but it was very different from you. That part of Julie was called Frightened, and when she's in that state she's not confident, as you are, Strong. Are you aware of this frightened state, Strong?

Julie: Yes, I know that part.

Counselor: Strong, I want you to think of the chair you're sitting in right now and how you feel sitting in that chair, and I will want to talk with you some more from this chair, but right now, Julie, I want you to move over to this other chair [pointing to the chair across from Julie], and as you sit down I want to hear from Frightened. As you sit down, I want to hear from the part of you that has had difficulty talking to your son recently. [Julie changes chairs.] Frightened, thank you for talking to me again. I know you've been finding it scary talking to your son lately, and I'm wondering what you think about this other part of Julie that she often experiences at work – this part called Strong.

Julie [frightened, spoken in a weaker voice]: That's a very different part from me. She always knows what to do.

Counselor: Frightened, you sound to me like a sensitive, caring part, and I'm sure there are things that you are very good at. I'm just not sure if you are the best part right now to deal with your son. What do you think?

Julie: I think you're right. He scares me now and I don't like talking with him.

Counselor: This may sound a bit funny, but Frightened, right now, I would like you to look over at Strong [pointing to the other chair] and ask Strong if she would be willing to help you when you are talking with your son.

Julie [looking a bit puzzled]: Will you help me, Strong?

Counselor: Now, Julie, move back to Strong's chair. [Points to the other chair. Julie changes chairs.] Strong, what do you think? Frightened would have difficulty doing your work, and she's quite different from you, isn't she?

Julie: Yes, she is much more emotional.

Counselor: How do you want to respond to Frightened? She's asking for your help.

Julie: Yes, I'm willing to help.

Counselor: That frightened part may not be the best part of Julie to be dealing with her son right now. You are very strong and confident and assertive. I wonder whether, when Julie knows how she wants to deal with her son, you can be the one to talk with him.

Julie: I could help.

Counselor: That's great. Thank you for talking with me, Strong. And thank you for helping. I will want to talk to you some more later.

Here, a resource of the client (her strong and confident work state) has been located, spoken with, and encouraged to help with one of Julie's needs: her need to communicate better with her son. Bringing resources to needs is an important aspect of counseling, although assisting the client with better handling a situation is not finished when a resource is located. She will need to have clarity about how she wants to handle the difficult situation. It would not be enough to only locate an assertive ego state. That state needs to be able to gain direction for dealing with her son.

4. Assist the client to determine how he or she would prefer to respond

The human personality and the parts that make it up are fascinating. Often, different parts or ego states of a client will hold different opinions regarding how a problem should be resolved. In the present example, we have located an ego state that is strong and confident, and quite capable of talking with Julie's son in an assertive fashion. Still, this ego state may not understand the dynamic nature of the relationship between Julie and her son. Therefore, it is important to spend time determining how Julie would prefer to talk with her son.

If the ego state called Strong were left to determine how Julie should communicate with her son, it is quite possible that he might be treated more like an employee at work than like a person whom she loves dearly and has raised. While hard and fast ultimatums might be appropriate for employees at work, they might not be appropriate for her son. It is the counselor's role to assist Julie in determining how she wants her relationship with her son to continue to develop.

Counselor: Julie, I have an important question for you, and I want you to look inside and think about it. What kind of relationship do you want with your son, now?

Julie: I want him to love me. I love him and I always have and always will. I don't want to lose our relationship. I don't want to lose him.

Counselor: I can see you really do care a lot for him. Given the way he's communicating with you now, how would you like to respond to him?

Julie: I know he's going through a lot. He will tell me about it. I don't think I help things by trying to make him feel guilty. It just makes him resent me. I guess I wish I could give him some space, but let him know I'm there for him.

Counselor: That sounds really wise. How would you like to do that?

Julie: I guess I could tell him what I'm thinking, if I could have the courage to do that.

Counselor: I don't think courage is going to be a problem for you. You have Strong, who is able and willing to talk with your son when you know what you want to say.

Julie: She is pretty strong.

Counselor: Yes, she is. And this part talking with me right now seems pretty wise. Is it OK with you if I call this part "Wise"?

Julie [smiling]: Sure.

5. Facilitate ego-state negotiation

Counselor: Julie, just close your eyes right now for a moment, and I would like Wise, that part who knows how you would like to relate to your son, and Strong to have a little internal conversation. See if Wise can communicate with Strong and let Strong know how you would like to communicate with your son, and see if Strong is willing to do that. [Pause.] What happened?

Julie: They worked it out.

Counselor: That sounds really good. Now, before you open your eyes again, I want you to imagine your son walking out to go to school. You don't know if he has thought about his lunch. You see him, and you see his mood. Remember, you have Wise, who knows about your son, and you have Strong, who is assertive. Tell me how you will handle this.

At this point, recall the scene the client described earlier when she said, "This morning he was leaving for school, and I just asked if he had his lunch. He turned and looked at me and said, 'As if you would care,' and slammed the door behind him. I just started crying. I don't know what to do. I don't know what I can do."

Julie [after a short pause]: I can see this is not the time to talk with him. He wouldn't be able to hear anything I would say before he leaves. I'll just say to him, "Have a good day."

Counselor: That sounds like a wise way to handle it. How do you feel when you say that?

Julie: In control.

Counselor: Now, let's go to a time when you do have a chance to speak with him. Remember, you have Wise and Strong. Where are you and what do you want to say?

Julie: He's in his room. It's nighttime, and I come to the door.

Counselor: Go ahead and open your eyes, and look across to the empty chair. Imagine the essence of your son sitting in the chair. What would you say, and how would you say it? Go ahead and speak to him now with him in the chair.

Julie: Andy, I know I haven't handled things the best lately. I know you're growing up, and it's hard for me to understand sometimes. You mean a lot to me. I love you. I really want a good relationship with you.

Counselor: That's very good. You really told Andy some things from your heart. Now, I want you to move over into Andy's chair [pointing], and as you sit down I want you to *be* Andy, hearing what you've just said as Andy heard it. [Julie changes chairs, and as she sits down.] Andy, your mother just said some things to you. How do you feel about what she said?

Julie: I don't know. She's always wanting something from me.

Counselor: It sounded to me like she really loves you, Andy. How do you feel about her?

Julie: I love her.

Counselor: I can see that. But I can also see that she's bothering you in some way. Tell me about that.

Julie: She just keeps wanting to run my life. I need more space.

Counselor: What could she do that would allow you to have space, and that at the same time would allow her to be your mother.

Julie: I don't know.

Counselor: Thank you for talking with me, Andy. Right now, I want to talk with your mother again. [Points to the other chair; Julie moves.] Boy, Julie, I can see how it can be difficult to communicate with Andy right now. Is there anything you learned from that?

Julie: That was really interesting. I didn't realize he felt so cornered. I really have to be careful how I talk with him.

Counselor: Yes, he does appear to have a need for some space. And I know you have your needs too. What would you like to say to him now? You can go ahead and say it now. [Points at the other chair.]

Julie: Andy, I know you need space, and I understand that. I'm sorry I haven't given you much space in the past. I will try to do that better, and it would help me if you try to speak nicely to me. I really do want a good relationship with you.

Counselor: You said that very well—clear and strong. How did you feel when you said that?

Julie: Good. I wasn't nervous.

Counselor: Let's see how he heard it. [Points for Julie to move to the other chair.] Andy, what do you think about what your mother just said to you?

Julie: Yeah, I can see she wants to get along. I have been a bit rough on her.

Counselor: That's really good, Andy, that you're able to see and say that. Now, I want to talk with your mother again. [Points for Julie to move to the other chair.]

6. Debrief with the client

Counselor [continuing]: Julie, how do you feel about how you're talking with Andy now?

Julie: I feel like there's been a shift. I'm not afraid, and it seems like I have more understanding.

Counselor: Remember, you have some really good resources. You have Wise, you have Strong, and at the right time if it's really safe you have Frightened, which could be a really good part of you to get a safe hug from Andy or from someone else whom you care about when you feel safe. You seem to be able to use your resources really well.

Julie [smiling]: I hope so.

Counselor: How do you feel about the session, and yourself?

Julie: The session was amazing. At times I thought it was a bit strange, but I think I was able to really get in touch with something important.

Counselor: What was that?

Julie: I don't know for sure. It just seems like with what we did I can see it so much better.

Counselor: That's really good. It will be good to see how your communication with Andy changes. [When possible it is good to give a positive suggestion about change. This can help empower the client to more easily achieve what is wanted.]

Julie: I hope it will be better.

Counselor: Do you have any questions?

Julie: What should I do to use this?

Counselor: It seems that you already have what you need to respond in a way you prefer. You know your resources better, your wise part and your strong part that you are aware of and that you can call on whenever you choose, when talking with Andy or at other times too.

Julie: I like that. I can use them with other people too.

Counselor: They are part of you, and you might as well use them in a way that is most helpful and preferred.

This example illustrated the steps involved in assisting a client to deal with a current-context-situational concern. Let us review the steps in this example. First, the counselor listened to the client and showed an understanding of the problem the client was presenting.

1. Hear and show understanding of the problem the client is presenting

Here, the client was having difficulty communicating with her teenage son. She was talking to him from an ego state that felt frightened and weak. He was speaking disrespectfully to her. Next, it was the counselor's role to find the ego state that was having problems with communication.

2. Determine the ego state that the client is in when the situational problem occurs

The counselor found and spoke with an ego state that gave itself the name "Frightened". This ego state was not speaking well with Andy and it was certainly not enjoying the communication. Therefore, it was important to find an ego state that felt stronger, and more able to speak with Andy.

3. Assist the client to find a more appropriate ego state to deal with the problem

The client was asked when she felt strongly confident, and an ego state that was normally executive at work was found, and it named itself "Strong". This was a good resource that the client would be able to use when talking with her son. It was next important to work with the client to determine exactly how she wanted to communicate with her son.

4. Assist the client to determine how he or she would prefer to respond

The client was asked about the nature of her relationship with her son, and what she wanted in that relationship. She was able to respond from a caring ego state that was called "Wise". This ego state was clear that what was most important was a good relationship with her son. The state was willing to work with the strong state to facilitate a clear communication of care and respect.

5. Facilitate ego-state negotiation so that the client will be able to hear and understand the situational problem from an appropriate state, and so that the client will be able to respond from an appropriate state

The counselor facilitated ego-state negotiation so that the states Wise and Strong could better work together, and negotiation was also facilitated between the client and her introject of her son, Andy. When she was communicating with Andy, it was clear that she was able to speak from a strong state, as she felt clear and not nervous during the communication. This practice helped give her confidence that she would be able to bring her own resources to her needs when communicating with her son. Her communication with the introject of Andy also appeared to help give her a deeper understanding of the nature of communication required between herself and her son.

6. Debrief with the client

The counselor helped the client overview the session, and get an idea of how the work may be applied in her life. It is good to allow the client to ask any questions to have a chance to integrate the session with the counselor. Also included in this part of the session would be arrangements for further sessions, if agreed to.

At no time in this counseling interchange was any work done in relation to unresolved issues of the client. The focus of the entire session was placed on a current situational issue and bringing the resources of the client to meet that issue. The client was able to gain a clearer understanding of the problem and was able to gain an understanding of her own resources, and was better able to access her resources.

In the next section, discussion will focus on situational problems that relate to unresolved issues from the client's past. We will see how the course of therapy differs, depending on whether or not the client's reaction is merely to surface-situational cues, or is outside what would be a normal reaction to the surface-situational cues.

Therefore, it is the role of the counselor to listen to the client, and to gather information that will indicate whether it is solely a situation that is giving the client a problem, whether the client's response is in line with what would normally be expected for that type of situation, or whether the client's response is outside what would normally be expected for that type of situation. This is an important part of assessing the client's presenting concern. It is not difficult to make this assessment, as long as the counselor clearly understands the difference between a surface-situational problem and an underlying-situation problem.

Unresolved-issues-situational concern: trauma resolution

Everything that happens has a cause. When the cause of the stressful reaction cannot be accounted for by the situation at hand, the stressful reaction is being caused by something else. When the client responds to a situation in a manner that is not consistent with that situation, the client is responding because that situation is touching a tender spot somewhere in the psyche of the client. That tender spot is an ego state that needs resolution. This section discusses how the counselor and client can locate the cause of the negative response, and can resolve the issues associated with the cause so that the client is able to respond naturally, to the situation at hand.

It may be helpful to give examples of how unresolved issues can cause unwanted situational symptoms. An obvious example is the individual who has experienced a horrific car accident, then finds it too overwhelming to drive a car. This simple example illustrates how an ego state can be affected by trauma, and, when a situational cue brings that state into the executive, the same trauma is re-experienced. This example is somewhat unusual in that it is very clear when the unwanted response started and what caused the unwanted response.

Normally, when a client is experiencing an unwanted response to a situational cue, he or she either has no idea why that response is being experienced, or merely has a guess at why. An example of this is the client who found it impossible to speak in front of the group, even becoming too nervous to move to the front of the room. Using ego-state techniques, it was discovered that the traumatized ego state that came to the executive when the client would come close to speaking in front of a group had been traumatized when he was a boy working in a field with his father. His father had yelled at him for being incompetent. The state that had been verbally abused had received no resolution, and later, when the client thought about performing for others, this unresolved state would come to the executive filled with the same negative feelings it had experienced in the field when the boy was yelled at. When the client came to therapy for help in speaking in front of groups, he had no inclination that the incident in the field had anything to do with his inability to give a presentation. The boy-in-the-field ego state was able to gain resolution using techniques described below, and the client found and later reported that he could easily give group presentations.

Incidents that subconsciously remind the client of trauma can bring into the executive ego states that have not had resolution. When those ego states achieve resolution the same incidents will not bring the previously unresolved ego state into the executive, thus allowing the client to respond to the situation at hand with surface ego states.

There are five main steps involved in trauma resolution, illustrated in Figure 2, and a number of sub-steps.

1. Hear and show an understanding of the problem the client is presenting.

2. Determine the precipitating cause of the unwanted symptoms.
   a. Gather detailed information concerning:
      i.   when the problem was experienced;
      ii. multiple sensory cues associated with the problem; and
      iii. how the problem was experienced.
   b. Use the detailed information that was gathered to facilitate a current experience of the unwanted symptoms.
   c. Bridge from the current experience of unwanted symptoms to the origin of the problem.

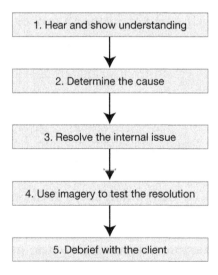

Figure 2: Steps to resolving a trauma

3. Facilitate a resolution to the trauma that the client has been carrying:
   a. Expression
   b. Removal
   c. Relief

4. Use imagery to test whether the trauma resolution has been successful in alleviating the unwanted symptoms.

5. Debrief with the client.

1. Hear and show an understanding of the problem the client is presenting

This is the same first step as was presented in the section, "Current-context-situational concern" above. It is in this step that the counselor makes a determination whether the problem being presented stems from a current-context-situational concern or from an unresolved-issues-situational concern. It is important that problems stemming from unresolved issues address those past issues. Otherwise, the steps taken in the session may be of limited benefit. For example, a client who is dealing with only a surface issue will be able to more easily bring to the executive ego states that have the ability to deal with those issues. But the client may not be able to bring to the executive talented ego states if, because of an unresolved issue, an ego state with negative feelings jumps into the executive. A client may not be able to bring a relaxed ego state to the executive when getting in an elevator if a traumatized ego state jumps into the executive causing fear and panic.

The purpose of this step is not to offer any solutions, but merely to hear, understand, and reveal an understanding to the client. This, in itself, can be therapeutic, because, in order to help the counselor understand, the client has to clarify a sometimes cloudy problem and may thereby better understand it themselves. Also, when the counselor demonstrates an understanding, the client can feel less alone in his or her concern.

2. Determine the precipitating cause of the unwanted symptoms

One of the most powerful and skillful aspects of counseling is determining the origin of the presenting problem. A client presents as having a reaction that is inconsistent with the situational cues of the problem because there is something that needs resolution.

Advanced Skills and Interventions in Therapeutic Counseling

One of the problems in counseling, and one of the aspects of counseling that prolong sessions, is the tendency for clients and counselors to talk about problems without addressing the cause of the problems. Clients often want to tell about when they had a problem and this is OK initially, but merely telling about a problem does little to resolve the problem. Clients need to experience empowerment.

It is easy to hear when clients are speaking in the third person, telling about their experience almost as if it were someone else's experience. When this happens, clients remain affectively unemotional and detached. Conversations such as these may continue for many sessions without having a noticeable impact upon the symptoms of the problem. In essence, what is happening is that an intellectual ego state is describing the experience of a different ego state that has unresolved issues. In order to make a direct impact upon the unwanted symptoms, it is necessary to bring out the ego state that has unresolved issues. It is only by working directly with the state where the cause of the problem is seated that resolution intervention can have the most impact on the unwanted symptoms.

This section will deal with the process of determining the precipitating cause of the presenting problem. The following section will deal with resolving the issue that causes the problem.

There are three steps involved in locating the precipitating cause. They will first be listed then explained in more detail.

i.   Gather detailed information concerning when the problem was experienced, multiple sensory cues associated with the problem, and how the problem was experienced.

ii. Use the detailed information that was gathered to facilitate a current experience of the unwanted symptoms.

iii. Bridge from the current experience of unwanted symptoms to the origin of the problem.

i. Gather detailed information concerning when the problem was experienced, multiple sensory cues associated with the problem, and how the problem was experienced.

The first step in trauma resolution is gaining a clear understanding about the client's problem. It is important to learn exactly what situations cause the unwanted response, and exactly what the unwanted response is.

The goal in locating the origin of the problem is to locate the ego state where that origin resides. It is imperative that the client talk from the unresolved ego state in order to resolve the unwanted symptoms. Detailed information about when and how the problem is experienced should be gathered.

For example, let's say a client, John, reports becoming extremely distressed each time he is criticized by his supervisor at work. While a common response to being criticized by a supervisor would not be positive, John reports becoming unable to speak, and practically unable to work for the rest of the day. He reports feeling physically ill with a sick stomach and a tightness in the chest. It is clear that John's reaction is tied to something beyond the situational criticism of his supervisor.

We will use John's reaction as an example to illustrate the process of getting the detailed information to facilitate the emergence of the unresolved ego state.

When the problem was experienced:

Counselor: John, I want you to tell me either the last time you felt criticized by your boss in this way, or about the time that sticks out in your memory?

John: It happens all the time. Pretty much every time he criticizes me I just feel like going home.

Counselor: I can understand why this is something you're really ready to change. What I need to hear right now is about one time, one specific time, that you would like to tell me about.

John: Well, on Monday of this week he came into my office and asked me where Friday's report was. I had finished the report, and he wasn't upset, but when he asked me that I just felt like I was in real trouble.

(It is much more effective, when wanting to bring out an unresolved ego state, to work with a specific incident, rather than to allow the client to talk about a theme of incidents. When clients talk about a theme of incidents, or a trend, they tend to be talking about that trend from an intellectual ego state that has been able to generalize. But, when clients talk in detail about a specific incident, it is easier for them to enter into the distressed state that experienced that specific incident.)

Multiple sensory cues associated with the problem:

Counselor: John, I'm going to want to know about your experience when he asked you for the report, but first I want you to tell me some things about where this took place. Describe your office to me, where you were in the office, and where your supervisor was.

John: I was sitting behind my desk. He came in and stood right in front of my desk to talk to me.

Counselor: What kind of desk do you have in your office? Is it wooden, or metal, large or small?

John: It's a large wooden desk with lots of papers on it. I'm not very good at keeping things put away.

Counselor: Is the door your supervisor came through straight across from your desk or at one side?

John: The door's on the right-hand-side wall from my desk. There's a big window straight across from my desk.

Counselor: And does the light come only from the window, or was there a light on over-head also?

John: It was in the middle of the day. So I didn't need the overhead light on.

Counselor: What were you and your supervisor wearing, John? Or, if you can't remember, what type of clothes would you normally be wearing at work?

John: I had on black pants and a blue shirt. He always wears a suit, with a white shirt and tie.

(Getting detailed information about the setting helps place the client into the setting and prepares him or her to enter the unresolved ego state when telling about the negative experience.)

How the problem was experienced:

Counselor: Exactly how did you feel when he asked you for Friday's report? How did you feel both emotionally and physically.

John: Well, he said he hadn't been able to find Friday's report, and the instant he said that I know my face must have gotten white, and it was like I had a big lump in my throat that would not move if I tried to talk.

Counselor: What emotions were you having?

John: I just felt little, like I was in real trouble, and like if I said the wrong thing I was going to be in even more trouble.

Counselor: It sounds like you were really afraid.

John: I guess I was. It's like I couldn't move. It's like everything shut down on the inside.

Counselor: Tell me as much as you can about what it felt like in your body. How did you physically experience this?

John: Now that I think about it. I felt it more in my head, shoulders, and arms. It was like there was something thick in my head and I couldn't think. And it was like I had no power in my shoulders and arms. I was powerless.

Counselor: Was the powerlessness an emotional feeling you are having also?

John: Yes, very much so.

(Often, when a client tells some specifics about their experience of a problem they automatically enter into the ego state that is unresolved. By the end of this first step of getting information most clients are at least closer to experiencing the unresolved ego state.)

This type of questioning is extremely important in finding the origin of the problem. John's response to his supervisor was not consistent with a mature adult's response to this situation. Therefore, with his supervisor speaking in an authoritarian fashion, something tender in John was touched, something unresolved. The result was a flush of emotions and a response that was undesired. Finding that tender spot is finding the ego state that is unresolved. Our ability to find and bring out that ego state is much dependent on the thoroughness, sensitivity, and artful fashion that information gathering is carried out.

We are now ready for the next step. It is important to take detailed notes during the information-gathering phase. These notes will be extensively used during this next step.

ii. Use the detailed information that was gathered to facilitate a current experience of the unwanted symptoms.

Steps ii and iii often work best if clients are first asked to allow their eyes to close. It is not necessary that clients close their eyes, but this can help facilitate their further entry into the unresolved state, and the bridging to the original cause of that lack of resolution. It is by finding that tender spot, that unresolved state, that real change can occur.

It cannot be overstressed how important it is for the client to be in the unresolved state before there is an attempt to bridge to the original problem. Counselors often make the mistake of attempting to bridge too early. This is a waste of time. It is not difficult to tell when the client is in the unresolved state. Emotions can be seen. Therefore, Step ii lasts as long as it needs to last. That is, until it is easy to see the client is currently experiencing the negative emotions that are unwanted. If the client is only *telling about* those emotions it is not time to go to Step iii, to bridge to where the negative feelings come from. It may be that after, Step i, it is clear to see the client is experiencing the unresolved emotions. If so, bridging may occur immediately. If not, the detailed information that was gathered in Step i is used to help the client to experience the unwanted symptom, so bridging to the original cause may occur.

John's example will continue to illustrate this.

Counselor: John, right now I want you to close your eyes and imagine sitting behind your desk in your office. You are sitting behind your desk, a large wooden desk with quite a lot of papers on it. You can look across and see a large window opposite your desk, and your boss is entering the door on the right hand side. You can see him with his suit, tie and white shirt, and you already know he's going to ask about the report. John, sitting there at your desk with your supervisor there in your office, tell me what you're feeling.

John: Nervous. He makes me nervous. I don't really want to be here.

Counselor: On the scale of zero to one hundred, how nervous are you feeling right now?

John: Pretty nervous. About sixty.

Counselor: See if you can have courage to get that feeling of nervousness up maybe to seventy. Your boss is asking, "Where is the report?" Think about your head, shoulders and arms. What are you feeling right now?

John: I'm feeling awful, like he's way bigger than me.

iii. Bridge from the current experience of unwanted symptoms to the origin of the problem

Counselor: Right now, feeling awful, like he's way bigger. What age or size comes to you? How old or big do you feel?

John: Not very big. About eight or nine.

Counselor: I want you to be eight or nine right now, and go to the time you felt awful, like "he's way bigger". Right there, feeling awful, are you inside a building or outside?

John: I'm outside.

Counselor: Are you alone or with someone else?

John: There are other people there.

(These questions, "Are you inside a building or outside?" and "Are you alone or with someone else?", help zero in on the traumatic occurrence.)

Counselor: Tell me exactly what is happening. [The client has his eyes closed and is showing signs of being extremely nervous.]

John: It's Ted Mavis. He says I have to give him my badge. I'd don't want to give him my badge. I just earned it.

Counselor: I'm right here with you, John. Who is Ted, and how big is he?

John: He's a ninth-grader, and he's always picking on me. I hate him.

Counselor: So you're eight or nine, and he's a ninth-grader. He must be a lot bigger than you.

John: He is. He's gigantic.

The origin of John's negative responses at work has been located. His feelings of being small and powerless in the face of an authority were the feelings of a child ego state that had experienced bullying and was never able to gain a sense of resolution. Later, throughout life, when this bullied ego state was reminded of the original trauma, that ego state would come to the executive with the same unresolved feelings of the original trauma. Even though John had not consciously thought about this bullying experience for many years, he carried his lack of resolution within him.

The work to assist John to not re-experience these unwanted feelings is only half finished. If counseling were to end at this point, John would have the insight of why he responds to authority figures in the way that he does, but he would still feel small and helpless. Therefore, it is important to continue to the next step of resolution.

3. Facilitate a resolution to the trauma the client has been carrying

There are three steps in facilitating a resolution of the trauma after the traumatic incident has been located. They are expression, removal, and relief.

Expression is when the client is able to rise above fear and say everything he or she would like to say. By rising above fear, rising above what had in the past seemed too big to face, the fear is disempowered, and the client is empowered.

Removal is when the provocative factor that had caused the fear is removed, or becomes no longer provocative. It is sometimes the case that a provocative factor, such as an angry person, may be asked to leave, after the first step of expression has taken place. This is one way the client can achieve removal. Remember, the client is working with a fear and image that is part of his or her current experience. The past is past and cannot be changed, but the client can alter the present experience and become empowered in the present. There will always be the memory of the past, but it becomes a healed memory, not a continuously festering sore.

Another way the provocative factor may be removed is for the client to achieve a new understanding of that factor. For example, if a loving parent had been expressing anger toward the child, removal of the provocative factor might occur by having that loving parent express love for the child. What is imperative for removal to occur is for there to be nothing left that is continuing to cause a problem for the previously traumatized state.

Relief refers to the moment when the previously traumatized state becomes comfortable and happy. After the steps of expression and removal, it is good to ask the state, "What do you need now?" If the ego state responds by saying that it needs a friend to play with, then a playful ego state may be found to come and play with the previously traumatized state, thus leaving it happy and content. (See the section, "When the client has difficulty finding an ego state that can help another state" on page 210 for a further discussion pertinent to relief.)

The steps of **expression**, **removal**, and **relief** will be illustrated with John's client example.

> **Counselor**: So you're eight or nine, and he's a ninth-grader. He must be a lot bigger than you.
>
> **John**: He is. He's gigantic.
>
> **Counselor**: Right there, with Ted in front of you, what term or name fits you? What can I call you there that seems to fit? [It is important to get a name for the ego state to help the client stay in that state during the conversation, and to provide a reference for the state in other conversations.]
>
> **John**: You can call me "Scared". I feel really scared.
>
> **Counselor**: OK, for now I will call you "Scared".

Facilitating expression

> **Counselor**: I want to tell you something, Scared. I know he's gigantic, but this isn't really happening right now, so right now you can say absolutely anything you want to him, and I'm here with you on your side. What you want to say to him?
>
> **John**: I want to tell him to leave me alone. But he's too big.
>
> **Counselor**: I'm here with you right now, Scared. He cannot hurt you now. Go ahead, and tell them to leave you alone. Tell him loud so he can hear you. Say it out loud so I can hear you too.
>
> **John**: Stop bothering me. I don't want to give you my badge.
>
> **Counselor**: That's good. No matter what happened at the time, you don't have to give him your badge now. What else do you want to say to him?
>
> **John**: I want to tell him to stop bothering my friends too, but I don't know if he's going to listen to me.

Counselor: What's he doing now?

John: He's just standing there looking at me like he owns the place.

Counselor: Is it OK if I tell him something? [It is good to help empower the client by speaking directly to the introject of a provocateur, although it is important that they later say what they need to say to rise above the fear they have held.]

John: Sure.

Counselor [loudly, and with authority]: Ted, get that stupid look off your face. You have no power here. Just give it up. You've been bullying too long, and it's not going to happen anymore. When you try to look mean you just look that much more stupid.

Facilitating removal

Counselor [continuing]: Now, Scared, tell him anything else you want to, and, if you don't want him there anymore, just tell him to leave.

John: I'm tired of you. Just get out. Go away. I don't want you here anymore.

Counselor: That was really good. What's happening?

John: He's gone!

Counselor: That's great. You really told him to get out and he left. That was really good. How do you feel now?

John: I feel good.

Facilitating relief

Counselor: Think about exactly how you feel right now. Is there any way that you don't feel as good as you could?

John: I'm still a little scared to be here.

Counselor: I can understand that. And at the same time you've been really brave telling Ted to get lost. I want to get a stronger part to be there with you to help you feel safe. Right now, I want to talk to a more mature part of John, a part that would like to be nurturing to an eight- or nine-year-old boy, a part that could help Scared feel safe. This may be a part that has helped children before. Just say "I'm here" when you're ready to speak.

John: Yes, I'm here.

Counselor: What can I call you, part?

John: You can call me "Helper".

Counselor: Thank you for talking with me, Helper. Would you like to help Scared feel more safe? [It is very important that the assisting part wants to help, otherwise it will not continue to do so. If a part says that it will help, but it doesn't really want to, then it is important to find another part that wants to help so the treatment will be lasting. When a helping part gets something out of helping, and enjoys it, that part will continue to help.]

John: Yes.

Counselor: That's great. Go to Scared now, right there where he is, and let him know that you're going to be there with him to help him, making him feel safe. You can always be there and still do everything else you do. [Pause.] Scared, what's happening now? Is Helper there with you?

John: Yes, he's here.

Counselor: Is that good?

John: Yes, he's much bigger than I am.

Counselor: Will he always be there with you?

John: I don't know.

Counselor: Ask him. Ask him if he will always be there for you, and always help you to feel safe. [Pause.] What did he say?

John: He said he would always be here.

Counselor: Do you feel like telling him thank you?

John: Yes.

Counselor: You can go ahead and do that. He likes helping. Is there anything else you need?

John: No, I feel really good now.

Counselor: Scared, I want to ask you something. You don't seem very scared right now. Do you still want to be called Scared, or do you want to be called something else?

John: I think it would like to be called something else.

Counselor: What would be a good name for you now?

John: I would like to be called, "Friend".

Counselor: That sounds like a great name, Friend. From now on I will call you that. When it feels safe you may want to come out in John's present life and be friends with someone and play. That would be good for you and for John. I want to say thank you to you, Friend. You have been very brave and you have accepted Helper as a friend so you can always feel safe. And I want to say thank you to Helper for agreeing to always be with Friend and help him feel safe. I think you will both get something positive out of this.

John has been able to rise above the fear he had carried in the ego state, Scared, for many years. This child state had never been able to let go of the fear of the bigger boy, Ted. There had been no resolution at the time, and there had been no resolution later, thus leaving a fearful state injured and unresolved. Throughout John's life, at times when an authority figure showed disapproval, this unresolved state would be activated with the same feelings it had in facing Ted, the bully. The bridging from the negative feelings John was experiencing at work allowed John and the counselor to discover where these feelings were coming from. No interpretation was required to discover this.

With the help of the counselor, John was able to face the bully, rise above his fear, and tell the bully what he had been afraid to tell him before. Once John rose above his fear and expressed himself, the fear was no longer bigger than he was. His own bravery dissolved his fear. Next, John was able to tell the bully to leave. Because he had already been able to rise above his fear of the bully, the bully had no choice but to leave. The bully that John had carried with him for years was disempowered.

The final step in the process of resolving trauma was making sure that the ego state that had carried fear was able to become relaxed and comfortable. In order to facilitate the relief step of resolution, the ego state, Scared, was asked what it needed to be relaxed and happy. It said that it still felt a little scared, so a mature ego state of John's was asked to stay with the scared state so that it could feel comfortable and secure. At this point, when the ego state felt safe, because it had chosen a negative name for itself, it was asked if it wanted a new name. It chose the name Friend.

A part of John, an ego state, that had felt unresolved, that had carried fear, was able to rise above fear, remove the provocative element that it had carried, and gain the feelings of safety and friendship. Inner healing such as this is lasting and profound for the client. If the same ego state were checked on years later it would normally be found comfortable, secure, and still enjoying the friendship of Helper.

What difference does this make in the way John is able to respond to authority figures? When an authority figure speaks to John, after the fearful ego state has gained resolution, that state will no longer jump into the executive with those feelings of fear. It will most likely not come to the executive at all to deal with authority figures. This will allow John, as an adult, to respond in the way he feels best when he is confronted. This does not mean that he will enjoy confrontation, but it does mean that he will be able to respond from mature surface states. He should be able to respond, no longer feeling out of control, but in a way that makes sense to him as an adult.

The case history of John is a realistic example of resolving trauma, once the traumatized ego state has been located. Of course, there are a number of variations that are sometimes necessary depending on how clients respond. For example, while it is normal for a client to respond readily when asked for another state that would like to help, it is not unusual for a client to have difficulty locating such a state. A client who has not been around children may not have a nurturing ego state that would like to help a child. When a client has difficulty in locating an ego state that could be helpful, some additional techniques can be useful (see the section "When the client has difficulty finding an ego state that can help another state" on page 210).

Occasionally, the bridging from the emotions of the original incident to the source of the unwanted emotional reactions locates an unresolved trauma that is not the wellspring for the presenting concern. Resolving this unrelated trauma, although still very good therapy and helpful to the client, would not result in eliminating the presenting concern. Therefore, it is always good to use imagery to test that the resolution has had a direct impact on the presenting concern.

4. Use imagery to test whether the trauma resolution has been successful

It is not difficult to use the same information as was gathered to help with bridging to test to see if the trauma resolution has had a direct impact on the unwanted emotional reactions. Information that was gathered as "multiple sensory cues associated with the problem" (above) is precisely what is needed to test the effectiveness of the treatment. It is important to take good notes so they may be referred to at times such as these. Some counselors do not like taking notes because they feel it separates them from the client, but note taking allows the client to understand that what they're saying is seen as important and it allows the counselor to have an important record of what was said, so it may be used in counseling. It would be impossible for most counselors to remember enough detail within the session, or between sessions, to be able to rebuild a scene in the client's words in order to facilitate change.

By looking back at the notes, the counselor will be able to see detail describing John's presenting problem. John was at work sitting behind a large wooden desk with lots of papers on it. There was a large window straight across from his desk, and a door on the right that his boss came through. There was no overhead light, with light coming through only the large window. John was wearing black pants and a blue shirt, and a supervisor was dressed, as normal, with a suit and white shirt and tie. John's supervisor came into his office and asked where a report was that he had not been able to find. At that time, John had felt a big lump in his throat, had felt a little afraid and powerless.

For the purpose of this example, we will start back in the session where we left off.

John: I would like to be called "Friend".

Counselor: That sounds like a great name, Friend. From now on I will call you that. When it feels safe you may want to come out in John's present life and be friends with someone and play. That would be good for you and for John. I want to say thank you to you, Friend. You have been very brave and you have accepted Helper as a friend so you can always feel safe. And I want to say thank you to Helper for agreeing to always be with Friend and help him feel safe. I think you will both get something positive out of this.

Counselor [continuing]: Those parts can go ahead and settle into their new roles now. John, I want to ask you now to go back to your office. You are sitting behind your big wooden desk with lots of papers on it. There's no light on overhead because plenty of light is coming from the big window across from your desk. You hear your boss coming toward your door. You know he's going to ask about the report that he hasn't been able to find. He comes into your office wearing his suit, white shirt, and tie. He asks you about the report. How are you feeling?

John: It's funny. I just see him as my boss. He wants to know about a silly report. He just doesn't know where it is. I haven't done anything wrong. All I have to do is tell him where it is.

Counselor: So, your experience is very different now.

John: Completely. I don't know why I was afraid before. [John actually does have full memory of the whole session.]

5. Debrief with the client

Counselor: That's very good, John. You can go ahead and open your eyes. Now, I want you to think about your whole life. I want you to think about other times when you have felt the way that part of you that is now called Friend felt when it was scared. Have there been other times when that part affected your life?

John: Yes, I have felt that way many times.

Counselor: And now that part of you that was unresolved is feeling safe, and is protected.

John: Will this really work? Will I no longer be plagued by the fear I've had? [A question such as this often comes from a cautious ego state.]

Counselor: It will be good to see exactly how well it works. It's nice to be surprised. [When a client asks if the treatment will work it is best to refrain from giving a clearly positive response, as this can create a resistance in some clients, causing them to prove that it can't work as well as a counselor says. By giving a positive but non-committal response—"It will be good to see exactly how well it works"—the counselor leaves the client with a positive expectation without saying that it will definitely work. By adding that it is nice to be surprised, a suggestion is given that the treatment may work better than even the client may expect.]

John: What do I do now?

Counselor: You've been able to get a better understanding of what's been going on with you when you've had to deal with authority figures. You've also been able to rise above past fears showing you no longer fear them. A past fear that you have become fearless about is no longer a fear. That part of you that felt unresolved has achieved a feeling of comfort. Now, all you have to do is decide exactly how you, as an adult, want to respond in each situation.

John: That sounds pretty good, if I can do it.

Counselor: You demonstrated that you could in the imagery we used, and, as I said, it will be really good to see exactly how well it works.

John: Thank you. I've never done anything like that.

Counselor: You did very well.

This type of intervention can be used to assist clients who present with a wide variety of concerns. This book contains a number of other examples of the expression, removal, and relief system of helping clients who have situational problems that stem from past events. These techniques are particularly useful in assisting individuals with addictive personality concerns (see the section on addictions on page 170).

The fallacy of interpreting why symptoms occur

It is very common for clients to come to counseling, describe the problem they are having with some unwanted reactions to a situation, and then tell the counselor why they react the way they do. "I get frightened when I stay alone at home because my parents never let me stay alone when I was a child"; or, "I get frightened when I stay alone at home because my parents left me alone when I was a child."

It seems as though we have a need to give a reason for the things we do. And it is not only the clients who like to postulate on why they have the reactions they do. Counselors get caught in this trap too. Some of the terms in psychotherapy underline the propensity of therapists to want to interpret:

"analyst" and "psychoanalyst". Many counselors attempt to interpret why clients act the way they do.

When the counselor works with ego-state techniques and bridges from the unwanted emotion to the original event, interpretation about what causes the symptoms is unnecessary. It is interesting to note that clients who present the reasons they act the way they do are normally inaccurate in their appraisals. A client may say, "I'm nervous when talking to men because my mother never let me talk to men when I was a little girl." Then, when a bridge takes the client directly from the ego state that is nervous about talking to men to the trauma that that state is reflecting, it may be that an incident at school is the real reason the client had previously been nervous in talking to men. Once this bridge has been made it is obvious to the client, and to the counselor, why she had been nervous in the past.

If clients, with all they know about themselves and their histories, can rarely interpret accurately why they react the way they do, then how can a therapist hope to have accurate interpretations after spending only a number of hours with the client in a setting that does not accurately reflect the real life of the client? It is the contention put forward in this book that they cannot. Therapists' interpretations are normally wrong, and they have to be wrong because most often the real cause of negative reactions to situational stressors are small incidents that were not even remembered by the client prior to bridging.

Bridging from the unwanted reaction to the original cause of that reaction allows counseling to occur where it is needed the most. The number of sessions needed to resolve an unwanted reaction is greatly reduced when counseling can occur precisely where it is needed.

Therefore, the message presented here is: don't interpret why a client does something. It can feel powerful to be a Sherlock Holmes, to sift through the evidence from someone else's psyche, to try to deduce and say this is why, but don't. Most of the time you will be wrong, and, even if you are not, merely telling a client "why" would have limited value. To effect real change, a resolution needs to occur for the ego state that is carrying trauma, so merely telling an intellectual state of the client your theory of why he or she reacts in a certain way is of little change value.

Abreactions

An abreaction is an emotive response in therapy that is inconsistent with what would normally be expected in that current context. An abreaction might consist of heavy crying, uncontrolled body movements such as jerking, rocking, or shaking, or a dramatic fluctuation in speaking, such as extreme rapid speech or an inability to speak at all. An abreaction is similar to a panic attack outside of therapy, although it may be somewhat less overwhelming for the client because he or she has the support of the therapist. Both abreactions and panic attacks are associated with unresolved issues associated with underlying ego states.

The observation of an abreaction in therapy gives the counselor important information. When an abreaction is observed this means that the client is close to some unresolved issue. At the time of an abreaction the counselor is actually observing the ego state with this unresolved issue. This means a real opportunity exists to bring resolution to an ego state in need.

Abreactions themselves are not therapeutic. There is nothing about experiencing an abreaction that resolves an issue for a client. In fact, if a client experiences an abreaction, and no therapy is conducted to resolve the issue associated with that abreaction, then the client may be retraumatized. Following this abreaction, the client may feel almost as though he or she has lived through a trauma another time. Because of this, unless the counselor is able to deal with highly emotive clients, resolution of the trauma should not be attempted. If, though, the counselor is able and willing to deal with highly emotive situations, a real opportunity exists to resolve issues that may have troubled clients for years.

If the counselor assists the client in resolving the issue associated with the abreaction, then the abreaction will cease, the client will not be plagued by feelings associated with that abreacting ego state again, and no retraumatizing will occur. Therefore, abreactions may be viewed as indicators that the client is where work needs to be done. Abreactions can be seen as markers indicating that here is where expression, removal, and relief need to occur.

If the client has not yet become aware of what is causing an abreaction, a good question to ask when one is evident is, "Just as you are experiencing that [describe the abreaction seen], how big or how old do you feel?" This question can help the client to begin identifying the event that is associated with the abreaction.

If the client is able to give an indication of how big they feel, or how old they feel, it is good to instruct the client next, "Just allow your eyes to close for a little while." Then, tell the client, "I want you to think about being [the age that the client told you], with the bad feelings you are experiencing. Feeling that way and being [the age that the client told you], are you inside the building or outside the building?" For example, "I want you to think about being about five years old right now, feeling just as you are right now. With these bad feelings and being five years old right now, are you inside the building or outside the building?" This question helps the client zero in on the event associated with the abreaction.

The next question that can help the client zero in on this event is, "Are you alone or with someone else?"

If the client can answer this series of questions, he or she will be able to describe exactly what is happening, to describe the event where these negative feelings first came from. This is very important in helping the client to resolve these feelings that have caused the abreaction. A good instruction to help the client describe the event is, "Tell me exactly what is happening right now."

Remember, this is said after the client has been able to associate an age or size with the negative feelings, has been able to determine whether at that age they are indoors or outdoors, and whether they were alone or with someone else. And during all these questions the client has his or her eyes closed.

The same steps in associating an abreaction with the original activating event are discussed in the section on resolving trauma (see page 107). That section should be referred to for assistance in bringing a positive resolution to the ego state that was associated with an abreaction. It is the resolution of trauma that brings an end to the associated abreaction.

This is very important work, as the same negative feelings that are associated with an abreaction often return over and over again during the life of the client, at times when the associated ego state is brought to the executive. For example, when the client feels threatened in a social situation an ego state that has felt threatened in the past may come to the executive, giving the client the negative feelings associated with that ego state.

Chapter 8
Applications of Skills

This chapter discusses and illustrates ego-state counseling techniques for a number of presenting concerns. These presenting concerns are by no means illustrative of the full range of problems clients bring to counseling. It is hoped that the reader will gain conceptual understandings by studying this chapter so that techniques may be more broadly applied. The reader should remember that counseling is ethical only when the counselor is trained and feels competent in offering services for the concerns presented. A number of therapeutic examples are provided in an attempt to help clarify techniques for dealing with particular concerns.

Crisis intervention

Effective crisis intervention is important in order for the client to keep from having residual issues connected with the immediate trauma. Following a traumatic incident, when the effective crisis intervention does not occur, the client is left with an ego state holding fear and misunderstanding. This ego state will hang onto the fear and misunderstanding, thus creating a tender spot in the psyche of the person. Later, when a situational event subconsciously reminds the person of what is unresolved, this tender ego state will re-experience the fear and misunderstanding associated with the original trauma. Therefore, it is very important for each individual to be able to express, feel understood, and gain perspective after a traumatic event so that the negative feelings event will not continue to re-emerge in the future.

Often, effective crisis intervention occurs through the actions of a friend or family member. It is most important that a person who has experienced a traumatic event should be able to talk about that event to a respected person who can be understanding. It is also important for the person who has experienced a traumatic event to be able to gain a level of understanding about that event, so that person can feel secure that either another event of that type will not happen in the future, or there is a clear understanding of the potential for another event of that type to occur. Because it is normal for individuals who have experienced a traumatic event to talk about their experience, effective crisis intervention most often occurs through these conversations with family or friends.

Sometimes, for various reasons, individuals do not talk about the trauma they have experienced, or they do not talk about it enough to feel expressed and to gain perspective. Even adults may choose to hold the negative feelings inside themselves, and may be reluctant to revisit what gave rise to them, but children are the most likely persons to hold traumatic events inside. They may not have anyone they feel safe to talk with. They may also be instructed not to tell, by either another child or an adult. They may fear telling. Below are some examples of crisis events that may not be discussed, either by adults or children.

- A man who works in the convenience store is robbed at gunpoint. Later, he says, "It's no big deal. I would prefer not talk about it."
- A child is afraid in a room, and calls repeatedly for a parent to come. As the parent either does not hear or chooses not to come, the child becomes more and more afraid. Later, the child never tells anyone about the fear.
- A child or adult is the victim of sexual abuse or rape. Because of fear or embarrassment no one is told.
- A child almost drowns while swimming in a place that was forbidden. No one is told.
- A woman is stranded behind the car when a sniper is firing at the crowd. Afterward, it seems too difficult for her to talk about, so it is not processed.

Obviously, these represent only a small sampling of crises that should be addressed near the time of the event. When the crisis is addressed near the time of the event the work of the counselor is somewhat more simple than resolving the issue years later because no bridging is needed. An example may be beneficial.

A transcript of a client in *Ego State Therapy* (Emmerson, 2003) details the experience of a client who suffered from panic attacks for many years. She had difficulty getting on a crowded elevator when she would have to stand touching another person, she had difficulty in dark places, especially when other people were there; and she had difficulty at times when she felt the air was bad or that she might not be able to get enough air. She had no idea why panic attacks would occur at these times. During the attacks, she felt like ripping something away from her neck, and she said she just felt as if she had to get away. These panic attacks were caused by a traumatic event that had not been resolved, had not been talked about and understood.

By bringing out the negative feelings and bridging to the event that related to them, it was found that when she was ten years old she almost drowned. She was caught in an ocean riptide that kept her from being able to swim back to land. Her little cousin was hanging onto her around the neck, making it even more difficult for her to breathe and to keep her head above the water. Her face would go down into the dark "blue-black" of the ocean water. She experienced real fear of dying. After making it to land, she was afraid that she would be in trouble with her parents if they found out she had been swimming at that location. She never told them.

If she had told her parents or someone else who was respected about the event, and if she had expressed her fear, received understanding, and gained perspective on where it is safe to swim and where it may not be safe, it is likely that she would never have experienced panic attacks. Because she held these unresolved fears inside herself, she was unable to feel comfortable to swim again, and she experienced panic attacks during which she re-experienced the same unresolved feelings of the trauma.

Ego-state techniques were used to assist her to bring to the executive the ego state of the 10-year-old fearful child, to fully express herself, to gain understanding, and to gain perspective. Ego-state techniques were used to allow her to tell her parents about the incident—that is, to tell the introjects of the parents of the ten-year-old child. The ten-year-old ego state was able to let go of fear, feel empowered, and feel brave.

It was good that she was able to resolve issues that had troubled her for many years. But it would have been much better if effective crisis intervention could have occurred near the time of the crisis so that she would not have been troubled by the event in the way that she was.

Effective crisis intervention will not remove all fear associated with an event, but it can keep an event from causing a pathological recurrence of the fear to return in such a way as to interfere with the life of the client. An event may be remembered with sadness, and thinking about the event may cause pain, but the client should be able to attend to a full range of life situations without the negative emotions of the event interfering.

What are the elements of the effective crisis intervention?

Working to resolve the trauma of the crisis is much like working to resolve the trauma that occurred years before. A major difference is that no bridging is necessary. The fear and emotions associated with the trauma are held by surface ego states, so immediate work to resolve the trauma may begin, without the need to determine which incident is associated with the negative feelings. Before the steps presented below, it will be important for the counselor to hear whatever the client has to say about the traumatic event, but just listening is not enough. The client needs to be able to resolve the fears and fearful situation.

It is important for a client who has experienced a traumatic event to:

- be able to express all fears and say everything that was not said at the time of the traumatic event;
- gain a feeling of safety from the cause of the traumatic event; and
- gain a feeling of relief, a feeling that "now I have everything I need".

These steps of expression, removal, and relief are the same steps found in the section "Facilitate a resolution to the trauma that the client has been carrying" on page 107. They are applied in crisis intervention in a very similar way to that described in trauma resolution, with slight differences.

Expression

Because the traumatic event is much closer in time, it is even more important to continue to reassure the client, when speaking to an introject, "We know the introject is not really with us in the room right now."

For example, if a woman has been terrified by a sniper, it may be very threatening for her to think of the sniper, as an introject, as being in the room so that she can express herself to him. In this case, it would be preferable for the counselor to explain to her in some detail that she is very safe in the counseling room, that the exercise is to empower her, and to ask her where in the room she would like to imagine the sniper might be where she could feel safe and address him. She might want to imagine him in the far corner next door, behind bulletproof glass, or she might even want to imagine him to be thimble-sized. Obviously, it would not be good for the counselor to pull a chair next to her and ask her to invite the sniper into the chair. The following is an example of this first step in crisis intervention, and comes after the client has told the counselor about the crisis situation in detail.

> **Counselor**: Susan, I can't imagine how you must feel given the horrific things this sniper has done. I can understand that it must have been a terrifying experience. He doesn't deserve to continue to cause you fear. The fear that you're carrying with you is understandable, but it is no longer needed, now that you're safe. I would like for us

to do something to take the power away from the sniper, away from the image of the sniper that you carry with you, now. What do you think about that?

Susan: That would be good, but I don't know what you mean. How can I do that?

Counselor: Here in the counseling room, where it's safe, I want you to be able to say exactly what you would like to say to that sniper. I'm going to be right here with you, and I'm going to support you. We both know that he's not really here, and that you can say anything you want in this room safely. So, where in the room would you like to imagine him, so you can say what you would like to say? [Here, the counselor directs the client straight into a situation where expression can occur. Rather than ask the client if she would like to talk to the sniper now, the counselor assists the client to rise above fear so that she will not have to carry the fear with her into the future.]

Susan: I don't know. I guess over in that corner.

Counselor: That's great. Just think about the essence of the sniper standing right in that corner. He is looking at you, and I'm here with you. You are safe and can say anything you want. What do you want to say to him?

Susan: I'm not sure I can do this.

Counselor: Would you like me to say something to him first?

Susan: Yes.

Counselor [to the sniper, spoken loudly and with conviction]: You poor, stupid man! You have no idea what you've done! I can't believe someone could do what you did. You have no power now. You just listen to what we have to say. [To Susan] OK, Susan, go ahead and say anything you want to him!

Susan: I want to ask why he would do such a horrible thing.

Counselor: That's good. Just look at him now, and go ahead and ask him that directly. There's nothing to fear here.

Susan: Why did you shoot all those people? Why would you do such a thing?

Counselor: What is he doing now?

Susan: He's just standing there. I think he's confused.

Counselor: How you feel about him? Go ahead and tell him how you feel about him. You can say anything you want. Absolutely anything!

Susan: I hate you! I wish you had never been born! I wish I had never seen you!

Counselor: That's really good. Is there anything else you want to say to him? If there is, go ahead and say it!

Susan: You have ruined so many people's lives. You have no idea how much pain you have caused. I just want to cry when I think about you.

Counselor: You're doing a great job. Is there anything else you want to say.

Susan: No, I just hate him.

Counselor: What is he doing right now, there in the corner?

Susan: He's just standing there looking dumbstruck.

Counselor: That's good. You've really told him what you think.

Removal

Counselor [continuing]: Do you want him to stay in the room now, or you want him to leave? [After the client has been able to express, this helps the client feel empowered over the object of fear.]

Susan: I don't want him here. I want him to leave.

Counselor: Tell him. Tell him to get out now!

Susan: You get out of this room right now! I don't want you here! Get out!

Counselor: That was wonderful! You really told him. I can't believe the things he did, either.

Relief

Counselor [continuing]: How are you feeling right now?

Susan: I have a lot of energy. I think I feel better.

Counselor: You really rose above your fear and told him what you thought. You had the control. That was very good. What's the difference in how you feel now and when you're very relaxed?

Susan: I guess I still feel a bit nervous.

Counselor: That's understandable. What do you need to feel more relaxed? What would help you feel more relaxed, normally, when you feel this way.

Susan: I don't know. I guess having someone with me who can make me feel safe.

Counselor: When you think of someone like that, someone who can make you feel safe, either the way they are now or the way they were some time earlier in your life, who do you think of?

Susan: My Grandpa Richards always made me feel safe. I knew he loved me.

Counselor: I want you to think of your Grandpa Richards the way he was at the time when he made you feel most safe. Right now, it doesn't matter if he's still living or not. I just want you to think of him the way he was when he made you feel most safe, and I want you to invite that Grandpa Richards right here in the chair next to you. [Pause.] I can see a smile on your face already. What would you like to say to him?

Susan: Hi, Grandpa.

Counselor: I'll tell you a secret. If he wants to, your Grandpa Richards, this essence of your Grandpa Richards that you know so well, can be with you any time you want and can help you feel safe. Ask him if he will help you feel safe when you need him. [Here the client is able to use the introject of her beloved grandfather to achieve a feeling of safety. She is bringing her resources to her needs.]

Susan: Will you help me feel safe, Grandpa?

Counselor: What did he say?

Susan: He said he would.

Counselor: What do you want to say to him?

Susan: Thank you, Grandpa.

Counselor: How do you feel about him?

Susan: I love him.

Counselor: It might be nice for you to tell him that now.

Susan: I love you, Grandpa.

Counselor: What did he say?

Susan [smiling]: He said he loves me too.

Counselor: That's really good. How do you feel right now?

Susan: I feel really good.

Counselor: You've done a great job. You have taken the sniper that you carried with you [the introject] and told him everything you want to say, and then you told him to leave. You rose above the fear you had. Then you invited the grandpa you carry with you to be with you and help you feel safe. He is yours, and always will be. Do you have any questions?

Susan: Will this help me keep from feeling the panic that I've been feeling?

Counselor: You experienced something really frightening. It's obvious that you will always wish that had not happened, but today you have been able to rise above the fear you have carried with you. I'm not sure exactly how much difference you'll experience. It's sometimes good just to have a nice surprise. [No commitment has been made about the level of change that will be experienced, but a suggestion has been given that the change may be surprisingly positive.]

This illustrates the use of expression, removal, and relief in crisis intervention. It is also good to make sure that the client understands any level of present danger. Occasionally, a crisis is ongoing. For example, a stalker may have caused a crisis situation to occur, and may still be a danger to the client. Current danger should not be diminished, but should be discussed with the client in relation to possible reactions to remain as safe as possible.

The method illustrated above utilizes the client's resource of introjects, in terms of working with both the agent of fear and positive introjects. Working with introjects is especially important in crisis intervention. As always with this work, it is important for the client to be directed to speak directly *to* the introject, rather than to speak *about* the introject. For example, it is not good enough for the client to say, "I think he did a bad thing." It is necessary for the client to say directly to the introject, "You did a bad thing." Speaking directly to the introject better facilitates the client's ability to remain in touch with the ego state that needs resolution.

In order to achieve the step of relief, the image of an introject can be used, as illustrated in this example with Susan's grandfather, or a more mature or strong ego state may be called upon to assist the previously traumatized ego state to feel safe and secure. The counselor can ask to talk with a part of the client that feels strong and that would like to help the part feeling insecure. It is always good to assist the client in understanding that the helping introject or ego state is a resource that will always be available.

When the crisis trauma does not involve another person

Sometimes the traumatic event in a crisis has nothing to do with another person. This does not change the need for the client to go through the steps of expression, removal, and relief. For example, the crisis event might be an earthquake or a fire, or even an attack by a wild animal. The crisis event might be the sinking of a boat or an avalanche while skiing.

While at first it may seem that expression would not be an important component of helping the client through a crisis where another person was not involved, it is still very important for the client to express. The purpose of expression is to assist the client to rise above the fear that is being carried.

Let's take as an example a client who is dealing with the aftermath of an earthquake. The client may have experienced great fear at seeing buildings shake and feeling the ground move. The physical devastation that the quake caused cannot be changed, but the internalization of the earthquake experience can be altered. The client will always be able to remember the earthquake as it happened, but the inner experience of that memory may be changed by facilitating the client to alter the experience that is being carried day by day.

An abbreviated example may help to illustrate the steps of expression, removal, and relief for this type of counseling. Remember, prior to these three steps, the counselor should allow the client to describe in detail what was experienced.

Counselor: Andrew, I really appreciate your telling me about your experience in the earthquake. I believe it is important for you to be able to express your feelings about what was going on during that time. In order to do that, what aspect of the earthquake stands out to you as central? Was it the things moving in the room, the ground shaking, the noise, or something else?

Andrew: I'm not exactly sure what you mean. What seemed strangest to me was that there was nothing I could hang onto. Somehow I have always thought that the ground was solid. I knew things like a chair might slide or move, but the ground would always be there and be solid. I don't know if I'm making any sense.

Counselor: Yes, you are. That makes perfect sense. If I am interpreting you right, it was the movement of the ground that was to you the most fearful aspect of the earthquake.

Andrew: I guess that's right.

Counselor: This is going to sound a bit strange, Andrew, but I want you to imagine the moving ground as being somewhere in this room. It doesn't have to be everywhere, as it was in the earthquake, but I want you to think about the moving ground as being somewhere in the room so we can focus on it. Where would you like to imagine it? [For a different type of crisis the client might think of a wild animal, of the ocean, or of whatever is centrally associated with a crisis.]

Expression

Andrew: Right over there, I guess. [Points to the other side of the room.]

Counselor: Good. Now, with the ground shaking over there on the other side of the room, what are you feeling about it?

Andrew: I don't like it. It should not be shaking. It's not supposed to shake.

Counselor: I want you to say that out loud to the shaking ground. Tell it exactly what you feel right now. Tell it as if it were person who could hear you.

Andrew: You shouldn't shake. I don't like you shaking. You're not supposed to do that. Stop it.

Counselor: That's excellent, Andrew. What are you feeling as you say that?

Andrew: A bit silly, but really nervous. I don't like this.

Counselor: Tell the ground you don't like it. Tell it that it should not make you afraid.

Andrew: I don't like your shaking. You shouldn't scare me like this.

Counselor: That's very good, Andrew. What is your sense of the ground and its ability to hear you right now?

Andrew: It can't hear me. It's the ground. It doesn't even know I'm talking to it.

Counselor: How does that make you feel?

Andrew: Like there's nothing I can do about it. No matter what I say, it can't hear me.

Counselor: So, it's not shaking because of you. In fact it has no real knowledge of you.

Andrew: That's right.

Counselor: You really mean nothing to it, no matter what you do.

Andrew: That's true.

Counselor: How does that make you feel, that nothing you say or do has any impact on it?

Andrew: Well, I guess it makes me feel good that it's not trying to hurt me, but it makes me feel powerless that I can't do anything about it.

Removal

Counselor: You're right. In reality you can't stop an earthquake. No one can. But we don't have a real earthquake in this room. The fear and frustration you feel right now about the ground shaking is not about anything happening in this room, because we both really know the ground is not really shaking here. So, the quake in this room is one you can stop, because it is totally yours. You can tell your earthquake to do anything you want it to. Go ahead and tell it now what you what to do.

Andrew: Stop shaking! I don't want you to shake any more.

Counselor: Yes, stop shaking, ground! You don't have our permission to move. Just be still. What's happening over there now?

Andrew: It's still. It stopped shaking.

Counselor: That's good. You have control over what you carry with you. You can't change what happened, but you can change what you carry with you. How do you feel now?

Andrew: Better. I didn't like its shaking.

Counselor: That's good that you're able to stop it. It was frightening enough to live through. There's no reason it should continue to have power, now that you've stopped it.

Relief

Counselor [continuing]: What do you need now to feel really relaxed?

Andrew: I need to be able to feel safe and relaxed.

Counselor: Is it OK if I call this part of you that I'm speaking with right now "Nervous"?

Andrew: Yes, I guess so.

Counselor: That's good. When I want to talk with this part or refer to it I will use the name "Nervous".

Andrew: OK.

Counselor: Nervous, I want to ask Andrew a question. Andrew, when in the past have you felt really safe and relaxed?

Andrew: I used to lie on the beach and listen to the surf. I could just let my mind go. I felt safe then.

Counselor: I can hear that feeling of safety in your voice right now. Is it OK with you if I call this part of you that can feel safe and relaxed "Beach Part"?

Andrew: Yes, I guess.

Counselor: Good. I want to address Beach Part directly now. Just that part of you that can lie on the sand, hear the surf, and feel safe and relaxed. Beach Part, how do you feel?

Andrew: Safe [pause], and relaxed.

Counselor: Beach Part, it sounds to me like you are very good at experiencing the sandy ground as something safe, at feeling the warm sun, and feeling very relaxed. There's another part of Andrew that could use your help: Nervous. Would you be willing to help Nervous in feeling more like you do, safe and relaxed?

Andrew: Yes, I guess.

Counselor: That's good. You are one of Andrew's resources, one of his important resources, and he needs you now. Right now, I want you to go to Nervous so he can benefit from feeling more safe and relaxed and help that part experience with you what you are so good at, as you hear the surf and feel the sand and sun. Go to that part now and see if it will let you help it. [Short pause.] And I want to ask Nervous, are you willing to allow Beach Part to help you feel safe?

Andrew: Yes.

Counselor: Good. I want those two parts just to communicate internally, quietly, and see if they can continue to work together for a feeling of safety and relaxation. [Pause.] What's happening now, Nervous?

Andrew: I feel good.

Counselor: Is there anything else you need?

Andrew: No, I feel safe now.

Counselor: That's excellent. You've been able to express what at the time of the earthquake was most frightening to you. You've been able to talk to your internal earthquake that you were carrying with you, and you've been able to stop it on the inside, still. And you've been able to bring some of your own excellent resources, your Beach Part, to your needs so you can continue to feel safe and relaxed.

It is easy to imagine how, given that a client can talk to a shaking floor, that a client can speak to a wild animal, or to any other object of fear from a time of crisis. Speaking directly to the focus of fear assists the client to enter into the ego state that was traumatized. It is by bringing this traumatized ego state into the executive that work can be done to resolve the feelings of trauma.

At the end of a crisis intervention the counselor should overview the session with the client, talk about what was accomplished in the session, and ask the client if there are any questions. It is important for the client to feel involved in the process of therapy, and to feel attended to and experience the sharing of information. Whenever possible, it is much preferred to see a client for a further session after crisis intervention appears finished. It is good for the counselor to express to the client a desire to make sure that he or she is at a point where there can be a feeling of appropriateness in the way he or she is handling the crisis situation. It is not the goal of crisis intervention for the client to feel as though nothing negative has happened. Just as grieving the death of a loved one is important and healthy, carrying the feelings about a crisis event is considered normal and appropriate in the grieving process. Therefore, it is the goal of crisis intervention to assist the client with perspective and with an ability to go into the future without the burden of unresolved trauma.

Working with grief and loss

There are a number of things to consider when working with clients who are having grief and loss issues. Possibly, more than any other group, these clients need education. It is not unusual for clients having grief and loss issues to have unrealistic expectations. It is also common for clients having these issues to believe that there's something wrong with them, or that they are not handling the loss or expected loss well, when they are actually going through a normal grieving experience.

A few years ago, a young woman came to see me reporting that she was having difficulty getting over the loss of her sister, who had been killed in a car accident. She said she was still crying and missing her sister terribly. When I asked her how long ago her sister had died, she replied, "Almost two months ago." Her expectation was that she should have been finished grieving almost immediately after her sister's death. After talking with her concerning her grieving process, and after describing to her what could normally be expected in grieving the loss of her sister, we both determined that she was actually doing an excellent job going through the difficult grieving process. She was relieved that there was not something wrong with her.

Therefore, it is important for clients in grieving to understand the normal range of feelings and behaviors that make up the grieving process. Grieving is like the healing of a deep wound. A level of pain is expected in the process of healing. At the end of the process, which will take different lengths of time for different people, a scar will be left. It is likely that there will always be sadness when one thinks about the loss, but, if grieving is done well, that sadness will not continue to negatively interfere with the ongoing life of the grieving person. Along with the sadness can be a real joy from having had the relationship, and many report that the relationship is an ongoing positive aspect of living. It is important that clients grieve appropriately to avoid complicated bereavement, and there are counseling techniques that can greatly assist clients throughout the grieving process.

It is also common for clients to come in who are suffering from complicated bereavement. Their grieving process may have lasted many years, sometimes decades, without their ability to feel any real closure of the type they would like. It is important for them to be able to gain a sense of healing, without having a sense of letting go something they want to hang onto.

This section on grief and loss is divided into "Grieving loss" and "Grieving future loss". The "Grieving loss" subsection focuses on the loss of a loved one. That may be a friend or family member who has died, it may be a beloved pet that has died or disappeared, or it may even be the loss of a relationship. There are many permutations of loss. Also included in that subsection is information on dealing with complicated bereavement. Ego-state techniques are excellent to help the client who is ready to move to a new phase of life, following a long bereavement.

The subsection "Grieving future loss" deals with both assisting the client who has found out that he or she has a terminal illness, and assisting the friends or relatives of the person who is terminally ill. There are also other permutations to grieving future loss. Some clients fear their own death, or the death of others, even when no illness or danger is evident. Often, a client who has a terminal illness will come to counseling at first in an attempt to live. Others will come to counseling because they find there is no one they can talk to about the issues they are experiencing that are associated with their dying.

Working with grieving clients is challenging, and wording is often extremely important. Possibly, more than with any other client, badly chosen words can cause the client to become angry or upset. Therefore, counselors who work with grieving clients need to be educated in relation to deep and sensitive issues faced in grief.

Grieving loss

Grief counseling entails a broad area in counseling. The techniques employed vary according to where the client is in the grieving process. A number of authors have theorized about the chronology of the grieving process and it is not considered necessary to illustrate those theories here. It is most important to point to places where counseling intervention is helpful, and to offer suggestions about the nature of appropriate interventions.

It is important to hear exactly where the grieving client is in his or her grief, and hear what the client wants. Good active-listening skills are an excellent tool to hear what the client has been experiencing, and to learn what the client is ready for. Obviously, it is imperative for the counselor to be sensitive concerning the loss, but even the most sensitive counselor may say things that the grieving client will hear in a negative way. There are some things that should not be said in working with clients who are grieving loss. The following is a selection of these inappropriate statements. To some counselors, items on this list will seem too obvious to mention, but it is surprising how often clients report that counselors have said them.

- It must have been God's will.
- Have you thought about having another child?
- There may be a good side to this.
- At least you didn't get to know the child.
- It was just a fetus.
- He shouldn't have been drinking while driving.
- You need to move on and let go.
- I know exactly how you feel.
- Do you think it might have been suicide?

Most of the items on this list diminish the loss of the client, screaming to the client that the counselor does not understand the tremendous gravity of the loss. A client who is feeling devastated and overwhelmed by what has been lost does not want to hear the counselor attempt to say that that loss was less than horrific. Counselors who attempt to diminish the meaning of the loss to the client are saying to the client, "I don't understand your pain." Rightfully, the client will wonder, "Why am I here talking to this person?"

The statement "You need to move on and let go" can anger a client who sees moving on as ending a cherished relationship. Some clients feel they never want to move on, and feel that attempting to do so would be dishonoring the relationship they had with their loved one. As with any client, these clients cannot be pushed, and should not be. Ultimately, it is their decision how they want to continue with the grieving process.

It is never good in counseling to say, "I know exactly how you feel." It is especially inappropriate to make this statement to a grieving client. The grieving client feels tremendous loss and knows that another person could not know his or her exact feelings. It is an insult to the client to say this, and it is an indication that the counselor is out of touch with the depth of the client's pain.

The last item on the list, "Do you think it might have been suicide?", may anger a client even if that client has had those same thoughts. If the client is phrasing sentences that indicate a concern that their loved one could have committed suicide it is much better to use active listening than direct questioning in order to allow the client to discuss this issue. For example, if the client says something like, "He was too good a driver to make a mistake like that," rather than ask the question, "Do you think it might have been suicide?", a better response would be, "I'm confused by, 'He was too good a driver …' " This type of statement allows the client to express feelings without feeling put on the spot by a direct question.

The most helpful statements to clients are those that assist them understand that you hear what they are saying and that you hear their pain.

- Your loss must be devastating. I can't imagine what you must be feeling.
- It's terrible how that happened. I can see why you would be having a really hard time with this.
- I'm honored that you're sharing this with me. I can't imagine how you feel.

While statements such as these, on the surface, may appear that they would cause the client to feel worse, they actually help the client feel heard and understood. The client who has felt that their pain was too much, and that it could not be understood by anyone, will be heartened by the knowledge that at some level it has been heard. This is an important aspect of helping a client through the grieving process.

How long does grieving take?

A common question that grieving clients ask is, "How long am I going to feel like this?" It would be nice if we could give them a simple answer. The best answer is, "I don't know, but I will tell you what I do know."

The grieving process lasts a different length of time for each person. Its length is not an indication of the love felt for the lost person or pet. The length of the grieving process can be complicated by other problems that the client has. For example, a client who has a tenuous psyche may find the grieving process takes much longer than the client who felt stable and mentally healthy prior to the loss.

It is OK to give ballpark figures to clients to give them an indication of how long the grieving process may last, but it should always be done with the caveat that the length of the process varies greatly among individuals. It is common for the grieving process to last one to two years following the loss of a close friend or family member, and five years or more following the loss of a spouse or child.

Clients seem to grieve somewhat in relation to how they saw the future for the individual who has been lost. Often, the loss of an aged parent or grandparent is easier than that of a younger person who the client expected would live for many years. The pain of grief also seems to relate to the importance to the client of the person lost, more so than to how well the client knew the person who has died. For example, a grandparent who has never met a grandchild living overseas may feel devastated to learn that the grandchild has died, while the loss of a coworker who has been seen practically every day may not result in as much pain.

It is also important to note that individuals grieve in vastly different ways. One person may cry a lot, while another person may grieve without tears. In a sense, crying does not have to entail tears. The important thing is that grieving should take place. It is OK if the client feels little loss following the death of a coworker, but, when loss is felt, as with any emotion, it should not be bottled. It should be released. It should be released through crying, through pain, through conversation. Some clients report that experiencing and releasing the pain of the loss of a loved one is a bittersweet experience, part pain and part loving appreciation.

The rest of this subsection will be divided into issues relating to clients in different stages of grieving: early-stage grieving, later-stage grieving, and complicated bereavement.

Early-stage grieving

An important aspect of helping clients in early-stage grieving is assisting them in understanding what is within a normal range of grieving responses. Clients often think there's something wrong with them because of some of the aspects of their grief. Common concerns grieving clients bring to counseling are:

- I just start crying and I'm not able to stop. I don't mind crying at home, but it's embarrassing at work. I should be able to control this better.
- I felt him come and sit at the edge of my bed.
- I think I'm going crazy. There are times I know she's in the room with me.
- I heard her speak to me. Sometimes she calls my name.
- I've seen her, physically, since she's died.
- I don't think this should still be bothering me. It's been over a year now and I'm still really bothered by his death.
- It sometimes comes over me and I feel like I can hardly breathe.
- I feel guilty because I'm actually relieved he's gone.
- I feel silly, but I've kept his shoes outside the back door.

All of the concerns above are normal reactions to grieving. Since no two people grieve in the same way, each person will have a different reaction, but it is very common for individuals not to be able to control their crying, to sense, hear, or see the lost loved one, to think the grieving process should take a shorter length of time than it does, to have varied and strange physical reactions, and feel guilt over feeling relieved that a loved one who could be difficult has died. Normalizing, helping these clients to understand that they are experiencing grief in a natural and healthy way, may be all some clients need.

Clients need to hear that their crying may be uncontrollable for a period of time. They may need a professional to assure them that this is normal and healthy. Some clients want to discard everything that reminds them of their loved one, while other clients may want to keep many keepsakes to remind them of their loved one. Either is fine. Some clients may need time to feel they can survive doing the practical things in life that their loved one took care of, and some clients may be excited at the things they will be able to do now that they no longer have to take care of their loved one. Either is fine.

The most important aspect of helping clients during the early stages of grieving is to be able to hear their pain, help them feel understood, and normalize their experiences. They should understand that you will be there for them, that the process they are going through is normal and healthy, and that there is a light at the end of the tunnel. There will be a time when the fog of pain and despair lifts and roses smell like roses again, when they can feel grounded and excited about living, when they can see a sunset and feel awed by the experience.

Later-stage grieving

A client in later-stage grieving is already aware of the grieving process. They are used to the experience of grieving. Clients at this stage may feel stuck and unable to continue the grieving process. Sometimes, these clients also need education as to the length of grieving and what can normally be expected. Often they may need a counseling intervention to help them continue naturally through the grieving process.

A client of mine whose husband had committed suicide found herself obsessing about his choosing to leave her in this fashion. She felt something might have been wrong with her that would cause him to take his life. She was in much pain, upset at herself and at her deceased husband.

Following an amount of time listening to her concerns, helping her feel heard, and exploring her personal issues, an empty chair was used to allow her to express her feelings to her husband. This process of using an empty chair was discussed with her, and counseling work was done to help her know exactly what she wanted to say to her husband before the empty chair was used. When she felt ready, an empty chair was placed in front of her and she was asked to invite the essence of her husband into the chair. She was encouraged to tell him, as if he were there, about all her feelings, her guilt, her anger, and her despair. After she finished expressing her feelings, she was asked to sit in the other chair and respond as if she were her husband. Speaking as if she were he, she responded (as the dead husband), saying that it was not her (the client's) fault, that she was loved, and that she needed to get on with her life. Upon returning to her chair (where she spoke as herself), she was able to thank her husband, and she was able to tell him that she was ready to live now. This is not to say that he would not continue to be an important part of her life, but that she was ready to embrace living.

136

A session using this technique is often cathartic for the client, and it was for this client. It is not recommended that this technique be used during the early stages of grieving, but, during the later stages of grieving or during complicated bereavement, allowing the client to speak directly to the introject of the lost person facilitates a more complete release of feelings, permits unsaid things to be said, and allows the person to gain permission to move forward. I have found that, after working in a number of sessions with clients discussing grieving issues, little change may be seen, but most often, following a conversation using an empty chair, rapid change may be made.

Complicated bereavement

Complicated bereavement is difficult to define, and probably should be defined only in general terms. Because each person grieves a different way, the line between normal bereavement and complicated bereavement is necessarily blurred. Therefore, it is best to talk around the concept of complicated bereavement to give the general impression of its meaning, rather than try to give a specific definition.

Clients who continue active grieving for a period easily exceeding what would normally be expected may be suffering from complicated bereavement. Because the normal expectation of grieving time varies among clients, the time in grieving must be extensive to be considered complicated bereavement. Often, these time periods may be several years, or even decades.

Mummification is an example of complicated bereavement. A man whose wife died when their daughter was three years old, fifteen years later still had his wife's makeup on the dresser, her clothes in the closet, and even the drawings of the three-year-old on the wall as they were when his wife died. He kept the same car and kept the house in the same way it was at the time she died. While this is an obvious case of complicated bereavement, it is common for individuals to keep items, or even rooms, that remind them of their loved ones, and this keeping of reminders is not considered complicated bereavement.

A lack of crying or grieving following the death of the loved one is often considered complicated bereavement. Individuals do need to grieve. Still, some people cry without tears and sometimes the death of someone who appeared to be a friend may actually have little consequence to the person.

The most common aspect of complicated bereavement is the difficulty in being able to progress through some aspect of the grieving process. This can be complicated by other psychological factors. The individual who is barely coping at the time of the death may find it more difficult to finish the grieving process. Examples of difficulty to get through some aspect of grieving include maintaining strong anger toward the person who died, toward someone else associated with a death, or even toward God. Statements such as, "I think about it several times every day" and "I just can't get over it; I can't get on with my life" may be indicators of complicated bereavement.

Another common aspect of complicated bereavement is the persistent feeling of unfinished business with the loved one who died. A common statement is, "I would give anything to have told him that I love him." Sometimes unfinished business even extends toward someone such as the perpetrator. A client may feel a loss from having unfinished business with the perpetrator.

A positive aspect of unfinished business is that the problem is actually within the client, and not between the client and a person who has died. Introjects do not die. When a client talks about unfinished business, that client is not talking about today's business, but about something that has happened in the past between the client and the person as they were in the past. This unfinished business is between the client and the introject of another person the client is manifesting internally. Therefore, therapy offers power to finish unfinished business.

It is important for clients to understand this concept, that they are the person in the room with the unfinished business, so the problem is within them. The problem is something they are carrying with them. Sometimes an example can be helpful in helping a client understand this concept. A person who was abused in the past may have anger toward the abuser as he or she was in the past, while having a better relationship in the present with that same person (the past abuser), who is now older. Sometimes, a person who has been abused tracks down an abuser to finally express to that person, and afterward feels incomplete because the person they were talking to looked older and unfamiliar, and did not seem like the real abuser.

The real power the client has to finish unfinished business is by having an interaction between the introject and each ego state of the client that feels unfinished. Once clients are able to understand that their resolution lies inside themselves, empty-chair work may proceed. It is empowering to understand that change can take place without having to access someone outside the counseling room. An example of this empty-chair work will be provided illustrating a client who had an abortion twenty years earlier. She continued to feel guilty and feel that she had made a decision that was not hers to make. (While some clients later question a decision such as abortion, others remain confident concerning such a decision.)

Counselor: I'm interested to hear some more about these feelings you've been having.

Alice: I just can't get Angie off my mind. You probably think it's silly that I named her, and it was probably the year after the abortion that I did that, but I kept thinking about her and she just needed a name.

Counselor: That seems very nice to me that you have a name you can associate with Angie. I can tell by your voice that you really do care a lot for her.

Alice: I do. I love her. I can't believe what I did to her, but even now, thinking back, I don't know how else it could've happened.

Counselor: It sounds like something is troubling you now about this, that something is interfering in your life.

Alice: I'm just tormented by what I did. Angie would be nineteen now. I've thought about when she would start school, when she would become interested in boys, about everything that would happen in her life.

Counselor: And the torment continues?

Alice: Yes. It's just as bad as it ever was. I want to get on with my life, but I don't know how.

Counselor: What do you want? What is your goal in this?

Alice: I'm not sure. I know I love her, but I guess I don't know how to love *me* after what I did to her.

Counselor: If you could talk to her, what would you want to say to her?

Alice: It would be really hard. I guess I would want to tell her that I'm sorry.

Counselor [pulling a chair to a position across from Alice]: I think you want to tell her some very good things, and I think it's time you have an opportunity to do that. I want you to imagine the essence of Alice right here in this chair, as if she were sitting right here. When you're ready, go ahead and tell her exactly what you would like to tell her. Speak to her directly.

Alice [looking at the counselor, then starting to cry]: You want me to talk with her right now?

Counselor: Yes, I'm here to support you. As soon as you're ready, just go ahead and tell her exactly what you want to. Speak to her directly, calling her name. Tell her what you want to tell her.

Alice: Angie, I'm so sorry. [Cries deeply.] I'm so sorry I didn't let you have a life. It was selfish of me. I know that.

Counselor: You're doing really well. Just continue to tell her anything you would like to. Tell her how you feel about her.

Alice: I love you, Angie. I have always loved you. I feel really bad about what I did.

Counselor [pointing to the other chair]: Now, go ahead and move over to Angie's chair, and, as you sit down, I want to talk directly with the essence of Angie. That's right, to sit right here. [Client moves.] Angie, it was very difficult for your mother to say the things she did. She has struggled with this for a long time. How do you feel about her, Angie, and about the things she said?

Alice: I love her, and I know she loves me. I know it was a hard decision for her and I don't blame her.

Counselor: Go ahead and tell her that directly, Angie. Speak directly to her, and you can call her Mother or Mom.

Alice: Mom, I love you. I want you to stop torturing yourself. You did what you had to. I don't blame you for that. I want you to get on with your life.

Counselor: And, Angie, how are you feeling? What else do you want to say?

Alice: I'm OK, Mom. I want you to be happy now.

Counselor: Thank you, Angie. I appreciate your talking with us. [Motions for Alice to move back to her chair.] Now, you can go ahead and move back to this chair, and as you sit down, Alice, I want to hear what that meant to you. It sounds to me like Angie would be happiest for you get on with your life. She loves you and wants you to be happy. What do you think? What do you want to say to Angie?

Alice: Thank you, Angie. I guess I just want to know if you can ever forgive me.

Counselor: Just close your eyes for a moment, and listen, and then tell me what she said.

Alice: She said, of course I forgive you. I always have.

Counselor: You can open your eyes, now. How does it make you feel?

Alice: Really special and, somehow, liberated, I guess.

Counselor: What do you want to say to Angie? What can you tell her about doing what she wants you to do, about getting on with your life and being happy?

Alice: Thank you, Angie. I will always love you. You know that. It helps to know that you don't hate me, and I know that now. I will try to get on with my life, and be happy.

Counselor: That was very good. How did she hear that?

Alice: She smiled.

Counselor: And, how are you feeling now?

Alice: Better. Better than I have in years. I feel lighter in some way. I had thought she hated me.

Counselor: She loves you.

Alice: I know.

This somewhat abbreviated presentation is an accurate illustration of this technique. When the client is ready, some of the most profound and rapid change I have seen in therapy occurs using this technique. It appears as though a client can have pent-up feelings and concerns for years without being able to express them fully. Determining when a client is ready for this technique involves sensitive negotiation between the counselor and client. Ultimately, it is the client who defines what is wanted as an outcome, and this defines the direction of therapy.

Clients have wonderful resources. They have the resource for expressing the feelings, and they have their introjects, internalized perceptions of the persons they love, and that can communicate with them.

I have often been asked by students about the possibility of a client getting 'angry and blaming' messages from the introject of a deceased child. This has never happened with one of my clients, and I have never had a student or colleague report that it has happened with one of their clients. This does not mean that it could never happen, but I believe it is unlikely. The client is communicating with an introject that is seen as a loving person. The client loves the introject. It makes sense that this loving introject would be forgiving and loving to the client. When the client can openly express bottled feelings directly to the introject, and hear from the introject acceptance, forgiveness, and love, a positive flow of feelings seems to wash through the client in a healing fashion.

Reports I have received back from clients indicate that this healing is not temporary. Years later, clients report having positive feelings about themselves in regard to the introject.

This technique can be used with a wide array of clients who have complicated bereavement issues. A common denominator of complicated bereavement appears to be bottled feelings and an inability to move forward. This technique assists the client in both these aspects of releasing feelings, and in having permission from the introject and from themselves to move forward.

Re-engaging in life

The decision as to when to re-engage in life can be an extremely difficult one for the client who has lost a loved one. Some clients will choose never to re-engage in life after the loss of the loved one, and a client who is not ready to engage can become angry at a therapist who suggests this is important. A counselor should not attempt to coerce a client to "let the loved one go". The counselor should be able to hear a client, and help him or her achieve what he or she is ready to achieve.

That said, many clients having issues of complicated bereavement will say that they would like to move on, that they would like to get on with their lives, but they have not been able to do this. When this is the case, it is important to negotiate with a client, making sure that the client is ready to re-engage in life. This does not mean that the client will stop loving the person, or that the person will become insignificant in the life of the client. It means the client will be able to live a life in the present without feeling most focused on a loving relationship that has been separated by death or loss.

When a client is ready to re-engage and live more fully in the present, the counselor can assist the client to tell the deceased loved one (personified in an empty chair) that it is time for that person to go where he or she needs to, and that the client is ready to engage in life and focus more fully on current relationships. This does not mean that the deceased loved one will necessarily stop being a part of the client's life, just that the client will be able to invest more in other relationships. It is important for the client to speak directly to the deceased loved one, rather than saying things like, "I would like to tell him that ..." If the client begins saying what he or she would like to tell the person, the counselor, rather than tell the person directly, should stop the client and instruct him or her to speak directly to the essence of the deceased loved one in the chair.

The counselor should be prepared for the client to be very emotional during this process. Following this process, clients will most often report an immediate change in their ability to move forward in life.

Some points to remember:

- A counselor should never coerce a client toward letting the deceased loved one go.
- Clients can become very distressed and angry if they feel the counselor wants them to re-engage in life before they are ready.
- Some clients will never be ready to re-engage, and that is their decision.
- Clients often feel stuck in the grieving process, and many clients want to let a deceased loved one go so they are able to engage more fully in current relationships.
- When a client feels that things have not been said to a deceased loved one, or when clients are ready to let the deceased loved one go, it can be cathartic for them to speak directly with the introject of the deceased loved one in an empty chair. (It is best not to use the term *introject* to the client.)

The normal sequence of using an empty chair for this purpose is as follows:

1. Use active listening to determine what the client wants to achieve in counseling, and to hear and show understanding for the experience of the client.

2. If the client clearly wants to re-engage in life and focus more on current relationships, talk with the client about what he or she would like to say to the deceased loved one. It is important that the client is ready to say three things: "I want you to move on to where you need to go"; "I want to focus my life on current relationships"; the client needs to say some type of "may peace be with you as you go" (goodbye), and needs to understand that a continued relationship with the deceased loved one is still possible.

   If it feels appropriate to the client, it can also be helpful for him or her to express positive feelings: "I love you." Depending on religious beliefs, the client can also be prepared to say other things, such as, "I look forward to seeing you when my time here is finished." This is also a good time for the client to say to the deceased loved one anything that has felt unsaid. The counselor should make a list of what the client wants to say, so the client can be helped to remember and say everything. Clients will vary in how much they want to maintain a relationship with the deceased loved one, and this is their decision.

3. Ask the client if he or she is ready to say the things that have been discussed, and offer the chance to invite the essence of the deceased loved one into the empty chair. This can be done by saying something like, "OK, now is the time for you to invite the essence of John into the chair. Just say, 'I'm ready' when you feel him there.

4. Encourage the client to speak directly to the deceased loved one in the chair, and, if the client forgets one of the things that were to be said, gently remind the client, "Did you want to tell John how you feel about him?"

5. After the client says goodbye, ask if the chair is now empty. When the client reports it is, support and congratulate the client for the difficult, loving work that has been done. Saying goodbye to a loved one does not mean they cannot visit.

6. As in any session, it is important to debrief the client at the end of the session. Clients should be encouraged to describe their views of the session, and should be encouraged to ask any questions.

7. When clients are working with ego states that are very emotional, it is especially important to help them bring a surface ego state into the executive before they leave the counseling office and walk back into the world. A good method to help the client bring a surface ego state into the executive at the end of the session is to ask questions about the current experience of the client in daily living. It will be a surface ego state that can tell about the daily experience of the client, and once the client is clearly experiencing life from a surface state then he or she is more ready to leave the counseling office.

Grieving future loss

Clients may have come to counseling for assistance in dealing with some future loss. This can be a terminally ill client who is dealing with the imminent prospect of dying. It may be a friend or relative of the person who is terminally ill. And, it may be that the client is dealing with prospect of the loss of a relationship or the loss of a pet.

The terminally ill client

Some of the loneliest people I have met in my career as a counselor are individuals who are facing their own death. They realize they will not be in this existence much longer, that they will be leaving all those who they know, and that they will be leaving alone. They often report that when they try to talk with friends and family about their own death that they have no success in finding anyone who will discuss it with them. They are facing, possibly, the biggest event of their life and often they find there is no one to talk to about it. It is little wonder they come to counseling.

It is a profound experience to be able to work with clients in counseling who are dying, hearing their fears and inner thoughts, while watching them become physically weaker with each meeting, seeing their bravery and weakness, and being one who is honored by their sharing their journey. They talk of anger, bargaining, wisdom, of wanting to see those closest to them, of wanting to leave something, and of their vision of meaning of life.

It is important to be able to hear them, to let them speak, to use active listening, and to allow them to define their own needs and their own ideas. It is important to be a resource to them, a person who will not stop them from talking, a person who will not say, "Let's not talk about that now," a person who can reflect a level of understanding without ever saying, "I know how you feel."

144

Obviously, it is important to allow them to have their own ideas about death. It is not the role the counselor to be a religious leader. Some clients will have definite religious beliefs about what to expect when they die; some clients will expect no life after death. It is common for clients to ask the counselor about this topic: "What do you think?" The counselor should never give a religious perspective in an attempt to sway the client to that perspective, unless the client has come for religious counseling expecting to be given religious guidance. While in counseling, I seldom give my personal perspectives on politics or religion, but I have not been able to tell a dying client who asks what I think that I will not tell them. I attempt to ensure that the client knows that my religious ideas are for me, and that it is important for the client to have religious ideas that work for him or her. Given that preface, if asked, I will tell dying clients my beliefs about life after death. I am not forwarding this instruction to readers of this book as the correct way to handle this situation, just that it seems right for me.

Therapeutically, from a skills perspective, working with a dying client is not a difficult task, although, depending on the counselor's own peace with the prospect of dying, it may be an impossible task. If the counselor is unable to talk about issues with the terminally ill client, that client should be referred to a counselor so issues can be aired. It is OK for the counselor to show emotion, to cry, or to show care. Dying is a very human experience, and the person facing that experience deserves a humane counselor, not a professional following a regimen.

A sensitive and ethical dilemma often occurs when a client who is terminally ill comes to counseling in an attempt to save his or her life by obtaining a higher level of mental health. While it appears that this is indeed a possibility, most clients who have been diagnosed as terminally ill do succumb to their illness. Therefore, with these clients who continue to deteriorate in terms of their health the question arises, "Should counseling continue with the goal of saving the life, or should counseling continue with the goal of helping the client face his or her death and assist the client in determining how to live the life that is left?"

There is no easy, or even correct, answer to this question. Possibly the best way to handle this situation is to continue to offer the client, in a sensitive fashion, the option of continuing to focus counseling work on physical wellness or on issues related to dying. It should always be the client's decision as to which of these two focuses should direct counseling.

When the terminally ill client has psychological issues that he or she wants to work on, techniques throughout this book may be used. The empty chair can be used for the client to express feelings to people from the past or the present, or to people who have died whom the client feels he or she may be meeting shortly. Occasionally, a client even asks to talk to God in the empty chair.

In many ways, the terminally ill client is an easy client to work with. This person is serious, sincere, mature, and motivated. It can be expected that, if you feel comfortable in working with clients who are terminally ill, the experience will be one that is full of growth for the client and for yourself.

The client grieving the future loss of a loved one

Anticipation can be a powerful force. Anticipating a trip can be as powerful as the trip itself. While anticipation can obviously be a positive or negative experience, anticipating the loss of a loved one can feel devastating to the client. It can also be a time of grieving that can moderate the length and pain of grief following the loss.

Clients who are facing future loss, just as clients who are grieving loss, often need education. Often these clients do not understand what grieving entails and/or do not understand that grieving future loss can be as difficult as grieving loss. It is not unusual for clients to say that their most painful grieving was *prior* to the death of their loved one. Clients should be made aware that grieving is a natural and healthy part of loss.

The counselor should be open and understanding, and should not diminish what the client reports. It is not unusual for clients to report things such as, "I can hear my father, who is unconscious, asking me in my head to let him die. I don't know if I can let him go. Do you think I'm going crazy?" It is the counselor's role to normalize experiences such as these by letting the client know they are common.

Clients often fear that they will not be able to cope without their loved one. These fears should be heard and not be diminished. A poor comment from the counselor would be, "You're a strong person. You'll be able to make it just fine." Statements such as these only tell the client that the counselor has no understanding of the depth of fear the client is experiencing. A much better response is, "I can see how that would be extremely frightening. I don't know how you will be able to cope. It must be frightening even to think about how you'll do that." These kinds of statements help clients feel heard and understood, and will result in their exploring personal resources.

It may well be that the client's life will be greatly diminished following the death of their loved one, the loss of their relationship, or the loss of a pet, and no person has a better sense of that than the client. The client is facing a real loss, and it is better for the counselor to show understanding of that loss than to attempt to diminish its impact to the client.

By being understanding, the counselor can demonstrate to the client that a support person is available who can hear, and who can be there for the client. Unlike the case with some other forms of counseling, the client who is facing the loss of a loved one will not leave the counseling room feeling normal and resolved. The client is in the midst of a process of grieving and it is the counselor's role to help the client understand that process and to help him or her feel heard and supported through the process. Often, clients have become tired of friends and relatives attempting to help them to be happier. The best way for the counselor to help the clients is to reflect an understanding of the pain and loss they are experiencing. These feelings of isolation diminish as clients gain a feeling of being heard and understood.

Therefore, clients who face the loss of loved ones need two things: they need to be educated about what normal grieving entails and they need to be heard and supported. They will be better able to hear that there is a light at the end of the tunnel with the counselor who tells them that he or she is able to be understanding about the darkness they currently experience.

Part of the education the counselor can offer is to encourage the client to say what he or she wants to say to the loved one prior to the loss. A good way to help the client determine what he or she would like to say is by asking the question, "If John was already gone now, is there anything that you haven't said to him that you wish he would have been able to hear?" The most common thing clients want to say is, "I love you." Many people have difficulty saying this and it can be extremely beneficial if the client is able to say it prior to the loss.

An empty chair may be used to help the client practice saying what he or she would like to say. This can be done even if the loved one is a beloved pet. An empty chair may also be used to allow the client to say things that he or she would like to say but for some reason does not feel that it would be appropriate to say to them directly. If it seems appropriate, the client may also be asked to sit in the chair of their loved one and respond to what was said. This process can be very enlightening and healing for the client.

It is sometimes the case that grieving the future loss of loved ones is complicated by other unresolved issues the client is facing. When this is the case it is appropriate to offer counseling to work on those issues.

Dealing with anger

Anger is a common emotion. It would be impossible to live without feeling anger. The acceptance of anger feelings and the proper expression of those feelings are positive and healthy. Anger becomes problematic when it is either not expressed or expressed inappropriately.

The problem with anger that is not expressed

Air is to the lungs what emotions are to the psyche. The lungs work best when they can take in and expel air unimpeded. The lungs are organs that thrive on the movement of air, and anything that prohibits that movement causes the lungs to feel constrained. If the psyche bottles emotions and they cannot flow in and out freely, there is also a constrained feeling.

Emotions are an elusive thing. We have little ability to choose the emotions we experience. We may want to love someone, but find that we can't. We may not want to be angry, but find that we are. It is important for us to be able to recognize our emotions and have an outlet for them. The psyche, and the body, can feel constrained when emotions are rejected or bottled. Studies have shown an association between cancer and our ability to recognize and express emotions (Cunningham and Watson, 2004; Temoshok, 1987, 2004), and further studies have shown an association between coronary disease and our ability or inability to appropriately express anger (Smith et al, 2004; Kubzansky and Kawachi, 2000).

Therefore, when emotions come into the body they need to be expressed. Bottled emotions can be problematic both psychologically and physiologically.

Anger is an emotion that is often repressed. When anger is repressed, an underlying ego state holds it internally until it can hold no more. Then, rage may result, a panic attack may result, or some other psychological or physiological expression. It is important that clients learn to recognize anger, and learn to express it appropriately.

The problem with anger that is expressed inappropriately

Some clients express anger, but do so in the manner that is problematic to them and those around them. Examples include screaming, violence, and passive-aggressive behavior. The person who says, "I don't care where we go eat," and then complains all evening about the choice exhibits passive-aggressive behavior. That person's anger is being released piecemeal and dishonestly by their continually psychologically jabbing others. This release of anger is painful for both the passive-aggressive individual and for those around that person.

Obviously, the person who screams and or becomes violent is releasing anger in an inappropriate fashion. Often, behavior such as this follows a feeling of lack of control, and may follow a period of not expressing angry feelings. This type of overt and aggressive behavior is normally unsatisfying both for the person inappropriately expressing anger and for those around that person.

Assertive behavior

Assertive behavior is a means of expressing feelings of anger or frustration in an appropriate fashion that maintains respect for the other person. It is much better to be able to say to someone immediately following an incident, "I'm upset about what you said to me" than to either bottle the feeling or become aggressive. It is possible for a client to say, "I'm really feeling angry with you right now" and explain why, then feel expressed without having the need to scream or to bottle the feelings.

It may be that individuals the client wants to express feelings of anger to in an assertive way have their own problems that make it difficult or impossible for the client to feel safe when expressing feelings. For example, if the client's boss is authoritarian and fragile, the client may fear retribution at work if appropriate expressions of anger were assertively offered. The client may be accurate in anticipating retribution from an authoritative and fragile boss, even when frustrations are expressed appropriately. Therefore, it may be important for the client to be able to express to friends or to a counselor those feelings that cannot be expressed to the fragile boss.

Understanding anger

In order to help clients with anger, it is important to have a good theoretical understanding of what anger is, where it comes from, and its nature. Different clients will need different solutions depending upon the nature of their anger. By understanding anger, the counselor will be better prepared to select appropriate interventions for the client.

Where does anger come from?

Anger is a normal and common emotion that results from our inability to accept discrepancies between what we would prefer and what we observe. We often observe things that do not meet our expectations without becoming angry. For example, we may prefer and expect a meal at a restaurant to be better than what we observe. We may expect a day with clear skies and bright sun, but observe a cloudy day with rain. These minor discrepancies between what we would prefer and what we observe are normally not enough to result in feelings of anger, rather feelings of slight disappointment—although, for some individuals, even these occurrences are enough to produce feelings of anger. Road rage may result even when a driver expects another driver to signal before turning, and observes no signaling.

Anger fragility

When two people observe the same incident, one may become angry and the other may not. This difference between individual responses to negative incidents is based in part on their respective levels of anger fragility. Consider a continuum of negative incidents from minor to severe. On the left side of the continuum are incidents such as breaking a pencil lead or dropping a bar of soap. Near the middle of the continuum are incidents such as someone walking across the carpet with muddy feet or having a flat tire on the way to work. Near the right side of the continuum are incidents such as being fired at work because of something someone else did or a bulldozer operator accidentally backing through the wall. Anger fragility refers to how negative an event has to be for a particular individual to experience anger. Colloquially, a person with high anger fragility could be said to have a short fuse. The person with high anger fragility would become angry nearer the left side of the negative incidents continuum, while it would take a more major incident before the person with lower anger fragility would feel anger – see Figure 3.

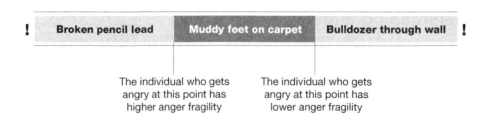

Figure 3: Negative-incidents continuum

Anger fragility seems to be based on a number of factors. Training, physiology, and aggregated negative feelings all interrelate to determine the level of anger fragility. Individuals who have been raised in households where anger is modeled tend to develop an ego state that can quickly become angry, so they tend to have higher anger fragility. They may feel a right or a responsibility to be angry at certain situations. Feeling physically tired, in pain, or sick can also raise an individual's level of anger fragility. And, if a person has not been expressing frustrations and anger previously, he or she will have an ego state that is burdened by negative feelings. Just as the straw can break the camel's back after enough weight has been accumulated, the person who is already burdened by negative feelings has higher anger fragility and it may take only a minor incident for that person to feel anger. This person could easily be a road-rager.

Blame and anger

Blame is often a component of anger. While it is difficult (not impossible) to attribute blame when a person becomes angry about the weather, most often individuals experiencing anger feel unfairly assailed, and they tend to focus anger on and blame who they feel treated them unfairly. They focus their anger at another individual. The road-rager focuses anger on another driver. The spouse whose partner has been unfaithful may focus anger on the partner and/or on the other party. The person who lost a loved one to cancer may focus anger on God.

Anger therapy techniques

It is important for clients to understand that anger is a common and natural emotion, and that the most healthy way of dealing with anger is to recognize it and release it appropriately. Some clients may present as a goal to not feel anger. These clients need to be educated about the nature of anger. Some clients may report that they never feel anger. Because anger is common and natural it is an emotion that everyone experiences. Clients who say they never feel anger are likely bottling those negative feelings, rather than releasing them in an appropriate manner.

Counselors need to be able to assist clients to prevent inappropriate expressions of anger or the bottling of anger, and help them with appropriate expressions of anger. They go hand in hand. Unless a client can learn to *appropriately* release anger that client will have to either release it *inappropriately* or bottle it.

All clients who have issues with anger need help to appropriately release that anger. This is the most important aspect of helping clients who have difficulty with anger. If clients are releasing anger in appropriate ways then the need will not exist to express anger aggressively or to bottle it.

Clients who release anger aggressively have two things to learn: (1) to stop the aggressive behavior and (2) to release anger in an appropriate way. Because these clients require facilitation for both these aspects an illustration will be given as to how to help a client having this difficulty. The following steps will be illustrated with the case example of the client who had difficulty controlling his aggressive behavior when angry.

Anger-management counseling

1. Hear the client's problem, showing understanding, and help the client to understand that anger is a common emotion that should be noticed and released in an assertive, not an aggressive, way.

2. Find when the client has been able to be assertive in the past, or have the client describe in detail what it would be like to be assertive.

3. Gather detailed information concerning:
    a. when the assertive behavior was experienced (or could be experienced);
    b. multiple sensory cues associated with the assertive behavior; and
    c. how the assertive behavior was experienced (or could be experienced).

4. Use the detailed information that was gathered to facilitate a current experience of the assertive ego state.

5. Negotiate with the assertive state, gaining assurance that this state is willing to take on a bigger role when the client holds negative feelings, so they can be released appropriately.

6. Gather detailed information concerning:
    a. when the anger was experienced;
    b. multiple sensory cues associated with the anger; and
    c. how the anger was experienced.

7. Use the detailed information that was gathered to facilitate a current experience of the unwanted symptoms (placing the client in the ego state that expresses anger aggressively).

8. Negotiate with the aggressive ego state to take on a lesser role and give permission for the assertive ego state to deal with more of the problems.

9. Negotiate with an intelligent state to call out either the assertive state or the aggressive state at the appropriate times.

10. Make sure all states agree with the arrangement.

11. Use imagery to test whether the negotiation has been successful in helping the client to release negative feelings in an appropriate manner.

12. Debrief with the client.

1. **Hear the client's problem, showing understanding, and help the client to understand that anger is a common emotion that should be noticed and released in an assertive, not an aggressive way.**

   Counselor: Thanks for coming in, Hank. What is it that you're ready to change today?

   Hank: I've got to get control of my anger. It's been pretty bad as long as I can remember it, but on the weekend I did something awful. It scared me and I have to get control of my anger before something worse happens.

   Counselor: You did something awful?

   Hank: Yes, I did. I killed my dog.

   Counselor: That *must* have been awful for you.

   Hank: It was. I can't believe I did it.

   Counselor: What happened?

   Hank: I had had a really bad day, and I was upset when I came home. I guess I was angry then. Then I saw where he had made a wet spot on the floor. I took him by the collar and dragged him over to the wet spot, and I went off on him. I yelled so loud he made another wet spot while I was holding him by the collar. Then I really went off. I got angry and slapped him on the head, and then I picked him up and threw him off the balcony. He hit hard, and he didn't get up. I can't believe I did that to him. He must have been terrified. I killed him.

   Counselor: Hank, I'm sorry. That must have been horrible for you, too. How are you doing now?

Hank: I just can't believe what I've done. I loved that dog. He meant the world to me.

Counselor: I can see that. You've lost something really important. I'm not sure if you would like to spend this time talking about your grief, or focusing on your issues with anger.

Hank: I really want to get on top of this anger thing. My girlfriend has been after me for a long time to get help for it, but now I can see I need to.

Counselor: OK, I'm happy to work with you on anger, but I want you to feel free to tell me about or ask questions about your loss at any time.

Hank: I will.

Counselor: I think it's important for you to understand that there's nothing wrong with feeling angry. It's what we do with the anger we feel that can cause a problem. There may have been nothing wrong with your feeling upset when you came home, but it became a problem when you dealt with it by becoming aggressive.

Hank: That's for sure. I want to get control of that, but I don't know if I can. I have tried.

Counselor: You have already taken a big step in gaining control by coming in here. I believe you already have the resources you need to respond to angry feelings in the right way. You just have not found how to use them. Do you know what I mean by being assertive?

Hank: That's like when you tell somebody what you think. You sort of give them a piece of your mind.

Counselor: You're on the right track, but that's not exactly it. There's a difference between being assertive and being aggressive. Being aggressive is like invading the other person's territory by attacking them. Being assertive is merely expressing yourself, saying how you feel so you can be heard, without attacking the other person. It would be aggressive for me to say to someone, "You're standing too close to me and you better back off," but it would be assertive for me to say, "I'm feeling crowded. Can you stand back a bit further?"

Hank: OK, but what if they don't listen to you?

Counselor: Then you could say, "I really am feeling crowded. It's important for me to have more room if I'm going to be able to be here." A key to being assertive is expressing your own needs clearly rather than blaming the other person, like, "You're standing too close to me." People find it easier to respond positively when you express your needs than they do when they feel blamed or attacked.

Hank: But the guy still may not want to move.

Counselor: That's true, and if that is the case then you have a decision to make. Would it be better to leave, or to become aggressive? There are times when aggressive behavior is appropriate. For example, if you should happen to be attacked by someone in an alleyway you might want to fight back and defend yourself. That would not be the time to say, "Excuse me, I really don't like being attacked." [Hank laughs.] Most of the time, though, assertive behavior works really well for you to express what you feel. Rather than bottle things up you tell the person exactly how what they're doing makes you feel. It takes practice to get really good at it, and some people take assertiveness training.

Hank: Is that what you think I need?

Counselor: I don't know if you'll decide that's something you want to do. I'm not thinking you need that right now. I expect there are times that you are assertive, or there are times that you have been assertive with someone in the past.

2. **Find when the client has been able to be assertive in the past, or have the client describe in detail what it would be like to be assertive.**

Counselor [continuing]: Think about yourself now, how you relate to people, and how you have related to people in the past. Tell me about a time that you have been assertive.

Hank: Well, I guess I'm assertive with my mother. She's always wanting me to come home and spend weekends there. I just tell her I have too many things to do here, and I tell her I love her.

Counselor: That sounds really good. It does sound like you're being assertive.

3. **Gather detailed information concerning:**

   a. when the assertive behavior was experienced (or could be experienced);

   b. multiple sensory cues associated with the assertive behavior; and

   c. how the assertive behavior was experienced (or could be experienced).

Counselor [continuing]: Where are you, Hank, when you're having one of these assertive conversations with your mother?

Hank: I'm at home on the telephone. She's a great person but she wants me to spend too much of my time at their house.

Counselor: I want to ask some questions that will help me bring out that assertive part of your personality. What room are you normally in when you talk to your mother on the telephone?

Hank: I'm in my living room.

Counselor: Standing or sitting?

Hank: I'm sitting on the couch.

Counselor: Is it normally daytime or nighttime when you're talking to your mother, and feeling assertive?

Hank: It's daytime.

Counselor: Tell me what kind of couch you're sitting on and what you might be wearing.

Hank: It's a black leather couch, and I've got jeans and a T-shirt on.

4. Use the detailed information that was gathered to facilitate a current experience of the assertive ego state.

Counselor: Good. And, as you're telling her that you won't be going to their house for the weekend, how are you feeling?

Hank: Good. I'm feeling relaxed, and I'm not afraid of her.

Counselor: It sounds like you're feeling strong and able to communicate. What name or term would fit with how you're feeling right now, really powerful and able to communicate without being aggressive?

Hank: I don't know, "Together".

5. Negotiate with the assertive state, gaining assurance that this state is willing to take on a bigger role when the client holds negative feelings, so they can be released appropriately.

Counselor: That's good. When I want to talk with this part of you that is strong and able to communicate clearly without being aggressive I will call it Together. I want to say something directly to that strong part of you now. Together, it sounds to me like you are a very good resource for Hank. As you know, Together, Hank has been having some problems in the way he expresses himself when he is angry. If you are given the opportunity, Together, would you be willing to play a bigger role and help Hank express himself in an assertive way, rather than in an aggressive way?

Hank: Yeah, I guess so.

6. Gather detailed information concerning:

a. when the anger was experienced;

b. multiple sensory cues associated with the anger; and

c. how the anger was experienced.

Counselor: Thank you for that, Together. I will want to talk with you again a bit later. Now, Hank, you have already told me about killing your dog. You've mentioned the wet spots on the carpet, and your throwing him off the balcony. Tell me something about that incident that comes to you now that you have not told me about before.

Hank: It was the look on his face. I'll never forget that. It's like there was two of me there, one really angry and yelling at him and another one noticing that sad look where he didn't understand what was going on. He was afraid of me and he wanted to please me. I hate myself for what I did.

7. **Use the detailed information that was gathered to facilitate a current experience of the unwanted symptoms (placing the client in the ego state that expresses anger aggressively).**

   Counselor: I am hearing those same two parts, Hank, that were there that night. I think when I hear you say that you hate yourself for what you did that that is coming from the part that noticed the sad look from your dog. Right now I'm really interested in knowing about the angry part that felt out of control. I want to talk directly with the angry part, that part that saw the wet spots on the floor and felt rage. Angry part, you can see the wet spot on the floor. What's happening with you?

   Hank: I can't believe he did this! I've had such a bad day, and now he does this!

   Counselor: It sounds like you feel everything is falling against you. It sounds like you feel you have to lash out to protect yourself.

   Hank: I have to! I can't let him do this and get away with it.

   Counselor: What can I call this part of you that feels angry and insecure?

   Hank: "Angry".

8. **Negotiate with the aggressive ego state to take on a lesser role and give permission for the assertive ego state to deal with more of the problems.**

   Counselor: Angry, I want to talk directly with you. Angry, are you aware that you are causing Hank problems? He's come to see me because he feels you are out of control.

   Hank: I know he's upset with me. But I have to get upset when things like this happen.

   Counselor: It sounds like it is your responsibility to get upset. Angry, can you help me understand this better?

   Hank: If it wasn't for me he would be taken advantage of. I have to protect him.

   Counselor: Angry, I was just talking with Together, and Together said that he is willing to help Hank express himself and not be taken advantage of. I know you are an important state, Angry, but wouldn't it be nice if the other states respected you and were happy about all the things you do? I know there are states that are upset with you, otherwise Hank would not be here now. I think you're important, and that you have a big role to play, but would you be willing to let Together help you so that the things you do can be respected by all states?

   Hank: What do you mean?

   Counselor: Well, I can see that you're powerful, and that you can be frightening. It seems like you would be a great state for Hank to use if he was threatened down the alleyway, or attacked by wild dogs. Your power and your strength would be of great use then, and I'm sure the other states would love for you to be there to help protect Hank. Would you be willing to be available during those important times, and let Together help Frank when he's not physically threatened?

Hank: Yes, I could do that. But, how can that happen?

9. Negotiate with an intelligent state to call out either the assertive state or the aggressive state at the appropriate times.

Counselor: It seems like it would be good if some intelligent part of Hank could determine when you are needed, or if Together is needed. Right now, I would like to talk to an intelligent part of Hank that could make that decision. Just say OK when you're ready to speak.

Hank: OK.

Counselor: What can I call you?

Hank: You can call me "Brain".

Counselor: Thank you for helping, Brain. When Hank is confronted with a situation where he feels angry, would you be willing to decide whether his anger could better be released by Together, or, if Hank is really physically threatened, if Anger needs to be called in?

Hank: Yes, I can do that.

10. Make sure all states agree with the arrangement.

Counselor: That's great, Brain. Now, Hank, just allow your eyes to close for a moment, and I would like all three parts, Together, Brain, and Anger, to have an internal conversation and see if all can agree on this solution. [Pause.] What happened?

Hank: They were all able to agree.

Counselor: That's great. How are you feeling now, Hank?

Hank: Good. More relaxed.

11. Use imagery to test whether the negotiation has been successful in helping the client to release negative feelings in an appropriate manner.

Counselor: That's good. Now, think about something, a situation that in the past would have caused you to lose control. Imagine experiencing that situation, and, as you do, see how Together, Brain, and Anger handle it. [Pause.] What happened?

Hank: It was like I have a choice. There was a moment there where I thought about how to handle it, and I decided not to become difficult.

12. Debrief with the client.

> **Counselor**: That's great, Hank. In truth, you have always had a choice. That choice was just not clear to you. There is always a decision that it is OK to be angry now, or it is not safe to be angry now. The difference is, Hank, now you are in control of that decision. Your resource, Brain, is helping to make that decision so you can react with people in a manner that you can be proud of. How do you feel about that?
>
> **Hank**: Really good. I think I can do this.
>
> **Counselor**: I think you can, too, Hank. Do you have any questions?
>
> **Hank**: No, I think I understand what's going on.

An important aspect of anger counseling to remember is that there is always an internal decision about how anger will be released, or, indeed, *whether* it will be released. One individual may get aggressively angry often at home, but practically never show anger at work. In this case, the decision is being made internally that it is safe to become angry at one time, but not at another time. After a decision is made to become overtly aggressive and angry, the individual may be out of control for a period of time. But the individual is in control, internally, before this decision to become overtly angry is made. Imagine an average-sized man becoming aggressively angry when a smaller or equal-sized man accidentally steps on his toe. This same average-sized man may not have become aggressively angry if a much larger man, a weightlifter, say, had accidentally stepped on his toe.

There is always an ego state that decides whether or not this is a good time to become aggressive. A key to helping individuals who become aggressive is to help the decision-making part to make wiser decisions as to how to respond to angry feelings. Before this negotiation takes place, it is helpful to locate resources that the client has that this decision-making part can be aware of. For example, it is important for the client to be aware of a part that can respond assertively so the decision-making part will be able to use assertiveness as an option, rather than aggressiveness.

Using this process, most clients respond rapidly to anger counseling. It is, of course, important that they want to change, but if they undergo a process of education, discovery of their own resources, and negotiation among ego states, this can result in rapid and dramatic change.

Relationship issues

Clients often present with issues related to the relationships in their lives. The goal of counseling in terms of relationship issues should not be to preserve the relationship at all cost. It should be for the client to become honest and assertive within the relationship, and for the client to be able to act in a manner that is satisfactory to the client, uninhibited by previous issues from the client's life. The client should not feel dependent upon the relationship, and should be able to enjoy the relationship with an understanding that neither party in a relationship can be perfect.

Understanding and working with ego states provides the counselor with excellent tools for facilitating stronger relationships. Relationship problems often result from a lack of communication. Almost always, when two people are not communicating well, they are communicating from ego states that are not the best states from which to communicate with each other.

For example, if John is angry and speaks in an angry voice to Mary (i.e. from an angry ego state), Mary may respond from a reactive ego state. This type of conversation, between angry and reactive ego states, can easily deteriorate into an argument where neither John nor Mary will feel heard and understood. But, if John is angry and speaks to Mary from an angry ego state, and if Mary is able to see John's anger and choose to respond from an intellectual ego state, then Mary will be able to hear John, John will feel heard, and the conversation can continue.

In order to help clients resolve relationship issues, empty chairs may be used so the client can speak directly to the introject of the person with whom they are having difficulty in a relationship. After a client has been able to express him- or herself to the introject in the empty chair, it is good for the client to sit in the introject's chair and respond, as the introject, to the client in order for the client to gain a better understanding of what the introject can hear and communicate. The client may be asked to move back and forth between the client's chair and the introject's chair a number of times to facilitate a better understanding of the possibilities of the relationship. An example of this type of intervention is illustrated on page 89.

Clients sometimes find it difficult to feel as though they can say the things they want to say while talking with the introject in counseling. When this happens, the counselor can ask the client when he or she has been able to communicate in the preferred way, with someone else. Ask the client to tell in detail about that time when the preferred types of responses were given to another person. While the client is in this more empowered ego state that has been able to give those preferred responses to another person, ask the client to name that part of themselves, i.e. that ego state, that can communicate in the preferred manner. Then, that ego state may be asked to help the client in responding to the more difficult individual.

For example, if Mary is having difficulty responding to John, Mary may be asked when she has been able to respond to a person in the manner that she would like to respond to John. Mary responds by saying that she can talk to her boss at work, Ruth, in the way that she would like to respond to John. Mary may then be asked to describe in detail a time when she has talked with Ruth. When the counselor can see that Mary is in the empowered ego state that she is in when she is talking with Ruth, the counselor may ask something like, "What can I call this part of you that is feeling you can say anything you would like." Mary may respond, "Talker." The counselor can then say something like, "Talker, I can see you are a powerful part of Mary. I wonder if you would be willing to help Mary when she's talking with John? She would like to be able to talk to John as you talk to Ruth. Would you be willing to help, Talker?"

By isolating and talking directly with Mary's ego state, Talker, Mary is better able to understand this part of herself and to call upon this part of herself when she wants to use it for her own purposes. Mary is training to bring her own resources to her own needs.

The next step is to ask Mary to speak to John in the empty chair, that is, to speak with John's introject. Mary may be asked to talk with John using her ego state, Talker. Allowing Mary to practice speaking with John using Talker gives Mary a chance both to practice and to gain confidence.

Clients need to gain an understanding that they have a number of different ego-state resources (a number of different ego states) and they need to understand that, once they become more familiar with their ego states, they can call upon them and use them at any time. There is no reason why clients should not be able to fully utilize their own resources to meet their own needs.

Sometimes a client has difficulty communicating because the person he or she wants to communicate with (such as an employer) brings out an underlying ego state of the client with unresolved issues. When this occurs, the client will feel out of control and will be unable to communicate appropriately with that person until the unresolved issues are attended to. To assist a client with this, the reader should refer to the section on resolving past issues on page 99.

Dealing with depression

The depressed client exhibits a low level of energy, making it appear that the executive ego state is *depleted* of energy. The opposite is actually the case. Normally, depression is the result of an ego state that has high levels of energy, and is unwilling to interact with the outside world. For example, an individual who has enjoyed success as an athlete will have an ego state with a high level of control over energy it has used to exercise, compete, and enjoy athletic pursuits. If this athletic individual is involved in a car accident, making it impossible to compete, the athletic ego state may become depressed, forlorn, and despondent. It can hang onto the high levels of energy it has controlled in the past, interfering with other ego states that would like to use this energy in positive ways by interacting with the outside world. The person will then experience a feeling of depression. This "athletic" ego state can dominate the personality and effectively block other states from pursuing their own interests. It is as if a huge truck were stalled across the freeway. It not only fails to move its own load, but slows other movement as well.

Another example is the person who has gained a strong identity as a parent. This person may have dedicated a life to parental pursuits, and when the last child leaves home the energy that has been invested in a parenting ego state may no longer be needed by that ego state. If the parenting ego state attempts to hold onto the energy, keeping it internal, it will not be able to be used, and this ego state may feel depressed and despondent over its loss of parenting interactions. Because this one ego state holds onto the large amount of energy it has previously used, the client experiences a low level of energy when attempting to interact with the outside world. Ego states that might have interest in volunteer work, in study, or in other pursuits do not have the advantage of a normal flow of energy among ego states, and therefore they have limited ability to act. Previously, the parenting ego state would have been a hub of interaction with other states, so when it shuts down that interaction ceases.

Depression, therefore, results from the blocking of a normal energy flow in the family of ego states. In order for the client to re-experience a feeling of having a movement of energy "to live", the ego state that is harboring a large amount of energy needs either to learn to use the energy itself in a new way or to share that energy among states that are eager to use it by interacting with the outside world.

Ego-state techniques can facilitate (a) an identification of the state that is harboring energy and blocking internal communication and (b) negotiation with that state to use or release that energy and negotiate with other states that would like to use energy to interact with the outside world. The conclusion of this negotiation can result in a rapid commencement of re-involvement with pursuits of interest to the client. The key to this negotiation is the ability of the counselor to persuade the ego state that is harboring energy to use it or to release it to other states.

Antidepressant medication

While antidepressants may sometimes be useful, they often act to distance the client from the ego state that is harboring energy. This can make it more difficult to gain contact with this ego state so that effective therapy can proceed. The use of antidepressants may allow a period of time for other ego states to gain a habit of interacting with the outside world, even though the issues held by the depressed ego state are not addressed. Following a course of antidepressants, the client may be able to continue interacting in a positive way with little interference from the depressed ego state, or may again become overwhelmed by the blocking of energy by this depressed state. In either case, it is recommended that, following a course of antidepressants, appropriate ego-state negotiation be used to facilitate reframing the role of the depressed state and a reintegration of the depressed state into the family of states. When possible, it is preferred to use ego-state negotiation with depressed clients prior to the decision to administer antidepressants. This gives the therapist and the client the best ability to have full access to the family of ego states, and to the issues they may have, and it may result in resolving the need for medication.

In order to assist the reader in understanding the progression of working with a depressed client, a list of steps is provided below. This list is presented as a guideline, and would rarely be followed in the chronological order it is presented.

Steps in working with the depressed client

1. Ask the client to focus on the symptomatic feelings of the depression.
2. Enhance the negative feelings until significant affect is demonstrated (this ensures that the client enters into the depressed ego state).
3. Get a name for the depressed ego state.

4. Talk directly with the depressed state to determine whether there is another way that it can use some of the energy it has previously used.

5. Ask to speak with a state that has had pursuits in the past that were unfulfilled, and get a name for this state. Repeat this step until at least two or three ego states wanting more energy and activity are found.

6. Talk with each state that has had pursuits in the past and make sure they are now willing to apply their interests in the outside world if more energy is made available.

7. Gain permission from the depressed state to share energy with these states that want to use it in the outside world.

8. Make sure all states agree with the negotiated sharing of energy.

9. Facilitate a more positive feeling for the depressed state. Help that state get what it needs to feel better.

10. Remind all states of the agreements that have been made, and express appreciation for their cooperation.

11. Use imagery so the client can imagine interacting in the outside world with energy and interest.

12. Debrief with the client.

The following is an example (Holopainen, Debbi, and Emmerson, 2002) of a work with a depressed client to help illustrate the steps above. The client, John, began exhibiting symptoms of depression after severe facial scarring from a burn accident. (This is a compilation example from a number of depressed clients. This abbreviated example is not meant to illustrate the entire counseling session.)

1. **Ask the client to focus on the symptomatic feelings of the depression.**

   Therapist: John, from what you've said, I understand that you've been feeling depressed. Tell me anything you feel may be important for me to understand about the way you have been feeling.

   John: Well, you can tell by looking at my face that I've had massive burn injuries. I was in a car accident and my face and upper body were badly burned. I used to go out with my friends a lot and have a good time. Now, I don't think they want to be with me, and I don't feel comfortable being with them. I just sit at home doing nothing, feeling bad.

   Therapist: Is that where you feel the worst, John, at home?

   John: Yes, I guess so.

Therapist: Tell me more about that experience of being at home, feeling depressed. When you think of that feeling, what room are you in, and what are you doing?

John: That's part of the problem. I don't feel like doing anything. I try to sit on the couch and watch TV, and I can never find anything that interests me. I just don't feel like doing anything.

Therapist: You said that you sit on the couch. What kind of couch is that, and what is the texture like. [Gathering information such as this helps place the client into the ego state that has the problem.]

John: It's a brown, soft couch made out of some kind of cloth material.

Therapist: Thanks, John. That's helpful for me to get a picture of when you're feeling most depressed.

2. **Enhance the negative feelings until significant affect is demonstrated (this ensures that the client enters into the depressed ego state).**

Therapist [continuing]: I want you to imagine being at home on your brown cloth couch, where you've told me you often feel very depressed. It's just as you've described it when you feel depressed. You've tried to watch TV but there's nothing that interests you and there's nothing you can think to do. You can feel the texture of the couch as you sit there, experiencing that feeling. Tell me exactly what that feels like in your body.

John: I don't know. I just don't want to do anything. I don't even want to get up.

Therapist: What do you feel like physically, right now?

John: It's like my head has walls around it and it's uncomfortable inside.

Therapist: Have the courage to really go into and experience that discomfort inside those walls. What can you tell me?

John: It's too much.

Therapist: What is too much? What's wrong?

John: I can't let anyone see me. I can't go out. My life is ruined!

3. **Get a name for the depressed ego state.**

Therapist: What can I call that part of you talking with me now, that part that feels your life is ruined?

John: I don't know, "Scared"?

Therapist: That's good. When I talk directly with this depressed part of you I will call it by the name, Scared. Thank you for talking with me, Scared. I realize you don't feel very good and I appreciate your talking with me. Scared, what did you like to do before the accident?

John: Go out with my friends and have a good time.

Therapist: And now you don't feel you can do that?

John: No. They don't want me to slow them down.

Therapist: That must feel bad, feeling rejected like that.

John: Yes, but there's nothing I can do about it. My life is over.

Therapist: Scared, there are two things I would like to help with. I want to help you feel better and I want to make sure that the energy you have is used for a really good use. Would you like that to happen?

John: I don't know. I guess.

4. **Talk directly with the depressed state to determine whether there is another way that it can use some of the energy it has previously used.**

Therapist: Scared, it sounds like in the past you've been good at socializing, good talking with and enjoying your friends. Is there any time now that you have an opportunity to enjoy communicating with other people?

John: Not really.

Therapist: What about when you talk to family members on the telephone?

John: They don't really want to talk to me. They just call me because they feel responsible.

Therapist: That may be true, and it may not be. But, Scared, since you have communication skills, I wonder if it would be possible for you to help them feel better. I'm not really sure if that is something you would like to do.

John: I don't know. I think they just feel sorry for me.

Therapist: Are you willing to consider using your communication skills sometime in the future to help your friends feel more comfortable? This is something you're good at, and, while it would not take as much energy to do this as the time you used to spend with your friends, it could be very helpful to other people. Is that something you can think about for the future?

John: Yes, I guess so.

Therapist: I really appreciate that, Scared. I know you've had a hard time, and that you used to be very busy. It would be good if some of that energy you've used in the past could be released so the other parts of this person could benefit from it. I do appreciate your talking with me, Scared.

5. **Ask to speak with a state that has had pursuits in the past that were unfulfilled, and get a name for this state. Repeat this step until at least two or three ego states wanting more energy and activity are found.** (Only one state wanting other pursuits will be presented here in this shortened example.)

> **Therapist**: Thank you. I want to talk now with a different part of John. I want you to think of the time when you have wished that you had more time for some activity. I want you to think of something that you've wanted to do in the past. It may seem like you don't want to do it now, but I want you to think of something that you would have really liked to do at sometime in the past. No matter how insignificant it may seem now, tell me about something that you have wished you could do if you had more time.

> **John**: Well, I used to want to do volunteer work at the hospital for children. That may seem funny but it appealed to me.

> **Therapist**: That doesn't seem funny at all. That seems like a really good thing to do. [Pulls an empty chair up across from the client.] Right now, I want you to move over to this other chair and as you sit in that chair I just want to talk to the part of you that would like to help children in the hospital. [Points to the other chair. John moves and sits in it.] That's good. Now, I just want to talk to the part of you, John, that would like to help children. What can I call you, part?

> **John**: You can call me "Helper". [A difference is noticed in John's affect.]

> **Therapist**: Thanks for talking with me, Helper. What would you like to do with more time and energy if you had more?

> **John**: There were a lot of kids in the burn unit. I would like to help them get through their hospital stay.

6. **Talk with each state that has had pursuits in the past and make sure they are now willing to apply their interests in the outside world if more energy is made available.**

> **Therapist**: If Scared would release some of his energy to you, would you make good use of it?

> **John**: Yes. I really think I could make a difference. I just have not been able to make myself move.

7. **Gain permission from the depressed state to share energy with these states that want to use it in the outside world.**

> **Therapist**: Let's ask Scared and see what he says. [John is directed to move back to the other chair.] Scared, you heard what Helper has said. He would really like to have some energy.

John: I heard.

Therapist: Would you be willing to release to Helper some of the energy you are not using so he can help the kids at the burn unit? It sounds like a really good thing to do.

John: That would be OK with me.

8. Make sure all states agree with the negotiated sharing of energy.

Therapist: Thanks, Scared. I want you and Helper to talk together internally now and see if you can work out a deal and exchange some energy. I don't need to hear. Just close your eyes for a moment and see if the two parts, Scared and Helper, can agree for Helper to have some of Scared's energy so he can help the kids in the burn unit. [Pause.] What happened?

John: Yeah, we have it worked out. Helper is taking some of my energy.

Therapist: Thank you, Scared. That's a great thing you've done. And I also want to thank Helper. I'm sure you will make really good use of the time and energy.

(This process of finding states that would like to do things and getting permission for them to have the energy to do them should continue in a counselling session until negotiation has established permission for three or four states to begin interacting in the outside world in the way they would like.)

9. Facilitate a more positive feeling for the depressed state. Help that state get what it needs to feel better.

Therapist [continuing]: Now, Scared, how do you feel? What do you need right now?

John: I feel tired and lonely.

Therapist: I can understand how you can feel lonely, given that you haven't been able to spend time with your friends. I want to speak with a nurturing part of John, a part that might like to make others feel better, a part that would like to come to Scared and help him to feel better. John, close your eyes for a moment and when a nurturing state is ready to speak just say, "I'm here" when you're ready to speak.

John: I'm here.

Therapist: What can I call you?

John: You can call me "John". [It is not unusual for an ego state to give itself the name of the client.]

Therapist: OK. Thanks, John. Would you like to go to Scared and put your arm around him and let him know that you will be there for him so he will never have to feel lonely?

John: Yes.

Therapist: Good. Go ahead and do that now. [Pause.] What's happening?

John: I have my arm around him.

Therapist: That's great! Scared, can you feel that?

John: Yes.

Therapist: How does that feel?

John: Really good.

Therapist: Ask John if he will always be there for you. [Pause.] What did he say?

John: He said he will.

Therapist: How do you feel now?

John: Better.

10. Remind all states of the agreements that have been made, and express appreciation for their cooperation.

Therapist [to Scared]: Is it all right with you to continue to allow Helper to put the energy to good use, and for you to continue to have the help of John?

John: Yes.

Therapist: Thank you. Do you still want to be called Scared, or do you want to be called something else? [Often the state chooses a new name, but it is not problematic if it wants to continue to be called by the original name.]

John: I want to be called "Loved".

Therapist: That's a very good name, and it reflects what you're getting now from John. I want to say thank you to John for helping the state that used to be called Scared and is now called Loved to feel loved, and I want to say thank you to Helper for agreeing to take some of Loved's energy so you can help the kids in the hospital, and I want to say thank you to Loved for agreeing to share some of energy with Helper. All states can now settle in with their new roles.

11. Use imagery so the client can imagine interacting in the outside world with energy and interest.

Therapist: Now, go ahead and open your eyes. You've done some good work. How are you feeling?

John: I'm feeling better, more settled, and I really think I will be able to go to the hospital and see if I can help children.

Therapist: That's great! Think about being at home in your living room, sitting on your brown cloth couch, thinking about the TV being switched on. How do you feel now?

John: Better. I think I might be able to watch some TV.

Therapist: Very good.

12. Debrief with the client.

> **Therapist**: That sounds great. What do you think about what we've done here?
>
> **John**: It was interesting. I think it's going to be helpful. What should I do? How should I use it?
>
> **Therapist**: You have some good resources that you're beginning to use now. It's understandable that the part of you that enjoys communicating would feel upset. But it is beginning to feel better now and may be able to enjoy communicating in some way in the future. You have a great part that wants to help out in the hospital and seems to have permission to do that now, and your other parts are working together to help you feel better on the inside. It will be good to see how well this works. [This leaves a suggestion that the intervention will work well.]

This type of intervention for depression attends to the state that has been harboring energy and has been blocking the flow of energy that other states might use. It helps the client locate internal resources—ego states that would like to interact with the outside world—and it helps negotiate an opportunity for them to begin that interaction. It further facilitates ego states to bring relief to the depressed, injured ego state that had been blocking the flow of energy. This intervention can result in a rapid affect change for the client, a rapid reintegration of the client with life pursuits, and a feeling of internal empowerment and peace. The above example should not be viewed as illustrative of a complete work in a session, but illustrative of the type of technique that can help the depressed client re-engage with life pursuits.

Working with addictions and obsessive-compulsive disorder

It is not unusual for clients to present with a type of addictive behavior. Addictive behavior, irrespective of the particular symptomology, stems from a common cause. Addictions are an attempt to escape from unresolved negative feelings.

Gambling

When a client has had difficulty staying away from poker machines, most normally that difficulty stems from unwanted negative feelings. While standing in front of the poker machine, with bright flashing lights, the client has an opportunity to zone out, to narrow the focus to the job at hand and forget about time and the past. When a person is plagued by unresolved emotional trauma, this escape to the poker machine, is understandable.

Drug addiction

Drug abuse is another example of addictive behavior. Physiologically, a particular drug is capable of blocking individual ego states. When a client finds his or her "drug of choice", the drug that blocks an unresolved ego state has been found. The difference between individuals who try drugs and leave them and those who become addicted to drugs is that the addicted persons need to block unresolved issues from the past. When the "drug of choice" has been found that can block out a painful ego state, it is extremely difficult for the person to stop taking this drug. This difficulty may be compounded by a physiological addiction or a sociological addiction, but the primary difficulty in breaking a drug addiction is dealing with the painful ego state or states that re-emerge when the individual ceases taking the drug.

It is easy to understand how addictive behavior can bring temporary relief to a person who feels painfully unsettled. It provides an escape, a refuge, a safe place, a place to which the person develops a need to return over and over again. Pathologies—such as obsessive-compulsive disorder—that have not previously been thought of as addictions also provide this escape.

Obsessive-compulsive disorder

An individual suffering from obsessive-compulsive disorder finds it difficult or impossible to refrain from compulsively acting out in some way. Often, this acting out takes the form of checking water taps or locks over and over again. Even though the person has checked the same locks a number of times in the same evening, he or she may have the need to compulsively recheck them several more times. While in the ego state that is checking the locks, the client is focused and centered and safe from negative feelings or pain held by other states. It is this ability to escape that provides an impetus to continue to enter into the compulsive behavior.

Because obsessive-compulsive disorder occurs as a means to escape internal pain, to a safe, "zoned-out" place, it is actually another form of addiction and should be treated therapeutically in the same manner. The techniques described below should be used to assist clients demonstrating obsessive-compulsive behavior to gain a resolution to the internal pain so the client no longer has the need to escape into the unwanted and uncontrolled behavior.

Self-harming behavior

People self-harm normally for one of two reasons. Sometimes it is a combination of the two. Some people who self-harm want and gain attention from their self-harming behavior. Other individuals who self-harm report going into a trancelike state while self-harming. They report feeling no pain while in this focused, safe state. Just like the flashing lights of the casino, the self-harming behavior facilitates for these individuals an ability to focus intently on what is happening, and to gain escape from the painful emotions of unresolved ego states.

Smoking

Smoking may be (1) an addictive behavior, (2) a behavior preferred by the individual even though there may be some desire to not smoke, or (3) merely a habit that is physiologically/sociologically difficult to break. If the smoker finds a need to smoke to escape, if while smoking the person enters a "safe zone" (common to addictive behaviors) away from the troubles of the past or present, then it is most likely an addictive behavior. If attempts to stop smoking result in neurotic reactions (reactions to life situations that would be unexpected reactions to those situations) it is also likely an addictive behavior.

The techniques presented in this section on working with clients for addictive behavior apply only to (1) above. Additional techniques to assist clients to stop smoking are presented below in the section, "Nonaddictive eating and smoking problems" on page 184.

It is important to note that, if the client is smoking because of an addictive personality, after the ego state that has been fueling the addiction has been resolved, the client can be further assisted in attempts to stop smoking by ego-state negotiations. An example of these negotiations will be given in the section referred to above. When smoking does result from an addictive personality, it is imperative that the ego-state work to break the addictive cycle be done first. Otherwise, any amount of negotiations between states that want to quit and want to smoke will be fruitless, because the client will continue to have an uncontrollable need to escape pain through smoking.

Compulsive eating

It is not uncommon for clients to present wanting help in controlling their diets. Just as is the case with smoking, difficulty in controlling the diet can be the result of an addictive personality. If the client seems to zone out when eating in an uncontrolled fashion, then eating may be being used as an escape from an unresolved ego state. When this is the case, work merely to control the diet will show few positive results. Just as it is almost impossible for the compulsive gambler to stop gambling without addressing the underlying issues, it can be almost impossible for the compulsive eater to curb eating without work on those issues. Therefore, when the client appears to eat in an attempt to escape, and when attempts to eat less result in distressing and uncomfortable symptoms, it is likely that an addictive personality is the core of the problem. After addressing unresolved issues that have fueled addictive behavior, work of the type presented in the section "Nonaddictive eating and smoking problems" (page 184) may begin.

What addictions have in common

There is a long list of addictive behaviors, each having the need to escape from negative feelings. An addictive personality is the psyche of the person who has not yet resolved past trauma, and has found a means to escape from that trauma by being able to zone out in some way, or in the case of drugs who has found a chemical substance that blocks the trauma-feeling ego state. Until this trauma is resolved, the person may go from one addiction to another, continually being dissatisfied with the addictions until an addiction is found that the person is able to live with. Compulsively working is an example of an addiction that some find compatible. Others include compulsively following a hobby, gardening, or any other activity that allows the person a safe escape from unresolved trauma.

Rather than continue with addictions that are problematic, or hiding in compatible compulsive behaviors, it is preferred to resolve the traumas from the past so the individual no longer has a need to escape the present. An ego state that has experienced a traumatic incident and has not been able to experience a resolution to that trauma has the potential for producing addictive behavior as a means of coping with the negative feelings. Once that ego state gains resolution, the client will no longer have a need to gain escape from that painful state through addictive behavior. Counselors should be aware that it is possible for a client to have more than one state that is associated with addictive behavior; therefore, trauma-resolution techniques may need to be applied to resolve more than a single trauma. The number of trauma-resolution procedures will relate to the number of ego states carrying trauma, not to the number of traumatic incidents in the life of the client.

Techniques for working with clients with addictive behavior

When working with clients with addictive behavior it is important to show respect for their inability to stop the behavior. Prior to coming to counseling they have most likely made many fruitless attempts to stop their addictive behavior. They often feel out of control and powerless. They may feel insecure about their lack of ability to control the behavior.

It is helpful for the counselor to show understanding for their addictive behavior, and to reflect that it is a normal coping mechanism that is easily understood. It is often relieving for the client to learn that their addictive behavior may have been their best coping mechanism for dealing with the problem at hand. It can also be encouraging for them to understand that their addictive behavior may no longer be needed once they are able to relieve the ego state or states that have felt unresolved.

It is often the case that they are unaware of any particular trauma that may be associated with their addictive behavior. They should be assured that this is common and that this does not pose any problem in counseling. (Clients should not be asked why they think they exhibit addictive behavior, since their interpretations are normally inaccurate and may inhibit an easy bridging.) They will likely be aware of their inability to feel settled and at peace when they have no means of escape, no addictive behavior.

These understandings can assist the client to feel accepted and understood, and to feel positive about possible changes, but they will not directly affect the client's addictive behavior. In order to impact upon the addictive behavior it will be necessary to do trauma counseling. The following steps are involved in helping a client extinguish addictive behavior. The steps are adapted for addictive behavior from the steps in the section, "Unresolved-issues-situational concern" on page 99.

1. Hear the client's problem, showing understanding, and help the client to understand that the addictive behavior has been a normal coping mechanism that will no longer be needed.

2. Determine the precipitating cause of the unwanted symptoms. (Here, it is important to gather information about the negative feelings that precede the behavior, rather than about the feelings the client has during the addictive behavior. Remember, the addictive behavior is an escape from painful feelings.)

   a. Gather detailed information concerning:

      i.   when the problem (painful feelings) was experienced;

      ii. multiple sensory cues associated with the problem; and

      iii. how the problem was experienced.

   b. Use the detailed information that was gathered to facilitate a current experience of the unwanted symptoms.

   c. Bridge from the current experience of unwanted symptoms to the origin of the problem.

3. Facilitate a resolution to the trauma that the client has been carrying:

   a. expression;

   b. removal;

   c. relief.

4. Use imagery to test whether the trauma resolution has been successful in alleviating the unwanted symptoms.

5. Debrief with the client.

The following is an example of working with a client with addictive behavior, problem gambling. It will illustrate the use of the above steps with this client.

1. **Hear the client's problem showing understanding and help the client to understand that the addictive behavior has been a normal coping mechanism that will no longer be needed.**

   Counselor: Jane, I'm interested in knowing what it is that you're ready to change.

   Jane: Well, for a number of years now I've had a problem with poker machines. It's been bad and worse than bad off and on, but it's always a problem. My husband tries to keep control of the money but I usually find a way of getting hold of it. We don't have money for anything.

   Counselor: I can hear the despair in your voice. That must be terrible, feeling out of control and wishing you had more control.

Jane: You don't know how terrible. Sometimes I just feel like ending it all. I just can't help myself.

Counselor: Jane, you said that sometimes you feel like ending at all. Is suicide something that you are seriously considering? [When a client makes a statement that could be interpreted as suicidal it is important to check out if suicide is seriously being considered. See the section, "Dealing with suicidal ideation" on page 197.]

Jane: No, not now. Sometimes I've felt like that, but I don't think I would ever do it.

Counselor: Just something I needed to check. I would like to hear more about your gambling.

Jane: I just can't stay away from it. I want to, and I tell myself I'll never go back into one of those pokie [poker machine] joints again, but then I'll be driving by, or I get a little bored, and I think I'll just go in for five or ten minutes.

Counselor: Then what happens?

Jane: Sometimes I think I can make some money. And sometimes I do hit jackpots, but I just keep going. It just seems like I can't stop.

Counselor: Are you aware of how long you have been there?

Jane: No, I lose all track of time. Sometimes I forget to pick up the kids at school. It's like that is the only place that exists, and I just need to keep doing what I'm doing.

Counselor: Sounds like you go into a bit of a zone when you lose track of time.

Jane: That's right! I am in a zone.

Counselor: What you're saying makes perfect sense to me. When you go into a zone and have a need to stay there you're escaping from something that feels bad. That need to go into a zone is a coping mechanism that helps you feel better. What you're doing is understandable, and it is understandable that you've had difficulty controlling your behavior, because your behavior is the best way you've found to cope. I understand that you don't like the way you've been coping because it has caused you and your family a lot of grief. We could look for another way to cope, but I think it's much better to resolve the bad feelings that cause you to need an escape place. What do you think about that?

Jane: How do we do that?

Counselor: We need to focus on what you feel like right before you go into a casino or a pokie. If you are ready for a change, we can start that right now. [Statements such as this help move therapy along by providing a means for the client to contract for change, and by leaving the suggestion that change will occur.]

Jane: Boy, am I ever ready! You don't know the hell this has been.

2. **Determine the precipitating cause of the unwanted symptoms.**
(Here, it is important to gather information about the negative feelings that precede the behavior, rather than about the feelings the client has during the addictive behavior. Remember, the addictive behavior is an escape from painful feelings.)

2.a. Gather detailed information concerning:

i.   when the problem (painful feelings) was experienced

Counselor: Great. Tell me about a time you can clearly remember when you went to the pokies. I especially want to hear exactly how you felt when you decided to go.

Jane: It's a bit embarrassing, but that's going to be easy. I went yesterday. I was on my way to the grocery store and I thought about driving a different direction so I wouldn't drive past the pub that has the poker machines, then I thought, "You can drive by that place." I couldn't. I found myself driving into the parking lot and going inside.

Counselor: So, while you were driving there was some pull or need you had that took control, and took you where at least part of you did not want to go.

Jane: That's right.

2.a. Gather detailed information concerning (continued):

ii.   multiple sensory cues associated with the problem (This helps the client get into the unresolved ego state that is necessary for bridging to the origin of the unresolved issue.)

Counselor: Jane, I would like for you to close your eyes for a moment and imagine yourself being in the car on the way to the grocery store. You have decided that it's OK to drive by the pub and as you approach the pub I want you to tell me all about your experience. Start by telling me what you see looking out of the car window, and what you are feeling. What do you see, and what kind of day is it?

Jane: Well, I see the creek before the pub, and it is a warm day with a bright sun.

Counselor: What are you wearing and what is in the car with you?

Jane: Just a pair of slacks and my cheap red top. I had just planned to go to the grocery store.

Counselor: And what else is in the car with you?

Jane: It's a bit messy. There are some toys in the seat and some papers that should have been carried in.

Advanced Skills and Interventions in Therapeutic Counseling

2.a. Gather detailed information concerning (continued):

iii. how the problem was experienced

Counselor: As you sit in that car with the toys and papers and look up and see the pub on this bright sunny day, emotionally, how are you feeling?

Jane: I am really feeling a need to go there. I can't keep myself from going there.

Counselor: I understand that is a powerful need you are feeling right now sitting in the car. Tell me how you experience that in your body. What is the difference between feeling that powerful need and feeling relaxed?

Jane: Actually, I feel a bit panicky. My chest and shoulders feel tense and I can feel that tension up the back of my head.

2.b. Use the detailed information that was gathered to facilitate a current experience of the unwanted symptoms.

Counselor: Just allow yourself the courage to go deeper into that feeling, that experience with tense chest and shoulders and tension in the back of your head. Tell me more about that experience you are feeling.

Jane: I really need to get into that pub.

2.c. Bridge from the current experience of unwanted symptoms to the origin of the problem.

The counselor notices that Jane is showing definite emotional distress. It is imperative for the client to be in the unresolved ego state in order for bridging to work. When the client shows definite emotional stress there has been a movement into the unresolved ego state.

Counselor: Right now, feeling just as you do with the stress in your chest, shoulders, and head, what number or age comes to mind? Or how old do you feel?

Jane: Young, really young. Not very old at all.

Counselor: About how old?

Jane: I don't know. About three or four.

Counselor: I want you to go to when you were about three or four feeling just like you are right now, uneasy and tense. Are you inside a building or outside?

Jane: I'm outside. [Shows more distress.]

Counselor: Are you alone or with someone else?

Jane: There are others.

Counselor: Tell me exactly what is happening.

Jane: It's awful.

Counselor: I'm with you to support you. Tell me about what is awful.

Jane: They've taken my panties away. I don't have any panties and I am on the playground with other kids all around me.

Counselor: I can understand why you're upset. Who took your panties?

Jane: It was Barbara and Ruth. They're always picking on me. They're bigger than me, and when I went to the toilet they pulled my panties off and put them somewhere. I don't know where they are and I don't have any panties on and I'm on the playground.

Counselor: I can understand you are upset, and I think you have a right to be upset. What can I call this part of you that is on the playground and upset? What name or term seems to fit you?

Jane: "Helpless"!

Counselor: OK, when I talk to this part of you I'm going to call you Helpless. Helpless, are you in kinder [kindergarten] or just at a park?

Jane [crying]: It's kinder.

3. Facilitate a resolution to the trauma that the client has been carrying:

3.a. Expression

Counselor: I see. Helpless, I have a secret I want to tell you. [Child states listen intently for secrets.] I know you're on the playground right now and that you're very upset because Barbara and Ruth have taken your panties, but the secret is that this is a memory and is not really happening now. It's something you are carrying with you, and while we can't change the past we can change what's happening on the playground, right now. Helpless, we have the power now, so we can do anything we want to. First, let's use some magic so you can have on a brand-new pair of panties right now, there on the playground. You can feel them on right now and feel how perfectly they fit. Is that better?

Jane [crying less]: Yes, I guess so.

Counselor: Can you feel them?

Jane: Yes.

Counselor: Good! Now remember, I'm on your side, and let's have Barbara and Ruth standing where they can hear you. Now is the time you can say anything you want to them, because it is safe now. What do you want to say to them, Helpless?

Jane: I don't know. I guess I want to know why they pick on me.

Counselor: You can go ahead and ask them that, right now. Ask them directly and out loud so I can hear you.

Jane: Why do you pick on me?

Counselor: That was good the way you asked them. What did they say?

Jane: They just laughed.

Counselor: Is it OK if I say something to them, too?

Jane: Sure.

Counselor: Barbara and Ruth, you are really stupid to stand there and laugh like you are! Get those stupid looks off your faces! Try to be mature enough to answer intelligent questions! Helpless, what are they doing now? [The counselor can help empower the client by acting as a support and saying things that help shift the balance of power in favor of the client. It is still important for the client to be able to express.]

Jane: They're just standing there now.

Counselor: Who are you focusing on the more, Barbara or Ruth?

Jane: Barbara.

Counselor: Do you want to tell Barbara not to pick on you anymore? Remember, this is our scene and we can do anything we want now.

Jane: Yes.

Counselor: Go ahead and tell her now.

Jane: Stop picking on me Barbara. I don't like it!

Counselor: That was really good. What is she doing now?

Jane: She's just standing there, looking at me.

Counselor: I want to talk to Barbara, directly. I want you to be Barbara standing there looking at Helpless. I want to hear directly from Barbara. [Pause.] Barbara, you have just been told to stop picking on Helpless. How do you feel?

Jane: She never told me that before. We were just having some fun.

Counselor: I understand that, Barbara, but it was really upsetting to Helpless. That was a mean thing you did, taking her panties. Do you understand that that was not a good thing to do?

Jane: Yes, I guess so.

Counselor: I don't know if you would like to tell Helpless you're sorry or not. Is that something that you would be able to do?

Jane: Yes, I didn't want to upset her so much.

Counselor: I really appreciate your help with this, Barbara. You can go ahead and tell her you're sorry now.

Jane: I'm sorry. I won't do it again.

Counselor: Thanks, Barbara. [Pause.] Helpless [pause], how do you feel about Barbara now?

Jane: I still don't like her.

3.b. Removal

Counselor: Do you want her to stay where you can see her or do you want her to leave now? If you want to you can even have her leave kinder for good because we can do anything we want now.

Jane: I want her gone for good.

Counselor: Tell her.

Jane: Barbara, leave and don't come back. I don't ever want to see you again.

Counselor: Boy, you really told her! What happened?

Jane: She left.

Counselor: And what about Ruth?

Jane: I don't want her here either!

Counselor: You are doing a great job. Tell her!

Jane: Ruth, you go too. I don't ever want to see you again!

Counselor: That was really good. What happened?

Jane: She left.

Counselor: That was great! You told them what you thought, and you decided you did not want them with you any more, so you told them to leave. That was very good.

3.c. Relief

Counselor [continuing]: You have all your clothes and you're safe on the playground. How do you feel now?

Jane: Much better.

Counselor: Is there anything else you need to feel totally comfortable? Would you like a more mature part to help protect you?

Jane: That would be good.

Counselor: Thank you for talking with me, Helpless. I'll want to talk with you again in a moment, but right now I want to talk to a mature nurturing part of Jane, a part that would like to help a young kinder girl feel safe. Just say, "I'm here" when you're ready to speak.

Jane: Yes, I'm here.

Counselor: Can I call this part, "Nurturer"?

Jane: Yes.

Counselor: Nurturer, would you like to go to Helpless and help her feel safe and let her know that you will always be there so she can always be safe?

Jane: Yes, I can do that.

Counselor: Good. Go to Helpless now and let her know you will always be there for her and that she will always be safe. [Pause.] Helpless, what's happening now? Is Nurturer there with you?

Jane: Yes, she's here.

Counselor: How does it feel?

Jane: It feels good.

Counselor: Ask her if she will always be there for you? You can ask her silently and then tell me what she says. [Pause.] What did she say?

Jane: She said she will always be here.

Counselor: Would you like to give her a hug?

Jane: Yes.

Counselor: You can go ahead and do that, now. How do you feel, now?

Jane: I feel really good.

Counselor: Is there anything else you need?

Jane: No, I feel really good.

Counselor: You have been really brave to say the things that you have, and to ask Barbara and Ruth to leave. Do you still want to be called Helpless, or do you want to be called something else?

Jane: I want to be called "Brave".

Counselor: I think that's a great name for you now, Brave. Tell me, Brave, in the past when you felt helpless, did that feeling have anything to do with the need to go to pokies? Was that the feeling that this person needed to escape from?

Jane: Yes, it was the same.

4. Use imagery to test whether the trauma resolution has been successful in alleviating the unwanted symptoms.

Counselor: And now, Brave, you feel comfortable and Nurturer is there to make sure you're safe. So, this adult person can respond to life the way she wants to. You can go ahead and settle in there with Nurturer. Thank you, Brave, and thank you, Nurturer. [Short pause.] Jane, I want you to imagine being in your car going to the grocery store. It's a sunny day and you can see toys and papers in the car. You can also see the pub on the left. Tell me how you're feeling.

Jane: It's OK. I can see the pub, but it's just a pub. I don't need to stop there.

Counselor: And think about other times that in the past you have been tempted to go to the pokies. Take a moment and place yourself in situations where you would have been tempted in the past. [Pause.] How did you go?

Jane: Good. I felt like I am in control.

Counselor: Very good. You can go ahead and open your eyes now.

5. Debrief with the client.

Counselor: How do you feel?

Jane: Really good. I had no idea that had anything to do with what happened when I was in kindergarten. That was so real. I was really upset. I felt awful.

Counselor: That would've been a really frightening experience. When you don't get a chance to get some kind of closure for an experience like that it can come back and bother you later.

Jane: I don't think I told anyone. I was too embarrassed.

Counselor: That's understandable. It would've been embarrassing, and not being able to talk about it with anyone kept you from being able to let it go into the past. That unresolved part kept coming up to get some resolution, and it was understandable for you to use pokies to try to escape its pain. Now, that part is feeling much better and that need to escape is no longer there.

Jane: Does this mean that I won't have any more trouble with gambling?

Counselor: We'll have to see exactly how you feel. It can be really nice to be surprised at how well these things can work.

Jane: What should I do?

Counselor: How did it feel when you imagined driving by the pub on the way to the grocery store?

Jane: That was easy. I didn't have any trouble at all driving by.

Counselor: So you have already had some practice in what to do.

Jane: I really think this may work. I have had this problem so long.

Counselor: I could hear that. I know it was hard in the past.

This illustration of working with the client for addictive behavior may be applied to any addiction. A key to this process working is to make sure that the client is experiencing the negative behavior that brings on the addictive behavior prior to bridging back to find the cause. When you are working with clients with drug addictions, it is important for them to have refrained from using drugs long enough for them to feel the need to escape the painful feelings of the unresolved state(s). It is the experience of feeling the need to escape that the client needs to experience in the counseling chair prior to bridging. When the client shows obvious emotional distress, shows a need for the addictive behavior, then the client is in the ego state that is unresolved. While the client is in this unresolved ego state, bridging back to the origin of the negative feelings is not difficult. But, if the client is merely *telling* about the negative feelings from a different state, then bridging back to the origin of the negative feelings is impossible.

Attempts to bridge while in the wrong ego state will cause the client to go to a time that he or she believes could be associated with the negative feelings. I have found that, when a client guesses the cause of a problem, the guess is normally wrong. I have found the same thing when a counselor interprets (guesses) the cause of a client's problem.

Nonaddictive eating and smoking problems

Work of the type presented in this section, with clients having eating and smoking issues, should be commenced only after the counselor determines that an addictive personality is not the cause of the problem. If the client "zones out" while eating or smoking, loses track of time, and seems to enter a "safe place", and, if the client experiences symptoms of severe anxiety when attempting to curb behavior, then that behavior is likely related to an addictive personality. Addictive personality is caused by unresolved issues that necessitate the client's seeking a safe zone from a painful or uncomfortable ego state. Refer to the previous section on dealing with addictions, "Working with addictions and obsessive-compulsive disorder" on page 170.

Many clients have eating or smoking problems but do not suffer from addictive personality. Work of the type presented in this section can begin with them immediately, or this work can follow the resolution of addictive behavior, as presented in the section on working with addictions.

Helping clients with eating and smoking problems is more difficult than helping them with problems such as inability to speak in front of a group. There is, normally, no ego state that enjoys being nervous in front of a group. But there are ego states that enjoy eating or smoking. Therefore, an internal dissension often exists between states that want to eat less and those that enjoy eating, and between states that want to stop smoking, and those that enjoy smoking.

It is important for an ego-state negotiation to assist states that have been unable to agree on these behaviors. Because the issues of eating and smoking are similar to each other in relation to an appropriate therapeutic response, an illustration will be provided to help a client stop smoking and the techniques of that illustration may be also applied to helping a client achieve a desired diet.

It is not unusual for a client to ask for help to stop smoking when that client has little commitment to the task. Statements such as "I want you to make me stop smoking" indicate a client who is not ready to quit smoking. This statement indicates a client whose ego state (or states) that wants to smoke is currently stronger than the ego state (or states) that wants to quit smoking.

Clients who want to quit smoking will have one or more ego states that do not want to smoke, and they will have one or more ego states that want to smoke, otherwise they would not present smoking as a problem. If all their states wanted to smoke they would not be considering stopping; or, if all their states did not want to smoke, it would be easy for them to stop smoking. They would not feel the pull to smoke.

Before a client can stop smoking there must be more energy with the non-smoking ego states than with the smoking ego states. If the client has ego states that truly enjoy smoking, and are more energized, or powerful, than the states that want to quit smoking for health, money, family members, or for any other reason, then that client is not ready to quit. Therefore, it is important to determine the relative desire of the state that smokes compared with the state that does not want to smoke. Using empty chairs is a good technique to determine this. Ask the client to sit in one chair and speak to all the reasons he or she does not want to smoke, and then to switch chairs and speak to all the reasons why smoking has been continued. As always, when using empty chairs, it is imperative for the client to be speaking directly from the ego states that you want to hear from. When the client is sitting in the "smoking" chair the words and tone should obviously favor smoking, otherwise this "smoking" ego state is not being heard, and negotiations will not work.

It is a good technique to encourage the smoking and nonsmoking ego states to communicate with each other, speaking directly to the other chair, in an attempt for the client to reach a positive conclusion. Because assisting a client to come to a resolution on smoking or eating involves resolving an internal dissent, the steps from the section "Helping the client resolve internal dissent" in Chapter 6 can be used for this illustration.

1. Get a clear understanding of the division and of the states involved.
2. Make clear which state will sit in each chair.
3. Listen to everything each state has to say.
4. Help each state to see the value of both states.
5. Suggest how nice it would be to have the respect of the other state.
6. Negotiate a way the states can work together.
7. Suggest that the states communicate directly with each other.
8. Thank each state for working together to achieve a solution.
9. Debrief with the client.

1. Get a clear understanding of the division and of the states involved.

Counselor: Amy, I understand you want to stop smoking. Can you tell me a little about what you want and what your history is?

Amy: Well, I've smoked since I was fifteen years old. I couldn't tell you how many times I tried to quit. My father died of lung cancer and I know I should not be smoking now.

Counselor: Tell me what happens when you try to quit.

Amy: Sometimes I can go for a few weeks, but there's usually something that happens at work, or at home, or someone offers me a cigarette while I'm drinking and I think, "What the hell!" and I have a cigarette. That's it. I'm smoking again.

Counselor: And, while you're having a cigarette, how do you feel?

Amy: I like the taste. I know that sounds strange given what it smells like, but I really do like the taste. And it helps me to relax.

Counselor: When you're relaxing with a cigarette do you lose track of time and sort of zone out?

Amy: No, not really. I just feel more relaxed.

Counselor: When you've tried to quit, during the times when you would normally have been smoking, how did you feel?

Amy: Well, there were nicotine withdrawals, but I can handle them. It's more like I got bored about smoking. I missed it and when I got a good excuse, any excuse really, I would go back to it.

(This client did not show traits of an addictive personality, zoning out during the symptom of the addiction or suffering severe anxiety during withdrawal.)

Counselor: I'm interested in hearing all the reasons you want to quit smoking. You've already told me about your dad's cancer, and your concern about health. Are there other reasons, too?

Amy: Yeah. My breath smells bad. I cough and have shortness of breath. It costs me a lot of money. It's embarrassing. I don't want to be a bad influence to my kids. Should I go on?

Counselor: I can see the part of you that's talking now really doesn't want to smoke.

Amy: You bet I don't!

Counselor [positioning another chair across from the client]: Amy, it's clear to me that there's a part of you that really doesn't want to smoke and a part of you that quite enjoys it. It seems to me like the arguing those two parts do has been pretty uncomfortable for you.

Amy: It's like a war in my head.

2. **Make clear which state will sit in each chair.**

Counselor: That's very well put. I want to be able to hear from each part and for the two parts to be able to agree on what's going to be done. Does the chair you're sitting in now seem to fit more the part that doesn't want to smoke, or the part that wants to smoke?

Amy: I think the part that doesn't want to smoke.

Counselor: Good. As I said, I want to be able to hear from both parts. They are both important, so when you're sitting in this chair I want to hear only about the reasons you don't want to smoke, like you were telling me earlier. I only want to hear directly from the part of you that does not want to smoke. I don't want to hear anything about how smoking is good. But, when you move and sit in the other chair, I only want to hear from the part that enjoys smoking. I will not want to hear from the part that is sitting in the chair you're in now. Do you understand?

Amy: Yes, I think so.

3. Listen to everything each state has to say.

Counselor: Good. It sounds like one of the reasons you want to be smoke-free is so your lungs will be clean, so is it OK with you if I call this part of you "Clean"? [It is good to call the part that does not want to smoke something other than "Nonsmoker", since terms including the word smoker continue to facilitate a focus on smoking.]

Amy: Yes.

Counselor: Clean, I think I heard from you a moment ago when Amy was telling me the reasons she doesn't want to smoke. Can you tell me some of those reasons again?

Amy: I want to be healthy, I want to live longer, and I don't want to be a bad influence on my kids.

Counselor: Clean, I can hear by your voice that you really do want to quit smoking.

Amy: I do. I've had enough of it.

Counselor: I can hear your determination there. I will want to talk with you more, Clean, but right now, Amy, go ahead and move over to the other chair. [Amy moves to the other chair.] Now, I want to hear directly from the part of you that enjoys smoking. Think about having a cigarette and tell me the good things about the experience.

Amy: I'm not sure there are any good things.

Counselor: Remember, you're sitting in the smoking chair now. I know you have a part that enjoys smoking, otherwise you would never smoke. I want to hear directly from that part now. Tell me what you enjoy when you smoke.

Amy: I like the taste. I like the feel of the smoke when it enters my lungs. I like the fact that it's my time, and that I get some rest from work. And I also like that I get to keep up with the gossip when other people come out and smoke with me.

Counselor: I can see that you really do enjoy smoking. It sounds to me like this part I'm talking to enjoys tasting, having time, and communication with friends. You sound like a part to me that really enjoys things. Is it OK with you, part, if I call you "Pleasure Seeker"? [It is good to call the smoking part something other than smoker. That way it can maintain its identity when the client no longer smokes.]

Amy: That's OK.

Counselor: Good. From now on when I'm talking directly to you I will call you Pleasure Seeker. Pleasure Seeker, it must have been difficult for you when Clean tried to keep you from smoking.

Amy: Yeah, she is a bit of a killjoy.

4. Help each state to see the value of both states.

Counselor: I get the sense that she doesn't understand how much you enjoyed smoking. That mustn't feel very good, not feeling understood by her.

Amy: I don't care that much. If I really want to smoke I go ahead and do it.

5. Suggest how nice it would be to have the respect of the other state.

Counselor: I can see that you're a really strong part, Pleasure Seeker. I think it's really important for you to do your job of making sure Amy gets some pleasure in life. I don't think anything should keep you from doing your job, but I do think it would be nice if you could do your job, making sure that Amy gets some pleasure in life, and at the same time be appreciated by all the other parts of Amy. I'm not sure if you realize how upset some of the other parts of Amy are with you. They really want her to be healthy, and they see you as a problem. They don't understand how important you are to make sure that Amy gets some pleasure out of life. I don't think I'm going to be able to help Amy without your help. You're very powerful and very important. Do you understand how some other parts of Amy don't understand and don't like you right now?

Amy: Yeah, I know they don't.

6. Negotiate a way the states can work together.

Counselor: That part of Amy that wants to have clean lungs is not a bad part. She just wants what she feels is best for Amy, just like you do. It would be nice if you could work together in some way.

Amy: I don't think she will ever like me.

Counselor: I think if we could find some way for you to make sure Amy gets the pleasure she needs without smoking, then Clean would like you just fine. Is it OK with you if I ask her about that?

Amy: Sure, go ahead.

Counselor [motioning Amy to move back to the other chair]: Clean, do you think you could like Pleasure Seeker if she could help with relaxation and pleasure in some way without smoking? Pleasure Seeker would still need some time to seek pleasure in some way. What do you think about that?

Amy: That would be great. I would really love to be able to stop smoking. I've tried for so long.

Counselor: So you don't have anything against Pleasure Seeker's helping with relaxation and pleasure? You just don't want to smoke anymore.

Amy: That's right. I just don't want to smoke anymore.

Counselor: Good. Amy, as strange as it may seem, it appears that there is a really good part of you that has wanted to help you by helping you relax and have pleasure, and that part has had something to do your smoking. We've been able to talk to that part, Pleasure Seeker, and I think it would be helpful if you could say directly to that part [pointing to the empty chair] that you can respect it, and appreciate it as long as it can help you without smoking. Just go ahead now and say what you would like to the Pleasure Seeker to help the part of you feel understood and cooperative. Speak out loud, so I can hear you.

Amy [looking a bit questioning]: I would love it if you would quit smoking and I do appreciate your wanting to help me with relaxation. I need that.

Counselor: Good. You're beginning positive communication, creating a peace within, with a part that in the past has felt unappreciated. That is a big step in cooperation. Now, Amy, move back to the other chair. I want to speak with Pleasure Seeker again. [Amy changes chairs.] Pleasure Seeker, it sounds to me like you can really be appreciated with helping Amy relax and have fun, by doing that in a way that does not involve smoking. What do you think of that?

Amy: That would be good, I guess. But, smoking is what I do. What else can I do?

Counselor: That's a good question. What would you like to do to help Amy relax and have fun? I think it's really important that you do something.

Amy: I'm not sure.

Counselor: What other things do you do to have fun and relax?

Amy: I like to surf the Internet, and to talk to friends.

Counselor: Is that something you could do in the times that you've smoked in the past? [It is important to refer to smoking as in the past, rather than saying "in the times that you smoke".]

Amy: I think so. Most of the time, I could do one or the other.

Counselor: That sounds good, then. And you may come up with other good ways of helping Amy relax and have fun, ways that will allow you to continue to be appreciated by the other parts. How does it feel to be accepted and appreciated?

Amy: Good. I didn't really think it would happen.

7. **Suggest that the states communicate directly with each other.**

Counselor: What do you think of Clean now?

Amy: She's OK.

Counselor: I think it would be good if you start communicating directly with Clean so you can help each other. You both do important work, and it would be nice for you to appreciate each other and work together. Just close your eyes for a moment and silently, where I can't hear you, have a little talk with Clean and see if the two of you can agree to continue to work together. [Pause.] What happened?

Amy: We are going to continue to work with each other.

Counselor: Pleasure Seeker, it will be important when Amy goes through a hard time for you to remember to work with Clean and to make sure you help Amy relax in some positive way. Do you think you can do that?

Amy: Yes, I think so.

8. Thank each state for working together to achieve a solution.

Counselor: That's great. Pleasure Seeker, you've been very helpful and cooperative. I want to thank you for that. I also want to thank Clean for working with Pleasure Seeker, for accepting Pleasure Seeker in the new role, and for continuing to be helpful. Now, Amy, go ahead and sit back in your original chair and as you do I would like Pleasure Seeker and Clean just to settle into their new roles, with their new understandings, so I can talk with you.

9. Debrief with the client.

Counselor [as Amy changes chairs]: Amy, what did you think of that?

Amy: It was really different. A bit strange, but I think it will work. I wouldn't have thought those different parts of myself could come out and talk like they're different people. Is that normal?

Counselor: Very normal. We all have different parts like that. Everyone has times when part of them wants to do one thing and another part wants to do something else. The best thing, though, is when our parts can agree, as yours are now, and we can have peace within.

Amy: It does feel like that.

Counselor: You did a very good job, Amy. Do you have any questions?

Amy: I don't think so. Will I just not smoke any more now?

Counselor: I think it will be easier for you to stop smoking, but it's still something that you will have to do. You may want to use nicotine patches or other ideas that you have to make it easier for you. You're the one quitting, and you will be able to take full credit for quitting. Coming here was one of the things you've done to quit.

Amy: Is there anything special I should do?

Counselor: You'll have full memories of what we've talked about. You seem to understand how your parts are communicating now, and how they're finding ways to work positively. This is your decision to quit smoking and you can use this information you have in any way that seems best for you. As I said before, you are the one in control.

Amy: That sounds good. I think I can do it.

Counselor: You have some excellent resources.

It is important with the different states that have been conflicting, in regards to smoking or overeating, to learn how to respect each other and work together for a common cause. When naming a state that has been eating in excess, it is better not to use terms such as "Overeater". It is better to use a positive term that incorporates the role that the overeating state has. In the example above the smoking state was called "Pleasure Seeker". A term such as this more easily allows the client to understand how the state can take on new roles, as compared with a state named "Smoker".

It is always important to be aware that addictive behavior may be involved in smoking or overeating. If, during the course of counseling, it becomes evident that the features of addictive behavior are present, as described in the section on addictions, then attention to addictive behavior must be made if the desired change in behavior is going to be lasting.

Dealing with sexual-abuse issues

It is a sad fact that sexual abuse is not a rare occurrence. It is not unusual for clients to present with sexual-abuse issues. While it is much more common for female clients to present with these issues, it is also not unusual for male clients to have been victims of sexual abuse. Working with clients on sexual-abuse issues requires sensitivity and an ability to hear whatever needs to be said. It is also important to be aware that both client and counselor often assume that current problems stem from a single cause (sexual abuse) for the client who has been abused. Just as clients who have never experienced sexual abuse have problems, clients who have experienced sexual abuse have problems that are not related to their abuse. The first part of this presentation cautions the counselor about focusing on abuse issues in a manner that fails to help the client, and that may actually negatively highlight the impact of the abuse. Following this, techniques for working with clients who have been abused are presented. The techniques presented in this section must be used with bridging and trauma resolution techniques illustrated in other sections, and not covered here.

Do not minimize or maximize the problem

The experience of sexual abuse is frightening and traumatic enough. A counselor should never increase the degree of trauma held by the client, by making statements that could cause the client to feel more victimized.

Clients will be affected very differently by traumatic events. Good crisis intervention can greatly moderate the effect an incident has in the life of a client. Because clients will be affected very differently by sexual abuse, it is important for the counselor to be able to provide the appropriate treatment for the amount of effect the client has experienced, and it is equally important for the counselor not to make the problem bigger than it is by making assumptions about how big it is for the client.

It is appropriate for the counselor to be able to hear what the client has to say, to be able to be understanding of what the client has to say, and to be able to reflect the level of pain the client reveals so that the client understands that the counselor understands. The counselor, with any problem, should never "awfulize" it, should never make it bigger than it is. The counselor should also never preconceive a reason for unwanted symptoms and attempt to link those symptoms to sexual abuse. Too often, counselors assume that the myriad problems a client has are linked to sexual abuse. It is true that sexual abuse may be a cause of many problems, but it should not be indiscriminately linked to negative symptomology.

A positive aspect about working with ego-state techniques is the ability of the techniques provided in this book to help determine the cause of negative symptoms (see the section "Bridging from the unwanted symptom to the cause of the problem" in Chapter 4). When a client has been sexually abused there is a tendency for him or her to blame almost every negative symptom on the experience of sexual abuse. The counselor should not automatically assume the client is correct in diagnosis and should not automatically focus therapy on the sexual abuse in order to help the client with the unwanted symptoms. If sexual abuse is not the cause of the unwanted symptom and if the counselor focuses therapy on sexual abuse, the unwanted symptom would continue and the client would be further reminded of the sexual abuse. The counselor should focus therapy on the negative symptom that the client presents, on what brought the client into therapy. If ego-state bridging techniques indicate that the unwanted symptom is linked to sexual abuse then ego-state work can focus directly on empowering and nurturing the abused ego state(s). But, if ego-state bridging techniques indicate that the unwanted symptom is linked to something else, then counseling work may focus directly on what is causing the unwanted symptoms.

If the unwanted symptoms are being caused by issues unrelated to sexual abuse, the client still may want to focus on sexual-abuse issues later in therapy, but this is a decision the client should be able to make, not the counselor. For the client who does want to deal with sexual-abuse issues, ego-state techniques provide an excellent opportunity for the client to gain the feeling of empowerment and nurturance.

Techniques for working with the sexually abused client

Be a fearless listener, but not a detective

If you are not able to hear what a client has a need to say about experiences of sexual abuse, that client should be referred to someone who is ready to listen completely. Clients may have a need to tell graphically about their sexual abuse (most often this is unnecessary). If the client has a need for someone to hear and understand what they have gone through, it is important to be able to use fearless active listening and allow the client to express fully. But it is absolutely not appropriate to coerce the client to tell details about sexual abuse. A good statement is, "I want to hear about absolutely anything you want to tell me, and I want you to feel free to tell me only about what you want to." The client should not be stopped from telling about abuse incidents, but it should be made clear that it is totally in the client's control as to what is discussed.

Therapeutically, it is important for the client to revisit only those incidents that are directly related to current unwanted symptomology. The negative symptoms the client is experiencing should be thought of as the beginning of the path to what needs to be resolved. Revisiting other incidents of sexual abuse may have little therapeutic value, and may result in the client's feeling retraumatized. Still, if the client expresses the need to tell about an incident, it is likely that that incident needs to be revisited so the client can become more empowered and nurtured. It is what the client expresses to the introject of the abuser that is important, not the details of the abuse.

If the client asks for guidance about what should be discussed, it is good to help them to focus on what is bothering them today. For example, if the client is unable to enjoy the sexual experience, that becomes the focus for therapy and a bridging technique may be used to determine the precise cause of the client's inability to enjoy the sexual experience. If the client presents with obsessing about memories of sexual abuse, then assisting the client to discuss those memories is the appropriate course of counseling. In either case, it is important for the client to be able to go through the process of detraumatizing using the techniques of expression, removal, and relief discussed in the subsection "Facilitate a resolution to the trauma that the client has been carrying" in Chapter 7.

Check for possible feelings of guilt

If sexual-abuse issues are discussed, it is important to allow the client to express any feelings of guilt that may be associated with the abuse. It is often the case that clients who have been sexually abused feel guilty themselves. The client may not volunteer that guilt has been a burden; therefore, it is important when working with sexual-abuse issues to allow the client an opportunity to define any level of guilt that has been assumed. Especially when sexual abuse has occurred over a period of time, the client may have at some point either enjoyed or encouraged some of the sexual behavior. The client needs to understand that it is the older person who is totally at fault. Absolutely no fault belongs with the person who has been abused.

The human body is designed to enjoy sexual stimulation. It may be the case that the client never once enjoyed sexual stimulation during abuse, but it is often the case that clients will have found some physical enjoyment during some aspect of the abuse, and the client may later feel extremely guilty because of this. It is easy for a counselor to want to avoid this issue for fear of insulting the client, but it is important to check for feelings of guilt that could be missed and remain to haunt the client. When clients have been abused over a period of time, guilt feelings are most often present and they can be pivotal to the client's progress.

It may also be the case that because of the positive feeling, or because of favors that were granted by the abuser, that the client may have encouraged incidents of sexual behavior. Here again, it is imperative that the client understand that any and all blame is rightfully placed on the abuser. How the client experienced the abuse and whether or not the client ever encouraged any of the sexual behavior has nothing to do with who is at blame. The client is "lily white", and while feelings of guilt are understandable, absolutely no blame belongs with the younger person who was abused.

When clients have an opportunity to express feelings of guilt and to gain a clarification that any positive sexual feeling or any encouragement of sexual incidents is completely normal and understandable, and that no blame lies with the person who was abused, they most often respond with an expression of real relief. They may have carried feelings of guilt for years, and it is therapeutic for a professional counselor to clarify with them that no blame rests with them.

Treat sexual abuse as a problem, not a defining problem

Too often, counselors talk to clients who have been sexually abused in a dis-empowering fashion. The message received by many clients says, "Oh, no, you're a victim of sexual abuse." Clients may already feel embarrassed or stained by underlying messages such as these. The counselor should only respond empathetically to the client, with an accurate reflection of the affect the client is demonstrating. The affect of the counselor should not be greater than the affect of the client. The counselor should speak with the client in a fashion that demonstrates an awareness that the client is "normal".

Do not assume sexual abuse unless the client remembers it

A number of studies have demonstrated that indirect suggestions can lead to false memories, especially if the client is in a hypnotic state (see the section on spontaneous hypnosis on page 214). Clients who are very emotional or highly focused are likely to be in a hypnotic state even when no formal "induction" has been used. It is, therefore, extremely important for the coun-selor to always avoid making statements that could lead a client to generate a false memory of sexual abuse. A statement such as "You may have been sexually abused, even if you don't remember it" is highly unethical. It may be the case that the counselor suspects that the client has been abused, but this suspicion should not be shared with the client.

Clients who are highly dissociated, toward the "multiple personality" end of the dissociation scale, will have major incidents in their lives that they can-not readily recall. Persons who have DID (dissociative-identity disorder) may be unable to remember events of their last hour, so obviously they may be unable to remember major incidents in their childhood. It is unlikely that a person with an average level of dissociation would fail to have access to sex-ual-abuse memories. Either average or highly dissociated persons can gener-ate false memories.

The best counseling techniques are to continue to hear the person and to use bridging techniques that connect the unwanted symptoms to the origi-nal cause. These techniques will work with clients who fall anywhere on the dissociation continuum. If sexual abuse is the cause, the client will discover that with bridging techniques, even if it was not remembered. There is no need to define the origins of clients' problems to them, and there is good reason not to. It has been surprising to me how often clients who present with an issue they believe must be caused by abuse discover that the issue is actually connected to some other aspect of their life.

Dealing with suicidal ideation

It is not unusual for clients to have thoughts of suicide. Some people speak in terms of the client's right to commit suicide. Existentialists sometimes say that the first step in accepting the self-control of one's life is to understand that suicide is an option, that the life that is being lived is in the total control of the person. The euthanasia debate has also clouded the issue of the client's right to commit suicide.

We will not enter into a debate on these issues here. It will be assumed that, when a client comes to see a therapist and expresses suicidal ideation, then that client is asking for help to live. This presentation will deal with understanding the suicidal client, techniques to assist that client through the critical period of suicidal ideation, and techniques to assist the client with the issues that brought on the suicidal ideation.

Understanding the suicidal client

Clients who talk about committing suicide have reached a point where the pain of life appears to exceed its benefits. They cannot see their lives improving. They are depressed, and, while the fact that they have come to a therapist indicates they want help, they can see no way out. They often feel as if they were on an island alone, and no one else understands them or their pain. When they think back on their life, because they are in a depressed ego state, they often think of only the times they were depressed. It is difficult for them to identify with happiness and joy. They often feel that there is something different about them that separates them from others, something that cannot be understood. Because these feelings of isolation are intense, it is easy to make some common mistakes in working with the suicidal client.

The suicidal ideation

One positive is that, while suicidal ideation is relatively common, a suicidal depression is more rare. In order to have a suicidal depression the client has to be depressed enough to want to commit suicide, and have enough energy to actually follow through with the suicidal action. Normally, when a client

197

is depressed, there is also a very low level of energy (mania). Therefore, even though the client might wish he or she were not here, there is no realistic thought of action.

There has been some debate in the literature about the role of antidepressant medication and suicide. Some therapists believe that antidepressants can increase the energy level of a depressed client more quickly than the depression level drops. This, they contend, may place a client in a suicidal depression. Other therapists contend that any temporary added risk of suicide brought on by the use of antidepressants is more than countered by the reduced risk of lowered levels of depression over time. This presentation will not attempt to enter this debate, but the debate does point out the interplay between depression and energy levels.

There is little disagreement that a suicidal depression can last only a relatively short period of time, normally no more than 48 hours. This is because it is so difficult to maintain the energy to carry through on suicide at the time that a high level of depression exists. If a therapist can assist the client through this 48-hour danger zone, then the immediate threat has passed. This is not to say that the same client will not go back into a suicidal depression in the near or late future. Because suicidal depressions normally last no more than 48 hours, techniques that will be presented below are, in part, to assist the client through this danger zone. Further techniques will be presented in order to help the client in the longer term.

Mistakes in working with the suicidal client

Suicidal clients need to be heard, and need to feel that their problems can be understood by another person. Statements that indicate that the counselor does not hear or understand the pain of the client can cause the client to feel more isolated and different.

Never say, "It is not that bad." This says to the client who is thinking of suicide, who is feeling very low and isolated, "I don't understand you." It says, "I do not hear your pain." It says that the counselor has no connection with what is being said by the client, that the counselor is another one of those people who cannot reach the isolated and painful island that the client inhabits. It may be that the client will present a problem that seems insignificant to the counselor. Clients may talk of suicide because of a sick cat, or because of a bad grade, or because of acne or some other minor medical concern. It is important to remember that, if the problem causes the client to contemplate suicide, then it is a big problem to the client and it should be taken seriously by the counselor. Never diminish a problem the client presents.

Show an understanding that it is a problem for the client, and that the client has a right to feel pain.

Do not be cheerful in an attempt to cheer the client up. This separates the counselor from the client and is a further indication to the client that the pain is not understood. The client sees a counselor as far away, in a far different mood state, and unable to demonstrate empathy. The client can become more frustrated, and feel more alone.

Do not fail to take talk about suicide seriously. While it is true that occasionally a client will talk about suicide in order to gain attention, it is also true that most people who commit suicide have talked about suicide to at least one other person. It is much preferable to take seriously every client who talks about suicide, and be wrong when one or more of those clients were not really serious, than not to take seriously the client who later commits suicide. Suicide is devastating to the family and friends, and can be to the counselor. The loss of a human life is a loss to society, and, while the best therapist when doing the best therapy can lose a client to suicide, every attempt should be made to prevent the loss. It could be very difficult to be a counselor who failed to take a client's suicidal talk seriously, if a client later proved to have been serious.

Techniques to assist the client through the critical period of suicidal ideation

The goal of the counselor working with a suicidal client is twofold: first, it is important for the counselor to show an understanding and a respect for the client's problem; second, it is important for the counselor to attempt to ensure that the client will not commit suicide during the suicidal depression. Therefore, a two-step process entails assisting the client through the critical period of suicidal ideation: (1) hearing and showing understanding; (2) making a suicide prevention contract.

Hearing and showing understanding

In order to help the client feel less isolated, the counselor needs to show an empathetic understanding of the problem being presented. Active listening, as presented in Chapter 3, is an excellent method to hear the suicidal client's concerns, show respect for those concerns, and show that those current concerns are understood. Examples of good and inappropriate responses to client statements may help illustrate this technique.

Client: If I can't pass this class, I can never be a doctor, and I don't want to live.

Poor responses:

I can see you are upset, but being a doctor isn't everything.

It's just one class. Don't you think you're going a bit overboard?

Good responses:

It seems like being a doctor is really central for you to feel worthwhile.

It must be terrible being so close to failing a class that is so very important to you.

The poor responses above indicate a low level of understanding. The counselor is taking a position different from that of the client, with the message being, "There's something wrong with the way you are feeling." The client would not contest that there could be something wrong with the way he or she was feeling, yet real feelings of pain are so deep that suicide seems to be the only answer. When the client hears the message from the counselor that there is something wrong in the way he or she is feeling, the client can become more despondent and feel even more isolated.

The good responses above indicate that the counselor has heard how important the issue is to the client. When the counselor says, "It must be terrible being so close to failing a class that is so very important to you," the client can feel relieved that someone else can understand how he or she could have terrible feelings. The counselor has stepped onto the client's island, and the client is no longer alone with the painful feelings. While at first it may seem that agreeing how difficult a problem can be could drive the client into a deeper depression, in actuality when the client feels understood there is a feeling of relief coming from being heard and understood, i.e. "Maybe I am not so crazy after all."

The counselor should continue to hear what the client has to say, and show understanding and empathy. The goal here is not to fix the problem but to understand and show care.

Contracting with a suicidal client

Suicidal ideation is very common. It appears to be the result of the client's current difficulties in life and tendency to consider suicide as a possible solution. Suicide rates increase following the report of suicides in the media, and a client who has had a friend or family member commit suicide is at more risk of committing suicide. Further, a school or locality may have a spate of suicides in a relatively short period of time. It appears as though the "highlighting" of suicide is a factor that increases suicide risks. This should not dissuade the counselor from appropriately asking a client if that client is serious about suicidal thoughts. It is most important for the counselor to become aware of the client's current risk in order to respond appropriately.

Because a suicidal depression normally lasts no more than 48 hours, it is important to attempt to ensure that the suicidal client will be safe during this 48-hour time span. The person who seeks therapy when considering suicide really does not want to commit suicide—as evidenced by the call for help. There is an underlying desire to live, but, at the moment, living is so hard it seems impossible. Therefore, what this client needs is a good reason why committing suicide cannot be done at this time. Contracting provides such a reason.

Contracting with a suicidal client is getting a promise from that client that he or she will not attempt suicide within the next 48 hours. When a client makes a promise to a counselor that no suicide attempt will be made, the client is given a reason not to attempt a suicide, i.e. "I can't kill myself because I've promised my counselor I would not do anything like that." Therefore, the client who could not see any way out, the client who had no reason to live, has been given a reason: "I've promised I will not kill myself."

Contracting will normally occur only when the client is currently in a suicidal depression, in the danger zone of committing suicide, when the depression is deep enough so the client does not want to live and the energy is high enough to act out. Otherwise, contracting could occur so often that its utility could be lost on the client who often talks about suicide. Therefore, it is good to ask a series of questions to determine whether a client is serious about suicide. Here is an illustration of the types of questions that may be asked.

Question 1

When a client makes a statement that may imply suicidal ideation, such as, "The world would be better off without me," the therapist should ask if the client is seriously thinking about suicide. For example, simply, **"Are you thinking about suicide?"** Do not be afraid to ask a direct question.

If the answer is no, therapy may continue as normal; but, if the answer is yes, go on to Question 2.

Question 2

In order to determine whether the client is eminently close to suicidal action, the following question can be asked: **"Have you thought about how you would commit suicide?"**

Clients who have not thought about suicide enough to consider how they would actually commit suicide generally are not an immediate threat, but if the client has decided on a manner of suicide, go on to Question 3.

Question 3

This question determines whether the client has the means for suicide. For example, if the client stated a plan involving a gun in Question 2, the next question could be, **"Do you have access to a gun?"**

Again, if the client has not acquired access or is not talking in terms of immediately acquiring access to the means of suicide, then the threat is not considered as great. If, though, the client does have access or immediate means of access, go on to Question 4, contracting.

Question 4

"Will you promise me that you won't make a suicide attempt for the next two days, and that if you have trouble keeping this promise you'll call me or call someone else?" It is good to give the client a number of a suicide-prevention hotline, or the number of another counselor as a backup to your own number.

When the client makes a suicide-prevention contract, they are given an excuse not to commit suicide. While nothing is ever certain, suicide-prevention contracts are very rarely broken. Mostly, at the end of two days, the suicidal depression has passed. If the client is not willing to make a contract, a breach of confidentiality is necessary. Obviously, client confidence should only very rarely be breached, but, if the therapist believes the client is a real threat to commit suicide, confidence should be breached. The appropriate family member and/or authority should be contacted immediately.

Techniques to assist the client with the issues that brought on the suicidal ideation

The techniques presented here are to assist clients who have suicidal ideation, but who are not currently in a suicidal depression. Clients who are in a suicidal depression should be dealt with immediately by understanding and contracting. More general counseling should follow only after the immediate threat has been addressed.

Because suicide seems to be the result of the client's current difficulties in life, suicide counseling must focus on assisting the client with current difficulties. There are some important aspects to working with suicidal clients in regard to their concerns.

There should be an attempt to discover the central cause of the suicidal depression. It is important to focus on what is immediately causing the client to prefer to give up on life. It is often the case that the client will point to an issue—such as "I'm afraid I will fail chemistry"—when the presenting issue is merely a reflection of a deeper problem, possibly, "I am a worthless person who will always let everyone down, and who could never be loved."

Ego-state techniques are excellent for discovering the central problem associated with suicidal ideation. It is often not difficult to bridge from the negative feelings to the core problem. This is because the suicidal client normally has little difficulty in experiencing the negative emotion, and that emotion is connected to the core problem. This negative emotion can act as a beacon to eliminate the client's real concern that is feeding the suicidal ideation.

Working with a client who has suicidal ideation involves:

- hearing and showing an understanding of the problem;
- locating the origin of the problem;
- working to internally resolve the problem (or the reaction to the problem); and
- only after working to internally resolve the problem, working to facilitate an engagement in the positive aspects of the client's life.

See the subsection "Determine the precipitating cause of the unwanted symptoms" on page 101 for detailed instructions on bridging techniques in order to connect the suicidal feelings with the ego state that is depressed so therapy may proceed with the correct ego state.

See also the subsection "Dealing with depression" on page 162 for instruction on facilitating a re-engagement with the positive aspects of living. It is important for the client to identify goals and projects that are positive where energy and focus may be placed, but this is often not possible before the overriding issue that is causing the feeling of depression is addressed.

Therefore, the four steps presented above to work with a client who has suicidal ideation should be followed chronologically.

What if one of your clients commits suicide?

The best way to protect yourself from self-blame should one of your clients commit suicide is to always take the client who talks about suicide seriously, and always do what you can to see if a contract is needed. If so, make a contract. Even if you do everything you can, a client can still commit suicide. Ultimately, while we as counselors need to do all we can professionally to guide our clients through a suicidal depression, it is the client who makes the final decision. While many who have been associated with a person who ultimately commits suicide will feel guilt, there is one person who is most responsible: the one who commits suicide.

If a client commits suicide, it is normal for the counselor to feel that something else could have or should have been done. It is normal to experience a deep sense of failure. Counselors, too, have a right to grieve. Depending on the workplace and clientele of the counselor, losing a client to suicide may be more or less common, and that frequency can impact on the period of grieving. Just as with any grieving, there should be a period of time when big decisions are put on hold. It is not the time to decide on a profession change, a relationship change, a move, or a major sale or purchase. It may be a time to see a professional counselor to discuss feelings and related issues. Obviously, there is nothing about being a counselor that precludes our being human and benefiting from the same kind of professional consultation that we offer others.

Chapter 9

More Training for Difficult Circumstances

The extra training in this chapter is presented to assist counselors having special problems working with the ego-state counseling techniques presented in this book. This chapter is not to help counselors who have not read the other chapters: it is presented to be helpful as additional material for counselors who have begun practicing with, or using, the techniques presented, and find they need further assistance for some of those techniques to work.

This chapter includes special problems that sometimes occur when working with this therapy. It was considered appropriate to present these unusual problems in a separate chapter, allowing the other chapters to be more straightforward and written in such a way as to capture the most common occurrences and counseling.

Examples of dialogue with ego states

COUNSELING PROBLEM: The counselor feels unprepared to speak directly with ego states, or does not understand the kinds of dialogues that can be useful when speaking with ego states.

Once the counselor is talking directly with ego states, there is some common information that is useful to get from states. You may not be interested in getting all this information from every state, but, depending on the type of work you are doing, this information is often useful. Some of the dialogue with ego states is useful for working with specific problems. If you have read the preceding chapters, a review of this dialogue will help consolidate the understanding of various techniques.

- **Make sure you get a name for each state you talk with.** This is necessary to be able to refer about that state when talking with another state, and to be able to provide the client with a reference point to that state. The name can be used to call that state into the executive later in order to talk more with it.

- **It is often useful to ask each state how it feels about each other state.** In other words, if you are using three chairs to talk with three separate ego states, it is good to ask each state how it feels about each of the other two states. This way the counselor can facilitate a better understanding and respect between the states. For example, a state that wants to get work done may have a negative opinion about a state that wants to rest, and the state that wants to rest may feel that the state that wants to get work done won't leave it alone.

- **What is your role?** This type of question helps define the purpose of each state, both to the counselor and to other states. For example, a state that wants to get work done may see a state that wants to watch TV as lazy and worthless. But, when talking to the state that watches TV, if the question is asked, "What is your role?" the response may be, "I have to make sure she gets some rest, otherwise she would work all the time and wind up breaking down." Getting this information is the first step in allowing other states to see the value of each.

- **What do you need?** It is often the case that ego states are unhappy. Whenever any ego state is unhappy, that means a part of the client is unhappy and, when the client experiences that ego states as executive, the client will feel unhappy. Therefore, it is good to see what an ego state needs in order to be at peace and be happy. Obviously, next it is appropriate to attempt to satisfy the needs of the ego state, as long as satisfying those needs would not interfere with other states in a negative way. For example, one state might say it would be happy if another state would just disappear (something that could not happen). In this case, negotiation and understanding would need to follow so each state can achieve roles that all states can value. It is important for all states to accept and respect all other states. If in response to the question, "What do you need?" an ego state responds, "I need to be loved," then the counselor can ask for the help of another ego state that would like to come and provide ongoing love.

- **What other parts do you know or work with?** It can be useful to determine the other states that an ego state commonly works with. For example, an ego state that expresses violent anger may be being called forward into the executive by another ego state that is fragile and fearful. In order to help the client resolve expressions of violent anger it can be useful to work with other states that commonly communicate with the violent state.

It can be useful to encourage those states to call forward an assertive state that is able to satisfy the needs of the client in a more positive manner.

- **I would like to talk with a part that would like to help.** This can be a very useful statement. For example, if the client is having difficulty talking with men and the ego state that is executive when she often tries to talk with men feels nervous and incompetent, it is possible to ask if another state is able and willing to help—a more assertive state that can be more expressive. Another example was alluded to above: when the ego state feels unloved, the counselor can ask to talk to a different ego state that would like to support and love the fragile state.

- **Say, "I'm here" when you are ready.** When calling for help from another ego state it is good to encourage that state to let you know that it is ready to talk. For example, the counselor may say, "I would like to speak directly with a part of you that has been able to be assertive sometime in the past, a part that has been able to say exactly what you want. Just say, "I'm here" when you're ready to speak." Then, when the client says, "I'm here" or "Yes" or something like that, the conversation with the assertive ego state can continue. When the state is instructed to say, "I'm here," the pacing of the interaction is given to the client.

- **Have the courage to feel that even more.** This is a good statement to make in helping a client bridge from a negative experience to the original occurrence that caused that experience. When a situational reaction stems from a past event it is important to facilitate a resolution of the past event so the client will not continue to re-experience the negative feelings associated with the original experience. Asking the client to experience that negative feeling more deeply can bring to the executive the ego state that experienced the original negative event. Bridging to the event will be the next step.

- **Tell me exactly what you're experiencing right now.** This is an excellent request that can be made at different times in counseling. Too often, counselors lose track of what is happening with the client. There's no reason the counselor should not be able to ask the client about his or her present experience. This reunites the counselor and the client, allowing both to have the same understanding. This is an especially good request when the counselor can see that the client is experiencing emotional turmoil. It not only allows the counselor to better understand the experience of the client, but it allows the client to understand that the counselor is there keeping track, and is understanding what is happening.

- **I know this really happened, but it's not really happening right now—now we have the power.** This can be a very empowering statement for a client to hear. When a client is recalling a traumatic event it can seem very real. Hearing the counselor say, "I know this really happened, but it's not really happening right now—now we have the power" can help the client understand that real change can be made. The fear that was experienced in the past does not have to be experienced in the present.

- **Say exactly what you want to say.** This is a good statement to make to the client who is speaking to an introject (in an empty chair). It can also be good to say that this is a safe time and you can say anything you want. These statements can help a client to rise above fear, and express things that may not have been expressed before. Once the client is able to rise above fear, the fear loses its power. The courage of the client has overpowered it.

- **Would you like me to say it first?** Sometimes when a client is speaking to an introject, he or she may at first have real difficulty in saying something. It is OK for the counselor to speak directly to the introject, with the permission of the client, and say something first. When this happens, it is important for the counselor to tell the client, "Now you say what you want to!" This way, clients have an opportunity to rise above their own fear and express themselves.

- **Thank you for talking with me.** It is good for the counselor to say to an introject, or to an ego state, "Thank you for talking with me." This helps facilitate a positive working relationship with all parts of the client. The dynamic personality of the client is respected in total.

- **Is there any part that would like to say something before we stop for today?** After you have worked with separate ego states, it is good to ask whether any part has something it would like to say before the counseling session stops. That is, before the part of the counseling session stops when ego states are being addressed separately. It is sometimes the case that an ego state is not happy with a resolution that has been agreed upon by other states. If this is the case the resolution may not hold, without first addressing the concerns of this dissatisfied state(s). For example, if two ego states have worked out an agreement whereby one state can have a specified amount of time to work and another state can have a specified amount of time to rest, a third state that has not been heard from may be concerned that it may have no time to play or read.

When the client has difficulty naming an ego state

COUNSELING PROBLEM: **"I asked the ego state what I could call it, and it said it did not know."**

A good initial question in asking for an ego state's name is, "What can I call this part of you? What name or term seems to fit this part of you?" Still, it is not unusual for clients to have difficulty coming up with a name for an ego state. Often, clients become better at naming states as more states are spoken with, but they may have difficulty in naming states at any time. The following are some examples of some statements that can assist clients in naming states if they are unable to respond to an initial question asking for a name.

- I want to say to you, to this part that I'm talking with, that you sound as if you're very good at feeling. Is it OK if I call you "Heart", or would another name the better?

- It's important that I get a name for this part that I am talking with right now, so that I can call it back and talk with it again later. What name or term will you recognize, so you will know the part I want to speak with?

- I hear you say you want to be called "Stupid". It's important for me to understand whether this part feels stupid or is a name that another part thinks about this part? I want this part to be happy with the name that I call it.

An important consideration when naming ego states is to make sure that during the process of naming you are talking directly with the ego state that is being named. It is important for the ego state that is being named to be the one that is naming itself, or that is agreeing with the name that is being suggested. It is not unusual for another ego state to suggest a name for a state. That name may not be a name that is acceptable for the ego state that is being named.

It is also preferable in naming ego states for the name that is agreed upon by that state and by the counselor to be a name that can more easily take on a positive role. For example, a smoking ego state is better named something like "Pleasure Seeker" or "Relaxer" than "Smoker". If the ego state is named "Pleasure Seeker", then other forms of pleasure may be able to satisfy the state, rather than smoking. It can also be better to name an aggressive state "Protector" than "Violent" for the same reason.

As stated earlier, it is important for ego states to get a name so that each state can be talked with later. It is also important for the counselor to keep good records of ego states' names and traits so that an ego state can be called upon in therapy either later in the same session or in later sessions.

When the client has difficulty finding an ego state that can help another state

COUNSELING PROBLEM: **"I said I would like to talk with an assertive state, and nothing happened."**

It is often the case that in order to assist a client it is beneficial to locate an ego state of a certain type that can help another state. The two most common types of ego states that are used to assist the client are nurturing states and assertive states. When a child state feels lonely or in need of love, that state can often be benefited by a more mature nurturing state that can come to its aid.

The client who has had difficulty with anger or expression can often benefit from an assertive state that can help him or her express in a clear, nonaggressive fashion. This state can allow the client to express feelings before they become built up over time. States other than nurturing or assertive that may be needed to help states in need include playful states, wise states, intellectual nonfeeling states, strong states, and spiritual states, among others. The same processes are used to locate any type of state.

In most cases when the counselor tells the client, "I would like to talk to a nurturing part of you, a part that would like to come and help this child state" or, " I would like to talk to an assertive part of you, a part that can speak clearly with determination, and without getting angry", the client is able to immediately respond from a nurturing or an assertive state. While this happens in most cases, it is not unusual for a client to have difficulty locating a nurturing or assertive state, or a state of the type that is needed.

In this section, I will list in order of my preference methods to access states that can be beneficial to clients, when those states do not respond initially. If the first method does not work in locating a state of the type I am looking for, I then move to the next method. Counselors may wish to review the list and may prefer to reorder these selections to suit their own preferences. A nurturing state will be sought in the following examples, although these same methods can be used to locate any kind of state.

Accessing the desired state

1. **Ask directly to talk with a state of the type that is needed to help the client.** Example: "I would like to talk and to a nurturing part of you, a part that would like to come and help this child state."

2. **Ask if the desired state is in the background.** Example: "There may be a state in the background that has not been out lately that is nurturing, a state that has been nurturing at sometime in the past. That state may want to play a bigger role now. I want to invite that state that may not have had much to do for some period of time to come forward and say, 'I'm here', so it can help at this time."

3. **Ask if a state that has not had the desired role would like to take on that role.** Example: "There may be a state that would like to be nurturing, but has not had that role in the past. If this state that would like to be nurturing and would like to have a bigger role now will say, 'I'm here', we can talk about the possibility of your taking a bigger role in helping this child state. Just say, 'I'm here' if you would like to do that."

4. **Ask if the client knows of another person (introject), living or dead, who the client can imagine would be helpful in a situation such as the present one.** Example: "I want you to think of all the people you know, either personally or people you know of such as a famous person, or people you have known in the past. Who can you think of that is assertive in the way that you would like to be assertive?"

   (Here, the client has the opportunity to describe the attributes of an introject. When the client is able to describe the attributes of an introject that means the client has already internalized those qualities in order to be able to describe them; therefore, the internalized introject may be used just as an ego state. This is one way of assisting the client to gain benefits from what he or she already has internalized.)

5. **Ask the client to imagine the type of person who would be helpful in the current situation.** Example: "I want you to imagine someone who

is assertive in the way you would like to be assertive. Imagine that person, then tell me about the qualities that person has."

(In order to build a picture of an assertive person, and in order to describe that person in detail, the client has to be able to have an internalized representation of the person. In essence, when the client builds a picture of an assertive person, the client is building an introject of the type of person that is needed for internal assistance. This introject can be used to help other ego states internally just as an ego state of the client can be helpful.)

It is a good practice to explain to the client that the ego state, the introject, or the newly constructed introject is a resource that has *come from* the client and *belongs* to the client. This resource is something that the client will always be able to use.

When the client is reluctant to speak to an empty chair

COUNSELING PROBLEM: **"I suggested that the client might talk to an empty chair, but the client was reluctant to do that."**

One of the most powerful aspects of counseling is when a client speaks either to a person, living or dead, imagined to be sitting in an empty chair, or to another ego state, imagined to be sitting in an empty chair. Occasionally, students will ask, "What if the client doesn't want to talk to an empty chair?"

A counselor is a professionally trained individual who is available to help the client achieve goals. If it is clear to the counselor that it is in the best interest of the client to bring feelings forward by speaking directly to an introject, rather than intellectually talking about that person, then it is important for the client to speak to an empty chair, imagining that the person is sitting in the chair.

A medical doctor would not say to a bleeding patient, "What do you think about holding your finger right here to stop the bleeding? Please hold the artery if it's not too much trouble, but if it is you don't have to." A good doctor would say something more like, "Put your finger right there, and hold tightly."

In the same way, a professional counselor needs to be able to be direct while working with a client. The counselor should not say to the client, "I have an idea of something we can try if you want to. What do you think about talking with your mother in the empty chair as if she were there?" It is much better for the client if the counselor shows professional knowledge and speaks directly and clearly to the client: "Right, now, I want you to imagine the essence of your mother sitting in this chair, as if she were really there. I want you to say to her exactly what you want to say to her. You know she's not really there so you can say anything, but imagine that she is there when you say it. I'm right here on your side. Go ahead and tell her exactly what you want to tell her."

When the counselor is clear, and directive the client will proceed with the session without pausing. Important feelings can be processed and rapid progress can be made. It is much better for the client to be able to work through feelings during the session than to talk around feelings and hang onto the negative aspects of those feelings at the end of the session. The client who hangs onto negative aspects of bottled and unexpressed feelings may have a difficult week between sessions. It is the responsibility of the counselor to assist the client to express those bottled feelings so the client can be free from the fear that kept them bottled.

When the client does not speak directly to the introject in the empty chair

COUNSELING PROBLEM: **"I asked the client to say what she wanted to say directly to her mother in the empty chair, and she told me what she wanted to say, rather than saying it to her mother."**

The introject is the client's internalized representation of another individual, as they are currently or as they were at some time in the life of the client. When the counselor asks the client to imagine the essence of another person, living or dead, in an empty chair, and further asks the client to express feelings directly to that person, it is sometimes the case that the client speaks to the counselor rather than to the introject.

It is extremely important that the client speak directly to the introject, in order to bring forward the ego state that needs to express to the introject. When the client says something like, "I would like to tell her that I love her" or, "I want her to know that I love her," it is important for the counselor to make sure the client speaks directly to the introject. "Yes, I can hear and see that you love her, but I want you to tell her that directly as she is sitting in the chair. Say it to her directly, not to me. Say it now."

The experience of talking directly with the introject needs to be as realistic as possible. In order to facilitate this real type experience, the counselor needs to talk to the client as if another person were actually sitting in the chair. Statements such as, "She really needs to hear it directly from you" and, "What is she doing now?" can help the client to create a more realistic communication with an introject.

When the client is able to speak with an introject in a realistic fashion, the unresolved ego state is then able to come to the executive and rise above fear and express things that have not previously been expressed. This is extremely therapeutic, and when this expression can take place in counseling, a place where appropriate processing can occur, feelings may be brought to the surface and expressed, freeing the client from what had previously been bottled and pent up.

The importance of having the client speak directly to the introject cannot be stressed too much. In the same way, when the client is speaking to the empty chair to another ego state it is imperative for the client to speak directly to that state, not to the counselor *about* that state.

The client looks to the counselor as professional, and will follow the instructions of the counselor when they are given in a professional and clear fashion. The statement made clearly, "No, speak directly to your mother as if she were in the chair," is better than the question, "Do you think you can speak to your mother as if she were in the empty chair?"

An important issue

Spontaneous hypnosis

It is important for every counselor to understand some issues relating to spontaneous hypnosis. Spontaneous hypnosis occurs frequently during counseling, and is not unusual outside of counseling. *Spontaneous hypnosis* refers to a hypnotic state that occurs spontaneously, without the use of a formal induction.

When an individual driving a car suddenly realizes that there is no memory of the last ten minutes, a state of spontaneous hypnosis has occurred. While in a hypnotic state, that individual has been able to access an underlying ego state. This underlying ego state was able to think, drive, and attend to the responsibilities of the road. The underlying ego state that was executive, driving the car, had little or no communication with normal surface states, so, when the individual returned to a surface state and came out of spontaneous hypnosis, there was no memory of what occurred while he or she was in the underlying state.

Another example of spontaneous hypnosis when amnesia is present is the individual who, while reading a book, finds there is no memory of having read the last two paragraphs or two pages. Here again, this person has spontaneously gone into a hypnotic state when an underlying state became executive, and little or no communication meant that the surface state did not have memories when the individual came out of hypnosis.

Hypnosis does not have to contain amnesia. Quite often individuals who are hypnotized, either through an induction or spontaneously, have a complete memory of the time spent in hypnosis.

Another example of spontaneous hypnosis is the individual who is listening to a speaker, attempting to hear what the speaker has to say, but drifts into a daydream. This undesired, clicking off, and drifting into a daydream is spontaneous hypnosis. If, on the other hand, the individual thought, "This person is boring—I want to think about what I'm going to do this afternoon", then no spontaneous hypnosis has occurred. Often, the individual who has experienced spontaneous hypnosis by involuntarily clicking off into a daydream will have complete memory of the daydream and the time spent while in hypnosis.

Hypnosis entails the narrowing of focus where the individual is no longer balancing a number of thought processes at one time. Concerns about things such as, "Did I leave the iron on; where did I park my car; what am I going to do tomorrow?" are generally suspended in favor of a more narrow focus on the current experience of daydream or action. This state occurs very frequently during counseling, and counselors should know about its occurrence and about some factors relating to hypnosis.

When the client tells a story in detail, and becomes involved in that story, and becomes in line with the emotions of the time, a state of hypnosis is likely being experienced. When a client becomes very emotional, and is lost in that emotion, a state of hypnosis is likely being experienced. At these times the focus of the client has narrowed, and the client is not experiencing general concerns about separate activities. The client is hypnotized. Most normally, the client will be able to remember everything said during the session, even though the state of hypnosis has been experienced.

There is nothing wrong with the client's experiencing spontaneous hypnosis. But there may be something wrong with the way some therapists react during this experience. During a state of hypnosis an individual is much more susceptible to suggestion (Durbin, 2003). A number of experiments have demonstrated how false memories can be created when direct or indirect suggestions are made while the individual is in a state of hypnosis. It is, therefore, easy to see how a client who is experiencing emotional distress, who is crying, who is experiencing spontaneous hypnosis, is vulnerable to suggestions of the counselor.

Occasionally, during a time when the client is experiencing spontaneous hypnosis, counselors will say things such as, "Even if you don't remember it, you may have been sexually abused. You demonstrate some aspects of someone who has been sexually abused." Suggestive statements such as these can create detailed false memories, especially if made while the client is in a state of hypnosis. They are, therefore, highly unethical. It is good practice to refrain from ever suggesting a past that the client does not present.

Spontaneous hypnosis occurs in all types of counseling. It should not be feared or avoided. During the free association of psychoanalytic therapy, clients often become highly focused, in a state of spontaneous hypnosis. During the processing of issues in person-centered and, especially, Gestalt therapy, clients will enter a state of spontaneous hypnosis. And, during any therapy when clients tell about an issue in detail and become highly focused, they enter a state of spontaneous hypnosis. Many of the techniques presented in this book will cause clients to become highly focused and enter a state of spontaneous hypnosis.

The counseling techniques presented in this book do not entail interpretation by the counselor. Therefore, the fact that clients are occasionally spontaneously hypnotized presents little concern. As stated above, spontaneous hypnosis is a part of everyday life. A client should be safer in therapy during these times than any other, as long as the counselor does not offer hypothesized suggestions based on a way the client reacts in a certain fashion.

Final thoughts

The process of therapeutic counseling is both simple and complex. At its most simple level, counseling is the interaction of two individuals where one presents a problem and the other attempts to hear, understand and help. When both these individuals approach this process with an honest and positive intent, the outcome is most commonly beneficial. The burdens of the troubled person are lessened and the counselor's desire to assist is at some level appeased.

At a more complex level, problems that are presented in counseling are often not clear, straightforward, or easily understood. The client and the counselor may feel unable to understand the internal dynamics that could create such problems. As therapeutic counseling has evolved, we have seen counseling theories that attempt to place problems into a single, layered, uni-dimensional understanding. Problems have been seen to stem from an environment that throttles open expression (person-centered), from faulty learning patterns (behavioral), from faulty thinking (cognitive), or from a lack of insight and interpretation (psychodynamic).

The theoretical perspective presented in this book is more complex. The reader has been asked to accept that the personality is not a homogeneous whole, but an assemblage of rather distinct parts. The notion that these parts can agree, disagree, fight, or find a peace is central to this theoretical perspective.

Accepting this more complex view of personality requires a more complex approach to counseling. Depending on the problem, counseling becomes a process of assisting the parts to work together, a process of locating the specific part where a problem is experienced in order to help resolve that problem at its base, or a process of assisting clients to better understand their specific internal resources so the best parts can be used at the best times in order to handle difficult issues. By assessing each issue with the assessment approach that has been presented, the counselor is guided to the appropriate course of intervention.

While this view of personality and this modality of counseling are more complex, I have found graduate students and practicing therapists able to achieve profound and positive change with their clients by its application. It is hoped that readers of this text have found a view of personality and counseling interventions that will likewise be helpful to themselves and to their clients.

Glossary

abreaction negative emotional or physical response in therapy that is related to an earlier trauma. Abreactions may occur while working through a trauma. In ego-state theory, the act of experiencing an abreaction is not therapeutic, but the act of resolving the trauma, which often entails abreactions, is therapeutic. When a trauma is resolved, no further abreactions associated with that trauma will occur. A panic attack can be thought of an abreaction outside of therapy.

affect bridge technique for discovering the origin of a neurotic symptom so a process of resolution can be initiated. Unwanted symptomatic emotions are brought to the experience of the hypnotized client, followed by questioning concerning those feelings and a request for the client to return to the first time those feelings were experienced.

alter personality state of someone with dissociative-identity disorder (multiple personality). While surface ego states of a nonpathological individual communicate well with each other, allowing the person to have relatively continuous daily memory, "alters" communicate poorly with each other, resulting in memory blackouts relating to times that other alters were executive.

conflicted ego states states that have a positive role but are uncooperative internally. A state that wants to work and a state that wants to rest may be conflicted. Ego state negotiation that results in conflicted states learning the value of each and learning to compromise and communicate can facilitate conflicted states to become normal functioning. If a conflicted state is vaded it will also benefit from trauma resolution. It is possible for a state to be conflicted, retro functioning and vaded.

dissociative-identity disorder (multiple personality) psychological disorder assumed to be caused by chronic childhood abuse. Normal personality segments (ego states) lose their ability to communicate with each other, becoming alters. An alter will often have no memory of the times other alters were executive.

ego state one of a group of similar states, each distinguished by a particular role, mood and mental function, which, when conscious, assumes first-person identity. Ego states are a normal part of a healthy psyche, and should not be confused with alters (multiple personalities in dissociative-identity disorder).

executive an ego state or alter is said to be executive when it is conscious and able to communicate or function external to the individual. For example, a state speaking with another person, petting a dog, or washing a car is executive. Some nonexecutive states will be able to hear a conversation while others will not, but only one state is in the executive at any given time. States may switch to and from the executive rapidly.

introject internal manifestation of a person significant in the life of the client. A five-year-old ego state (of an adult client) may have an introject of "Father" or "Mother" as they were at the time the client was five. An introject may also represent another person as he or she is currently. For example, there may be an introject of a partner, friend, or parent. Introjects may be of living or dead persons, of persons who were viewed as positive or negative, but they are of persons who are or have been meaningful in the life of the client.

malevolent ego state state that appears to act purposely in opposition to either other (ego) states of the person, or to the outside world. While all ego states are created to benefit or protect the individual, over time malevolent states have taken on a negative function. They are a type of retro functioning state, having a role that is opposed to other states or opposed to the benefit of the person. They may learn to assume a positive function, with ego-state therapy negotiation.

multiple personality see *dissociative-identity disorder*

neurotic reaction reaction in an inappropriate and neurotic manner to a given situation. An example of a neurotic reaction is, as part of a pattern, becoming emotionally distressed when criticized by an authority figure. Neurotic reactions are negative feelings of an underlying ego state—feelings from an unresolved issue. When a situational occurrence reminds this ego state of the original unresolved issue, that state temporarily becomes executive with the feelings of the original occurrence. The client is aware only of experiencing the unwanted reaction.

normal functioning states states that function with positive roles to the benefit of other states and the person. It is the goal of therapy for all states to become normal functioning. Pathological states are retro-functioning, vaded, or conflicted, i.e., not normal functioning.

obsessive-compulsive disorder psychological disorder characterized by obsessive thought and compulsive action. The client is often unable to control these thoughts and actions, which are often disruptive. For example, an obsessive-compulsive client may worry so much about whether the doors are locked and may check them repeatedly over a short period of time.

panic attack temporary sense of loss of control and fear, sometimes associated with an inability to have normal function. Panic attacks result when an ego state comes to the executive that has either unresolved trauma from a past experience, or has consistently absorbed frustration and anger owing to nonassertive expression. Panic attacks may also result from an interactive combination of these two. Each of the two situations can cause an ego state to feel overwhelmed and unable to cope, and, when this ego state comes to the executive, the severe loss of control is experienced.

protector states states formed to keep the person from experiencing pain. They often help protect fragile states from being hurt, by either keeping them from the executive or reacting in a defensive manner, such as with anger or withdrawal. Protector states may also attempt to protect surface states from pain held by underlying states by attempting to keep them buried.

psychosomatic symptom physical or medical condition caused by a psychological phenomenon.

retro-functioning ego states states that have roles that are opposed to other states or opposed to the benefit of the person. States that manifest uncontrolled anger, pathological lying, or psychosomatic symptoms are examples. Ego state negotiation can facilitate a retro functioning state to take on positive roles. It is possible for a state to be both retro-functioning and vaded, and when this is the case the state will also benefit from trauma resolution.

surface states states that are most often executive in normal daily function. They have good communication between each other. This means that a surface state that is cognitive and deliberate will remember what happened when a surface state that is more emotional was executive. Likewise, a surface emotional state will have good awareness of what happened when the cognitive state was executive. Daily routine is experienced by surface states. Clinically, surface states may be accessed without hypnosis.

switching when an ego state is in the executive and a different ego state becomes the executive state, switching has occurred.

underlying states states that come to the executive only rarely. They vary greatly in their relative closeness to the surface. Some have almost no communication with surface states. These states become executive only occasionally outside of therapy. The person who sees a type of wallpaper like that of a childhood room may experience an underlying ego state, bringing childhood feelings and memories. Some of these memories may have previously been unknown to the surface states. Clinically, underlying states are difficult to access without hypnosis. While most underlying states hold positive and pleasant memories, unresolved trauma is held in underlying states.

vaded ego states states that are overcome by negative experience to the point where they can no longer conduct their role. These states may interfere with the life of the individual when they come to the executive. If an ego state experiences a trauma, and is not able to receive some type of crisis intervention after the trauma (that is, talking with someone who understands, being able to more fully express, and gaining some perspective on the event), then that ego state becomes vaded, and while vaded, each time it comes to the executive that individual will re-experience negative emotions associated with the trauma. Trauma resolution can free a vaded ego state so it can resume its normal role and cease causing neurotic reactions.

References

Blakemore, C., and Price, D. J. (1987), "The organization and post-natal development of area 18 of the cat's visual cortex", *Journal of Physiology*, 384, pp. 293–309.

Buisseret, Pierre, Gary-Bobo, Elyane, and Imbert, Michel (1982), "Plasticity in the kitten's visual cortex: Effects of the suppression of visual experience upon the orientational properties of visual cortical cells", *Developmental Brain Research*, 4 (4), pp. 417–26.

Cunningham, A. J., and Watson, K. (2004), "How psychological therapy may prolong survival in cancer patients: new evidence and a simple theory", *Integrative Cancer Therapies*, 3 (3), pp. 214–29.

Durbin, Paul G. (2003), "Therapist: Beware of false memories", *Australian Journal of Clinical Hypnotherapy & Hypnosis*, 24 (1), pp. 35–44.

Emmerson, G. J. (2003), *Ego State Therapy* (Carmarthen, Wales: Crown House).

Emmerson, G. J. and Farmer, K. (1996), "Ego state therapy and menstrual migraine", *Australian Journal of Clinical Hypnotherapy & Hypnosis*, 17, pp. 7–14.

Ferdern, P. (1952), *Ego psychology and the psychoses* (E. Weiss, ed.) (New York: Basic Books).

Gainer, M. J. (1993), "Somatization of dissociated traumatic memories in a case of reflex sympathetic dystrophy", *American Journal of Clinical Hypnosis*, 36, pp. 124–31.

Harrison, Julie Anne (2001), "Behaviors, traits, and types: Exploring the hierarchical structure of personality disorders", *Dissertation Abstracts International: Section B: The Sciences & Engineering*, 61 (12-B), p. 6707.

Hilgard, E. R., and Hilgard, J. R. (1975), *Hypnosis in the Relief of Pain* (Los Altos, CA.: William Kaufmann).

Holopainen, Debbi, and Emmerson, Gordon J. (2002), "Ego State Therapy and the Treatment of Depression", *Australian Journal of Clinical Hypnotherapy & Hypnosis*, 23, pp. 89–100.

Kubzansky, L. D., and Kawachi, I. (2000), "Going to the heart of the matter: do negative emotions cause coronary heart disease?", *Journal of Psychosomatic Research*, 48, pp. 323–37.

McCabe, R., and Priebe, S. (2004), "The therapeutic relationship in the treatment of severe mental illness: A review of methods and findings", *International Journal of Social Psychiatry*, 50 (2), pp.115–28.

Muir, Darwin W., Dalhousie, U., and Mitchell, Donald E. (1973), "Visual resolution and experience: Acuity deficits in cats following early selective visual deprivation", *Science*. 180 (4084), pp. 420–2.

Parfitt, David B., et al. (2004), "Differential early rearing environments can accentuate or attenuate the responses to stress in male C57BL/6 mice", *Brain Research*, 1016 (1), pp. 111–19.

Perls, Frederick (1965), *Gestalt Therapy* (Oxford, UK: Dell).

Phillips, M. (1995), "Our bodies, our selves: treating the somatic expressions of trauma with ego-state therapy", *American Journal of Clinical Hypnosis*, 38 (2), pp. 109–21.

Rogers, C. R. (1951), *Client-Centered Therapy: Its current practice, implications, and theory* (Boston, MA: Houghton Mifflin).

Schrott, L. M. (1997), "Effect of training and environment on brain morphology and behavior", *Acta Paediatrica*, 422, pp. 45–7.

Smith, Timothy W., et al. (2004), "Hostility, Anger, Aggressiveness, and Coronary Heart Disease: An Interpersonal Perspective on Personality, Emotion, and Health", *Journal of Personality*, 72 (6), p. 1217-71.

Temoshok, L. (1987), "Personality, coping style, emotion and cancer: towards an integrative model", *Cancer Surveys*, 6 (3), pp. 545–67.

Temoshok, L. (2004), "Rethinking research on psychosocial interventions in biopsychosocial oncology: An essay written in honor of the scholarly contributions of Bernard H. Fox", *Psycho-Oncology*, 13 (7), pp. 460–8.

Wark, Robert C., and Peck, Carol K. (1982), "Behavioral consequences of early visual exposure to contours of a single orientation", *Developmental Brain Research*, 5 (2), pp. 218–21.

Watkins, J., and Watkins, H. (1990), "Dissociation and displacement: Where goes the 'ouch'?", *American Journal of Clinical Hypnosis*, 33 (1), pp. 1–10.

Watkins, J. G., and Watkins, H. H. (1997), *Ego States: Theory and Therapy* (New York, NY: W. W. Norton).

Watkins, John G. (1949), *Hypnotherapy of War Neuroses: A Clinical Psychologist's Casebook* (Oxford, UK: Ronald Press).

Watkins, John G. (2003), keynote presentation, First World Congress on Ego State Therapy at Bad Orb, Germany.

Weiss, E. (1957), "A comparative study of psychoanalytical ego concepts", *International Journal of Psychoanalysis*, 38 (3–4), pp. 209–22.

Wilkinson, Frances, and McGill, U. (1995), "Orientation, density and size as cues to texture segmentation in kittens", *Vision Research*, 35 (17), pp. 2463–78.

Wolpaw, Jonathan, R. (2001), "Activity-dependent spinal cord plasticity in health and disease", *Annual Review of Neuroscience*; 24 (1), pp. 807-843.

CPSIA information can be obtained at www.ICGtesting.com
Printed in the USA
BVOW04s0308160916

R7429300001B/R74293PG462069BVX2B/1/P